THE AUTHOR

Robert N. Van Wyk is Associate
Professor in Philosophy and Human-
ities at University of Pittsburgh,
Johnstown. He has a Ph.D. from
the University of Pittsburgh and a
M.Div. from Pittsburgh Theological
Seminary. Most of his writing has
been on ethics and religion.

INTRODUCTION TO ETHICS

INTRODUCTION TO ETHICS

Robert N. Van Wyk
University of Pittsburgh at Johnstown

St. Martin's Press   New York

Project management: G&H/Soho
Cover photo and design: Doug Steel

Library of Congress Catalog Card Number: 89-60981

For information, write:
St. Martin's Press, Inc.
175 Fifth Avenue
New York, NY 10010

ISBN 0-312-03682-5 cloth
ISBN 0-312-02731-1 paper

Library of Congress Cataloging-in-Publication Data

Van Wyk, Robert N.
  Introduction to ethics / Robert N. Van Wyk.
     p.   cm.
  ISBN 0-312-03682-5.—ISBN 0-312-02731-1 (pbk.)
  1. Ethics.   I. Title.
BJ1021.V36   1989
170—dc20   89-60981
                                                                            CIP

ACKNOWLEDGMENTS

Extracts from *The Altruistic Personality: Rescuers of Jews in Nazi Europe* by Samuel P. Oliner and Pearl M. Oliner, reprinted by permission of the Free Press, a division of Macmillan, Inc. Copyright © 1988 by Samuel P. Oliner and Pearl M. Oliner.

Extracts from *The Theory of Morality* by Alan Donagan, reprinted by permission of the University of Chicago Press. Copyright © 1977 by University of Chicago Press.

Extracts from "Moral Conventionalism," by John Kekes, *American Philosophical Quarterly*, 22 (January 1985), reprinted by permission. Copyright © 1985 by *American Philosophical Quarterly*.

Scripture quotations are from the Revised Standard Version of the Bible, copyright 1948 and 1962 by the Division of Christian Education of the National Council of Churches of Christ in the United States of America. Used by permission.

Chapter 10 of this book uses material from my "Perspectives on World Hunger and the Extent of Our Positive Duties." *Public Affairs Quarterly*, 2 (April 1988): 75–90. Copyright © 1988 by *Public Affairs Quarterly*. Used by permission.

This book is dedicated to my wife,
Audrey,
and to the memory of my parents,
Adrian and Gertrude Van Wyk.

Preface

I see the course in ethics as having a number of purposes. In this age of cultural illiteracy, one purpose is to acquaint students with the moral traditions that have influenced the Western world (and not only the Western world). Every college graduate should have some idea of who Aristotle was and what he thought about the good life. (College graduates should also know something about Plato. Unfortunately, not every worthwhile figure or topic could be included.) For the same reason, the Western religious tradition is treated more extensively here than is usual for introductory ethics texts.

A second purpose is to help students think about moral theory and moral issues for themselves, taking into consideration alternative points of view and the criticisms that have been made of them. A third purpose is to move beyond theory and to challenge students to ask questions about their own moral values and moral commitments, about whether they are well thought-out or have only been acquired by osmosis from the popular culture, and about whether they are adequate or inadequate. Neil Postman writes: "The school stands as the only mass medium capable of putting forward the case for what is not happening in society."[1] The more the assumptions of dominant cultural trends can be challenged and deflated, the less hold they may have on people, and the more likely it is that people will give open-minded thought to the alternatives and make rational and autonomous decisions. According to Daniel Callahan, one of the most prevalent attitudes in our society is what he calls "moral minimalism."[2] If Postman and Callahan are right, and I believe they are, then another legitimate purpose of an ethics course is to encourage students to reflect critically on the adequacy of "moral minimalism." I hope that this text will help accomplish these purposes.

This book differs from other ethics texts by giving some attention to feminist concerns. These have been addressed somewhat in anthologies on specific moral issues, but as of this writing they have not yet been dealt with to a great degree in single-author texts focusing on theory. Most of the important philosophers of the Western world wrote before feminists were raising the concerns that they are raising today. Nevertheless, the teachings of those philosophers and the concerns of feminists can often be discussed together. Sometimes feminist concerns can be addressed in the applications of traditional principles. Kant's principle of respect for persons is certainly relevant to criticism of the frequent mistreatment of women in contemporary society. Sometimes the observations of feminist writers can be used as a basis for exposing the inadequacy of traditional positions. For example, some of Carol Gilligan's observations on the different moral attitudes of men and women are relevant to discussing the adequacy of social contract views. Sometimes traditional approaches can be used to raise questions about the proposals of some feminist writers. For example, are radical feminist proposals for restructuring society likely to meet utilitarian criteria? There is no chapter on the varieties of feminist theory, but feminist concerns and some feminist theories are discussed in various places.

Even more noticeably, this book differs from some others in its more extensive treatment of religious ethics. Chapter 3 gives an exposition of Jewish, Christian, Islamic, and Buddhist ethics, along with some mention of Taoism, Confucianism, and Hinduism. It also deals with relationships between philosophical ethics and religious and theological ethics. Chapter 10, on virtue and vice, gives some attention to Jewish, Christian, Taoist, and Buddhist views on this subject. Some reference to these traditions appears in other chapters as well. Buddhism also finds its way into chapter 7.

Some ethics texts never mention religious ethics. Some express hostility to religion or give accounts of religious ethics that are largely unrecognizable by an educated person with religious sympathies. Some dismiss religious ethics as illegitimate or irrelevant, sometimes with clearly inadequate arguments. Others say that since the existence of God cannot be proved on the basis of reasons equally ascertainable to everyone, the ethics of theistic religions can be dismissed as irrelevant to discussing public issues. This overlooks the fact that ethics has to do with the individual's personal life as much as with public issues. But even when discussing public issues, personal values, including religious ones, may be relevant if those issues cannot be decided on the basis of available public reasons.[3]

What are likely to be the results of ethics courses that ignore or denigrate religious ethics? First, students with a secular upbringing may be left with a large area of cultural illiteracy. Second, many students come into classes having been nurtured in a particular religious tradition, or having made a personal commitment to one. Religious students who are used to approaching moral issues through religion alone may see moral philosophy as something irrelevant to their lives. Third, an opportunity may be lost to encourage religious students to examine their own religious ethic, instead of compartmentalizing it until after the course is over, when it may very well be brought back out of its box untouched and unbroadened. Fourth, dealing with religious ethics can encourage religious students to think critically about whether there is a lack of consistency between their religious beliefs and the morally minimalist views they often express when not explicitly thinking about religion. So this text takes religious ethics seriously and does not question the legitimacy of religious or theological ethics as a discipline for the believer. It seeks to show the student with religious convictions that philosophical ethics is also a legitimate discipline and one that he or she should be no less concerned with than the nonreligious student, and that religious grounds for moral positions and philosophical grounds for moral positions can interact and supplement one another.

When introducing a subject such as this, an author faces a number of choices. One can proceed topically, seeing how different persons or theories deal with a specific topic, or one can treat a certain theory or the views of a certain philosopher as a unit. One can proceed logically or historically. One can be noncommittal, or one can use the strong points (and the criticisms) of other positions as a foundation on which to develop one's own position. For the most part I proceed historically and treat the views of individual philosophers or schools of thought as units, except with respect to their views on virtue and vice, to which I devote a separate chapter. One result of this is that the views of Aristotle are split between the chapter on natural law theory, where they are referred to in preparing the way for St. Thomas, and the chapter on virtue and vice.

The book does attempt to present a continuing discussion, but the instructor has some flexibility in its use:

The final text section in chapter 2, on psychological egoism, could be omitted.
Chapters 2 and 3 could be reversed.
The sections of chapter 3 on the ethics of Asian religions could be omitted.
The last two sections in chapter 4 could be omitted.
If the course deals with contemporary moral problems after theory, chapter 10 could be read along with other writings on the issue of world hunger.

Some sections cannot be easily skipped. Chapter 11, on social justice, for example, refers back to chapter 8, on utilitarianism, for criticism of the utilitarian view of justice.

I do seek to develop my own views in the two chapters entitled "Toward an Adequate Moral Theory" (chapters 8 and 9) and in parts of the following chapters. My own position begins with a pluralistic view of value, similar to the views of John Finnis, Alan Brown, Joseph Raz, and numerous others. It proceeds to a view of moral duty that is contrasted with rights-based, social contract, and utility-maximizing approaches. It is influenced by such philosophers as Joseph Raz, Theodore Benditt, and Robert Goodin. Perhaps it can be called a natural law approach, if that term is understood broadly enough.

Another problem facing an author of an ethics text is how much weight to give to theory and how much, if any, to specific moral issues. I was advised by other teachers of introductory ethics not to stress specific moral problems, since they prefer to deal with these by using collections of readings representing different points of view, rather than by using a single-author text. Specific moral problems are not ignored completely, however. Chapter 9, on duties to the hungry, is included because of its contribution to an important question of moral theory, namely, how much sacrifice our positive duties to other people actually require us to make. Other specific moral issues are also dealt with along the way, including moral evaluations of the traditional family, rape, the unjust treatment of women, servility, and drug use. Chapter 11, on social justice, briefly relates each theory of justice discussed to the question of the just distribution of medical care within a society and to the question of the legitimacy of reverse discrimination or "strong" affirmative action. I hope that this text and associated readings in the primary sources will lead to a useful consideration of other specific moral issues.

I would like to acknowledge the useful suggestions of Don Reisman of St. Martin's Press, the considerable help from various anonymous reviewers for St. Martin's, the valuable work of copyeditor Janet Podell, and the proofreading assistance of Joanne McGahagan and Jeffrey Dandoy.

ROBERT N. VAN WYK
Johnstown, Pennsylvania

NOTES

1. Neil Postman, *Teaching as a Conserving Activity* (New York: Dell, 1979), 12.
2. Daniel Callahan, "Minimalist Ethics: On the Pacification of Morality," *Hastings Center Report 11* (October 1981): 14–25; reprinted in *Vice and Virtue in Everyday Life*, ed. Christina Hoff Sommers (New York: Harcourt Brace Jovanovich, 1985), 638.
3. See Kent Greenawalt, *Religious Convictions and Political Choice* (New York: Oxford University Press, 1988).

Contents

INTRODUCTION TO ETHICS

1

Introduction: The Discussion of Moral Issues in Today's World

MORAL ISSUES AND MORAL CONSIDERATIONS

This book talks about *ethics*, or *morality*. We frequently say that something or other is, or is not, a moral issue. It is a moral issue if moral considerations are relevant to it. But what are moral considerations? Many people think in terms of the violation of a rule in some code of ethics. A person has done something morally wrong if such a rule has been broken. The moral code of a primitive tribe may prohibit killing another member of the tribe, but not members of other tribes. If a member of the tribe kills someone, he or she is regarded as morally blameworthy only if that killing explicitly violates the tribe's code. Many people think that way today, especially within the sphere of professional ethics. In recent years there has been constant discussion of the ethics of public officials and others in the public eye. A government official, a lawyer, a banker, a doctor, or a nurse is regarded as unethical if he or she has violated the established code of ethics for the tribe of government officials, lawyers, bankers, doctors, or nurses. So a steady stream of people accused of unethical behavior appears before congressional committees and grand juries claiming that even if they used "poor judgment," they did not violate the code of ethics that applied to them.

But there must be more to ethics or morality than this, since we are often unconvinced by these defenses. Presumably the rules are part of the code because they were thought, rightly or wrongly, to represent certain more general principles (e.g., people in positions of power should not use their advantageous positions to take advantage of the vulnerable). So we

1

feel that the violation of such a general principle is a reason to judge behavior to be unethical or immoral even if no specific rule was explicitly violated.

The possession, use, and intended use of weapons of mass destruction are considered by many to be among the most crucial *moral* issues of our time. People who discuss these issues are not thinking about the violation of some precise code, but about more general principles. So we hear the following sorts of moral arguments:

> We ought never to kill the innocent intentionally. Furthermore, if it is wrong to do something, it is wrong to intend to do it. But targeting civilian populations indicates an intention to slaughter innocent civilians if we are sufficiently provoked. It is, therefore, morally unacceptable.

> We ought never to be first to use greater violence than has henceforth been used. Neither ought we plan to do so. Targeting nuclear missiles at enemy missile silos violates this principle, since it only makes sense if we intend to attack first (otherwise our missiles would be hitting empty silos).

> Since both of the preceding arguments are sound, there is no permissible way of targeting nuclear missiles. Therefore we ought to get rid of them.

> One side's unilaterally doing away with its nuclear missiles would destabilize the international situation and make nuclear war more likely. Such a policy is, therefore, morally impermissible since it cannot be right to do something which increases the possibility of some great evil occurring.

The issues are not simple. Other principles can also be appealed to, and principles can be applied in various ways. Which of these principles are sound and which applications are justifiable are difficult ethical questions that have been debated at great length.

Of course, we face moral issues in our personal lives as well. Moral issues are those to which moral considerations are relevant. But what sort of considerations are moral considerations? Moral issues would at the very least seem to involve considerations other than just personal preference. Whether we play softball or basketball, whether we eat cheeseburgers or salad, may not seem to be moral issues. But these can become moral issues. Perhaps I have high cholesterol and have promised my wife to stop eating cheeseburgers. Perhaps by not changing my diet I am endangering my life. Perhaps I am thus also endangering the future financial security of my children. Under such conditions everyday acts may become moral issues. If what I do affects the interests or welfare of other human beings or perhaps even of myself, then we have raised moral considerations. (And yet not every act that disregards the welfare of other human beings is automatically a candidate for moral evaluation on those grounds. If Martha and Steven choose to get married, the fact that this may adversely affect the happiness of other people who may have wished to marry either Martha or

Steven does not in itself seem to instill Martha's and Steven's choices with great moral significance.)

If there is a conflict of wills, moral considerations may be relevant even if no vital human interests are involved. If Mike loves basketball and Bill loves softball, then Mike's willingness or unwillingness to play softball after Bill has repeatedly agreed to play basketball would seem to be a moral issue. At an early age, children begin to appeal to a principle of fairness as a way of resolving those conflicts, as Bill is likely to do in the above situation.

Consider the following case. Elizabeth and Arthur are expecting their second child. One (does it matter which one?) thinks that Arthur should interrupt his career to stay home and take care of the infant so Elizabeth can pursue her career with only a minor interruption. Perhaps one appeals to fairness. Elizabeth interrupted her career for the first child, now it is Arthur's turn. People involved in a common enterprise should share burdens equally. But what is or is not a burden may depend on what people want. One parent may have a stronger desire to stay home (or not to stay home) than the other. Perhaps they should seek to satisfy the most numerous and strongest desires or preferences.

But then again, perhaps all desires are not equally worthy of consideration. Perhaps someone might argue that a desire that Elizabeth not stay home should be disregarded because it goes against what is natural (i.e., a mother devoting more of her time to her children), or because it is contrary to tradition, or because it goes against the Bible, which teaches (according to some interpretations) that wives should be subservient to their husbands. Perhaps someone might argue that if Elizabeth has a desire to stay home because she has been indoctrinated by her culture not to think of any other possibility, then her desire is "inauthentic" and should be disregarded. Perhaps someone might argue that if she has a desire not to stay home just because she has been indoctrinated by feminist friends, then that desire is "inauthentic" and should be disregarded.

Perhaps certain desires should be disregarded because they spring from undesirable character traits. Someone might ask Elizabeth whether her desire to stay home or not to stay home might not be displaying the undesirable characteristic of selfishness. Of course, Elizabeth can ask whether Arthur is not displaying the same characteristic. Could selfishness be more of a vice for one gender than it is for the other? Perhaps everyone's personal desires should be overlooked, and the decision should be made in terms of which alternative would have the best long-term consequences for the future prospects of the child, the family income, the good of society, and so on.

In fact, various people have appealed to arguments similar to all of these. Suppose a number of these considerations are legitimate moral considerations? Is there some one principle that should be decisive, or, if not, is there some one right way of weighing them against each other? What might moral considerations tell us: that there is one right thing for everyone to do, that there is one right thing for these particular people to do, that there are a range of morally acceptable alternatives, or that some alternatives are definitely morally wrong? Sometimes confusion occurs because when people ask "Is that the right thing to do?" they are usually using the word "right" to mean "morally required."

MORAL ISSUES AND MORAL PHILOSOPHY

Moral Philosophy and the Discussion of Moral Issues

We have been posing various questions, and we will be considering many more. *Applied moral philosophy*, also called *applied ethics*, seeks to use reason to answer these questions to the degree that it is possible to do so. When people discuss moral issues, they are often inconsistent. An individual may appeal to one principle when discussing the issue of abortion and a totally different one when thinking about the ethics of war. Moral philosophy differs from ordinary discussion of moral issues in that it seeks to avoid this sort of error by thinking more rationally, carefully, and consistently than people generally do.

One way in which philosophers seek to be consistent is to come up with one moral theory that will tie these various questions together, answer them in some coherent way, and provide moral guidance on a wide range of specific moral issues. Perhaps the most prevalent way of defending such a theory is by using reason to point out the inadequacies and inconsistencies of competing theories and to reply to charges that one's own theory is inadequate or inconsistent. This is the *theoretical* (as opposed to the applied) part of moral philosophy or philosophical ethics. This book will deal with such theories, with the ways in which they have been attacked, and with the ways in which they have been defended.

The kind of ethics that we have been talking about, whether theoretical or applied, is also called *normative ethics*. Another part of moral philosophy, called *metaethics*, will be touched on in chapters 2 and 8, but it will not play a central role in this book.

Moral Considerations and Moral Philosophy

We have already noted that almost everyone could agree on this simple definition of moral issues: They are issues for which there is some reason to believe that certain considerations other than purely personal preference are relevant. But which considerations? Whether an action violates some kind of rule such as "You must not kill," or some principle such as "Do unto others as you would have them do unto you," would seem to be a moral consideration. Whether an action adversely affects the interests of other human beings would seem to be another. Whether it can be correctly described as exhibiting a certain kind of character trait, such as selfishness, may be another.

But which rules and principles are correct, and which character traits are undesirable, and which ways of affecting the interests of other people are relevant? To some extent this depends on what moral theory one thinks is most plausible. For example, in the discussion between Arthur and Elizabeth, reference might have been made to "what is natural." According to some moral theories, such a consideration is totally irrelevant. According to one theory, it is of crucial importance.

To some extent what morality is depends on which theory of morality is most plausible, and one cannot decide that without first looking at what the alternatives are. What we hope to accomplish in this book includes looking at and evaluating such theories.

Moral Philosophy as Philosophy

This book deals primarily with *philosophy*. Philosophy means love (in Greek, *philia*) of wisdom (*sophia*). At one time the word "philosophy" was applied to any serious intellectual endeavor or academic discipline. What we think of as the physical sciences were called "natural philosophy."

We might think of philosophy today as the attempt to use reason to answer those questions that cannot be answered by the methods of the specific sciences. They include questions of meaning, such as "What is a scientific law?" or "What is a right?" or "What is happiness?" They also include questions of evaluation. The physical sciences, for example, may increasingly give human beings the ability to select the sex of their children. The social sciences may increasingly be able to predict the consequences of one policy or another. But neither the physical sciences nor the social sciences can tell us whether the consequences of alternative policies concerning the use of such techniques are good or bad. Neither do they tell us to what degree the goodness or badness of those consequences should be a reason for adopting one policy rather than another. These are philosophical questions.

Philosophical Ethics and Religious Ethics

Religious thinkers and theologians also discuss moral issues and deal with many of the same questions. Religion has been defined as "an expression of basic evaluations and ultimate loyalties."[1] Those who use reason to work out the implications of those "basic evaluations and ultimate loyalties" for particular issues of life are engaging in the discipline of theological ethics.

One difference between religion and philosophy is, as William Temple put it, that "the primary assurances of religion are the ultimate questions of philosophy."[2] Thus a difference between religious ethics and philosophical ethics is that while religious ethics begins with certain "primary assurances" or unquestioned commitments, philosophical ethics does not. This is not to say that philosophers do not work from presuppositions and have commitments. But from the philosophical point of view, such presuppositions and commitments are open to investigation, modification, and rejection. Philosophy seeks to go as far as reason can in making clear the options and establishing what can be said in favor of and against those options. Chapter 3 will continue the discussion of the relationship between religious ethics and philosophical ethics.

SOME ADDITIONAL MORAL ISSUES

Many times moral questions are about what is permissible or impermissible. Is it ever morally permissible to deliberately kill an innocent person? Many moral codes tell us what *types* of actions are, according to that code, prohibited. Thus the moral code of ancient Israel says: "You must not commit murder" (Exod. 20). We can ask, for example, whether it is universally, or at least usually, wrong to remove someone from life-sustaining equipment, or to have an abortion.

Morality is also concerned about what is permissible or impermissible in a particular situation. If the answer to the question about life-sustaining equipment and abortion is no or maybe, then we can go on to ask additional questions: "Is it morally permissible for Dr. Jones to remove Mr. Smith from life-sustaining equipment, given their particular circumstances?" "Is it morally permissible for Alice to have an abortion in her particular circumstances?"

RIGHTS, LIBERTIES, POSITIVE AND NEGATIVE DUTIES, AND MORAL MINIMALISM

Sample Cases in Which People Appeal to Rights

We have looked at a few moral issues. The consideration of some of these issues may go on primarily within a person as he or she considers what is best. But people may discuss these issues with each other. When they do engage in the discussion of moral issues with others, they often do so to defend their behavior when it is challenged. Consider some of the following cases.

Case 1: Hester discovers she is pregnant. Barbara says it would be wrong for her to have an abortion, but Hester argues that she has a right to an abortion.

Case 2: Carla is wasting her term, getting high on drugs and not doing her schoolwork. Donald argues with her that what she is doing is morally wrong, but Carla defends her behavior, claiming she has a right to do what she wants to do.

Case 3: Michael is about to drop out of school because his pay was stolen and he cannot pay his bills. The students in his dorm take up a collection, asking every student to contribute five dollars so Michael can stay in school. Fred, although he could give five dollars without missing it, refuses to do so, claiming that it is his money and he has a right to do with it as he wants. Fred's roommate, Tom, accuses Fred of selfishness.

Case 4: James becomes a pimp and makes his living recruiting runaway girls, including Sally, for prostitution. When challenged, he claims that he has a right to do what he is doing.

Case 5: Edward gets through school by handing in term papers written by other people. Walter challenges his behavior.

Case 6: Kimberly and Frank, who work for a chemical company, refuse to sign a statement saying that a certain product is safe when in fact the tests were rigged. Fellow workers appeal to their loyalty to the company, but Frank continues to refuse on the grounds of his duty to uphold professional standards, and Kimberly appeals to her duty to people who might be harmed.

Case 7: Zachary refuses to register for the draft because he is a Christian who believes that Jesus commanded the complete rejection of violence. His refusal is a disappointment to his father, a retired army officer who is also a Christian, but who reads the Christian moral tradition in a different way.

Case 8: Paul is in the air force and has an opportunity to become a bomber pilot, but turns it down on the grounds that in past wars, bomber crews have often been called on to drop bombs on targets that were of questionable military value and destructive of the lives of civilians. He argues that he cannot violate the right to life of noncombatants.

Rights and the Discussion of Moral Issues

In different cultures and periods of history, discussions of moral issues take different forms and use somewhat different concepts. *Virtue* and *vice* are such concepts. Someone asks Elizabeth whether she might be displaying the vice of selfishness. Tom, in case 3, accuses Fred of selfishness.

Another concept is that of *duty*. In the last three cases mentioned above, Kimberly, Frank, Zachary, and Paul defend their behavior by reference to duties they believe they have.

In the United States today, debates about morality are more often carried on in terms of *rights* than in terms of virtues or duties. We hear about civil rights, women's rights, gay rights, the rights of the fetus, reproductive rights, welfare rights, and so forth. In the first four cases described above, someone appeals to his or her rights. We can talk about *legal rights*, which are rights which people have because of what the law says. We can also talk about *moral rights*. Antiabortionists say that a fetus has a moral right to life whatever the law says, and proabortionists say that a woman always has a moral right to do what she wants with her body whatever the law said in the past or may say in the future.[3]

There are three ways that references to rights appear in the discussion of moral issues. One approach refers to rights only at the end of a discussion of a moral issue. After we weigh all the moral considerations, we conclude that Hester does or does not have a specific right to an abortion, or that Carla does or does not have a right to do what she is doing, or that civilians in general, or certain civilians, do or do not have a right not to be targets in time of war. A second approach is to think of people as having certain general rights. We think about a moral issue by balancing the rights of the various people involved. So we decide whether abortion is morally justified in a particular case by taking into consideration the perhaps conflicting rights of the woman, the father, and the fetus. No one individual's rights are necessarily decisive.

A third approach also begins with rights that people are thought of as having. However, with this approach an appeal to a right also terminates the discussion. In this view, having a right is like having the ace of trump in a card game.[4] If I have the ace of trump, I take the trick regardless of what other cards are played. Similarly, if I can appeal to a right, then I win the moral argument no matter what good reasons other people may give. So for many antiabortionists, the argument about abortion is totally settled by an appeal to the right to life of the fetus, and for many defenders of abortion, the abortion issue is totally settled by an appeal to the woman's right to do what she chooses with her own body. A major problem with this third approach is that discussion ends as soon as it begins and there is no way to find areas of compromise.[5] In the first three cases above, Hester, Carla, and Fred seem to be thinking of rights as trumps that settle an issue abruptly.

Types of Moral Minimalism

We see that Paul (case 8) uses the word "right." The right to life of innocent people is the foundation of a duty that other people have to refrain from deliberately or recklessly killing them. It is fear of being asked to violate that duty that leads Paul to refuse to become a bomber pilot. This sort of right can be called a *claim right*, since it is the basis of claims on the behavior of other people. When Hester, Carla, Fred, and the others use the word "right," they speak of having a right to do something. This is called a *liberty right* (or *discretionary right*), since they are saying that they are at liberty to do that thing. They have no duty to do it and no duty not to do it, and thus they should be immune from coercion or criticism whatever they do.

An approach to ethics that emphasizes liberty rights, or the duties one does not have rather than the duties one does have, might be called a minimalist view of ethics. *Ethical minimalism* is a phrase used by one writer, Daniel Callahan, as a name for what he regards as a prevalent way of thinking in contemporary American society. The people referred to in the first five cases are concerned with telling others what duties they do not have, not because they have some conflicting duty, but because they have no duties in the matter at all. If asked why they think that they have such a liberty right, some of their answers could be minimalist answers. What might some of these answers be?

(a) One possible answer is that they have no duty to refrain from behavior they are engaged in because nobody has any duties at all. This position rejects ethics or morality altogether. It can be called *amoralism*. If this position is correct, the rest of this book is irrelevant.

(b) Another answer is that our only duty in life is to further our own good. So Hester might claim that since refraining from an abortion would not further her own good, she has no duty to refrain. This is a position called *ethical egoism*. Some versions of egoism leave room for debate about what a person's good really is and what furthers it. So Tom (case 3) might argue that what Fred is doing is causing others to dislike him, and that being disliked is not to one's advantage.

(c) When it is pointed out to Carla (case 2) that she is not furthering her own good, she might answer that the only duties she should live by are ones that she personally adopts and believes in, and that nothing she is doing violates her own personal ideals. Carla is taking a position called *subjectivism* or *personal relativism*. Carla can also be seen as placing a high value on *autonomy*, or choosing one's own way of life.

(d) Another minimalist approach recognizes duties to other people, but they are all "negative duties," that is, duties not to do certain things, such as harming other human beings. We hear people say: "If I'm not harming another person, then I'm not doing anything wrong." Hester may claim that she is harming a fetus, not a person; Carla may claim that she is not harming anyone else, only herself; Fred may claim that he is not harming anyone, only refusing to help. If we define harming people as violating their rights, then James may also claim that since Sally works for him voluntarily, he is not violating her rights, and so is not harming her.

(e) Suppose someone promised to do something for Hester, Carla, or Fred. Wouldn't they insist that that person has a positive duty, that is, a duty to do something, and not just the negative duty of not harming? Another view is that we have such positive duties if and only if we have done something to incur such a duty, such as making a promise, borrowing money, getting married, having children, and so on. By avoiding making promises, borrowing anything, or doing anything else to incur a duty, we can avoid having any positive duties. This view, like the preceding ones, puts a high value on individual freedom or *autonomy*, since no one has any positive duties he or she has not freely chosen to have. This position, which could be called *voluntarism*, also represents a type of minimalism. The positions advanced in paragraphs (d) and (e) together make up a position called *libertarianism*, which says that we have negative duties not to harm, but no positive duties to aid anyone, other than those duties we have freely accepted.

Beyond Minimalism

Many people have thought that morality demands more of them than this. Perhaps there are other important considerations that have not been referred to by Hester, James, Fred, and the others. In other ages, these considerations were widely regarded as more important than liberty rights and autonomy. Perhaps it is wrong to do that which would not be done by a person of good character, or which tends to corrupt one's own character or that of another. What would James or Fred do if they had a good moral character? Do they have a duty to oppose the deterioration of their own characters, and even to further their development? Possibly James's behavior is wrong because it involves corrupting his own character as well as the character of another. Perhaps it is irrelevant whether the other person consents to such harm. Perhaps Carla is violating a duty of gratitude to her parents, who have invested much in her life and are paying for her education.

Perhaps we also have duties to other human beings apart from such factors as gratitude. If that is so, then Edward and Zachary, even if they are not harming any specific individuals, may be violating duties of fairness to other people who abide by the rules of honesty in education, or who abide by the laws of the land. Perhaps we have positive duties to help others that are not based on our doing anything to incur those duties. So Fred may have a duty to help Michael. Perhaps people have duties to respect or promote certain values, such as knowledge, wisdom, or beauty.

What, for example, does morality have to say about choosing a career? Should a young college graduate take into consideration whether she may end up contributing to the harm of other people—for instance, by manufacturing or marketing harmful products such as dangerous insecticides that are banned in the United States but that chemical companies still export to Third World countries? Should she take into consideration harm to herself? Suppose she knows that she has a weakness toward being overly enthralled with the life-styles of the rich and famous. Should she then, as a way of protecting her character from corruption, avoid professions in which she would be surrounded by the temptation to become totally obsessed with money? Should she take into consideration the interests of other people and the positive contribution she can make to the world (for example, in a career of public service)? Should she consider whether a certain choice would waste her talents (artistic, musical, medical)? A religious person will (or should) regard wasting such talents as violating a sacred trust. There have been times and places in the recent history of the United States in which many young people made career plans with at least some of these considerations in mind.

We can think of minimalist morality as that which leaves out all of the sorts of considerations mentioned in the previous two paragraphs. Our college graduate would be taking a minimalist approach if she said:

> As long as I don't choose to be a drug dealer or a bank robber it is all right for me (I have a liberty right) to choose whatever career I feel like without bothering my head about all of those other questions. I don't have any duty to think about those other questions, and it's nobody else's business. Other people should not have opinions on the subject, and if they do, they should keep their opinions to themselves.

Daniel Callahan claims that minimalist morality has been pervasive in American society in recent years. He describes it in this way:

> What has been that morality? It has been one that stressed the transcendence of the individual over the community, the need to tolerate all moral viewpoints, the autonomy of the self as the highest human good, the informed consent contract as the model of human relationships. We are obliged under the most generous reading of a minimalist ethic only to honor our voluntarily undertaken family obligations, to keep our promises, and to respect contracts freely entered into with other freely consenting adults. Beyond those minimal standards, we are free to do as we like, guided by nothing other than our private standards of good and evil.[6]

Callahan goes on to criticize the minimalist approach to ethics in the following way:

> Hard times require self-sacrifice and altruism—but there is nothing in an ethic of moral autonomy to sustain or nourish those values. Hard times necessitate a sense of community and the common good—but the putative

virtues of autonomy are primarily directed toward the cultivation of independent selfhood. . . . Hard times need a broad sense of duty toward others, especially those out of sight—but an ethic of autonomy stresses responsibility only for one's freely chosen consenting-adult relationships.[7]

Is Callahan right about today's society? If he is, is much of the moral thinking in today's society inadequate? Are there reasons for believing that various forms of minimalism, amoralism, ethical egoism, or subjectivism are true or false? Are considerations about moral character, duties to further good character, duties of gratitude, and duties to help people in need, even distant people, being neglected today? Are these considerations nevertheless legitimate and important? Is there some general theory that will account for all of our duties just as one general scientific theory may account for various physical phenomena? Can such duties be sometimes/always/never overridden by religious conviction? Suppose a father of three dependent children is in danger of dying because he refuses a blood transfusion in accordance with his belief that blood transfusions are against the will of God.

We have asked many questions without providing answers. Brilliant minds have pondered many of these questions for many centuries. Socrates devoted his attention to such questions at the end of the fifth century B.C., and philosophers have been writing about them at least since Plato and Aristotle in the fourth century B.C. It would be presumptuous to believe that we would be likely to come up with very satisfactory answers to these questions without considering the answers given by those who have devoted their attention to such questions in the past. In this book we will look at some approaches to finding answers to these questions. We will also consider the strengths and weaknesses of these approaches.

QUESTIONS

1. What does Daniel Callahan mean by "ethical minimalism"? Perhaps it is difficult to answer the following question, since you have never lived in any age other than the one in which you in fact live. But do you agree or disagree with the claim that ethical minimalism is particularly characteristic of the present age? If so, why might this be true?

2. In several classes, students were asked if they thought that Fred was doing anything wrong in case 3. Most took the position that in some sense Fred "ought" to give five dollars, but that he was not violating any duty, or doing anything wrong, if he did not. Do you agree or disagree with these students? Why? Would it make any difference to your answer if the question was phrased this way: "Would you be doing anything wrong if you acted the way that Fred did?" (Perhaps you might think that what was permissible for Fred would not necessarily be permissible for you, since you may have different ideals, commitments, or religious beliefs than Fred.)

3. What do you regard as the considerations that a person should take into account when choosing a career? Are some of these moral considerations? Which ones? Is the person who takes such considerations seriously a morally better person than one who does not?

4. In sample case 8, Paul referred to the claim rights of innocent people as a basis for a duty not to kill them. The right not to be killed unjustly could be called a *negative right*. The duty not to kill someone is often called a *negative duty* since it is a duty to *refrain from doing* something. My specific right to be paid back by someone who owes me money could be called a *positive right*, since it is the basis of a duty someone has to *do* something—in this case, to pay me back. Are there also general human rights that are positive rights, that is, rights that are the foundation for duties to *do* certain things, such as feed the hungry? What would they be?

5. Distinguish between claim rights and liberty rights, legal rights and moral rights, positive claim rights and negative claim rights, and positive duties and negative duties. Give an example of each (other than those in the previous question). One example can serve to represent several types of rights (e.g., it can be an example of a moral right, a positive right, and a claim right).

6. The expression "No one should criticize what I am doing since I'm not hurting anybody else" is one that might be considered typical of ethical minimalism. What, if anything, do you think is wrong with what is stated or implied in that statement? Suppose it is true that this person is not harming any specific individual who could be pointed to, except perhaps himself or herself. In your opinion, could this person still be falling short morally? In what ways?

7. Distinguish between amoralism, egoism, subjectivism and voluntarism, and libertarianism in terms of how adherents of these positions answer four questions: Do we have duties to ourselves? Can we have duties to others because of our own choices and values? Do we have negative duties to others regardless of our own choices and values? Do we have positive duties to others regardless of our own choices and values?

8. *Some* pro-choice advocates seem to base their views primarily on the simple claim that "it's my body so I may do what I want with it." Is this an example of modern moral minimalism? Much of the social pathology of our time has been blamed in part on the effect on children of the breakdown of the traditional family. It has been claimed that the American idea of no-fault divorce has come to mean for many Americans "no-responsibility divorce," in which the welfare of children is likely to be overlooked.[8] Is this another undesirable effect of a moral minimalism that emphasizes rights at the expense of duties or responsibilities? Discuss.

FURTHER READING

Discussions of minimalism and of the proper place of rights in the analysis of moral issues include the following:

Callahan, Daniel. "Minimalist Ethics: On the Pacification of Morality." *Hastings Center Report* 11 (October 1981): 19–25. Reprinted in *Vice and Virtue in*

Everyday Life, edited by Christina Hoff Sommers, 636–52. New York: Harcourt Brace Jovanovich, 1985.

Churchill, Larry R., and José Jorge Simon. "Abortion and the Rhetoric of Individual Rights." *Hastings Center Report* 12 (February 1982): 9–11.

Perry, Michael. *Morality, Politics, and Law*. New York: Oxford University Press, 1988. See appendix A, "Not Taking Rights-Talk Too Seriously."

Wolgast, Elizabeth. *The Grammar of Justice*. Ithaca, N.Y.: Cornell University Press, 1987. See chap. 2, "Wrong Rights."

A discussion of ethics and career choice may be found in:

Care, Normans. "Career Choice." *Ethics* 94 (January 1984): 283–302.

NOTES

1. Samuel M. Thompson, *A Modern Philosophy of Religion* (Chicago: Regnery, 1955), 25.

2. William Temple, *Nature, Man, and God* (London: Macmillan, 1934), 35.

3. I deliberately avoid the labels "pro-choice" and "pro-life," which have been advanced by the advocates on either side and which are arguably question-begging and self-serving.

4. See Ronald Dworkin, *Taking Rights Seriously* (Cambridge, Mass.: Harvard University Press, 1977), xi.

5. See, for example, Larry R. Churchill and José Jorge Simon, "Abortion and the Rhetoric of Individual Rights," *Hastings Center Report* 12 (February 1982): 9–11.

6. Daniel Callahan, "Minimalist Ethics: On the Pacification of Morality," *Hastings Center Report* 11 (October 1981): 19–25; reprinted in *Vice and Virtue in Everyday Life*, ed. Christina Hoff Sommers (New York: Harcourt Brace Jovanovich, 1982), 638.

7. Ibid.

8. Mary Ann Glendon, *State, Law, and Family* (Amsterdam and New York: North Holland, 1977), 232; Glendon, interview with Bill Moyers in PBS television series "Bill Moyers and the World of Ideas."

2

Relativism, Subjectivism, Minimalism, and Egoism

The expression *moral relativism* is used in various ways. What it is right or wrong for someone to do may depend on circumstances. Among those circumstances would be the moral beliefs of the individual and his or her society. Thus what is right or wrong to some extent depends on, or is *relative to*, the moral beliefs of the individual and of a particular society.

There are extreme forms of moral relativism that substitute "completely" for "to some extent" in this statement. The *social form* of (extreme) moral relativism says there is no standard of right and wrong that is not completely *relative to* the views of a particular society. Furthermore, it says, the standards of various societies are all equally valid or justified. So what is really right for people in society X is whatever society X believes is right.

The *individual form* of (extreme) moral relativism regards all moral judgments as just a matter of the personal taste of the individual. Some who take this approach might say that whatever is right for individual X is whatever individual X believes is right. This approach is more likely to say that because moral judgments are a matter of taste, they are all equally invalid or unjustified. This individual form of relativism is also called *subjectivism* or *skepticism*.

In general terms, moral relativism is the theory that various moral standards are equally valid or equally invalid, and that there is no objective standard of right and wrong or good and evil that transcends the opinions of different individuals or different societies. The denial of relativism is called *objectivism*, which maintains that there is a transcultural standard that has objective validity, that is, that is valid regardless of what

15

particular individuals or societies happen to believe. Much of the rest of this book asks what such an objective standard might be. Thus, if either extreme form of relativism were in fact true, then much of this book would be irrelevant.

RELATIVISM AND SOCIETY

Relativism and Anthropology

Since ancient times it has been known that what one culture regarded as morally good, others regarded as morally bad. Modern anthropology has multiplied the examples of such moral differences. Some examples suggest that what would be regarded as an extreme abnormality in one culture may be thought of as the cornerstone of the social order in another.[1] Some anthropologists, such as Ruth Benedict, have argued that this shows that whether a person's actions are morally right or not depends completely on what culture that person is in. This view is one form of moral relativism.

Such philosophers as W. T. Stace have replied that the anthropologists' argument for relativism really amounts to something like this: Some cultures have moral beliefs radically different from the moral beliefs of other cultures; therefore, there is no absolute moral code. But, Stace maintains, this argument is no better than the following one: Some cultures believe that the world is flat and so have cosmological beliefs radically different from others; therefore, there is no absolute cosmology and the world is flat in some cultures and round in others.[2] So Stace shows that Benedict's observations about cultural differences do not prove anything about moral objectivism and moral relativism.

Other anthropologists have disagreed with Benedict and have stressed the similarities between the moral codes and values of widely different societies.[3] In fact, many of the differences in values and morality between societies turn out to be based on differences in nonmoral beliefs. When, for example, a society is discovered in which it is considered morally right to kill middle-aged parents, this seems to imply a great difference in values and morality from Western society. But when it is discovered that the people of this society believe that those who die will have only as much health and vigor in the next world as they had when they left this life, it becomes clear that this difference in practice is not really based on a difference in basic moral principles. These people are doing what they believe will be best for their parents. So how deep the disagreements about basic moral values among various societies really are is a matter of dispute.

Some philosophers have argued that the anthropological arguments stressing similarities between cultures and those stressing differences between cultures are equally irrelevant to the philosophical question of whether there are objective standards for determining what is right and wrong.[4] It seems to this author, however, that they may not be completely irrelevant. Suppose people are looking at an object from different perspectives and cannot agree as to its shape. This does not prove that it has no definite shape. On the other hand, suppose people looking at an object from many different perspectives do agree as to its shape. This would seem to be *some* indication that it has the shape they believe it has. So also, if people who look at something from different perspectives because they have been conditioned by different societies still agree on something, this would seem to give *some* support to the belief that these claims have some objective validity.

Arguments for the Social Form of Moral Relativism

What reasons would someone have to accept the social form of moral relativism? We may come across good reasons for a person to regard the values of his or her own society as a criterion for deciding what is right or wrong. But why should one regard the standards of one's society as the only standard of right and wrong?

First Reason to Accept Moral Relativism.   The reason that is given by Ruth Benedict is that when people use the expression "morally right," they simply mean "approved by my culture."

Reply to the First Reason.   Now it may be true that isolated primitive people generally see no difference between "morally right" and "approved by my culture," but once a person begins to live with one foot in one culture and one in another, and then asks which of conflicting moral views are more likely to be preferable, he or she cannot think that "right" and "approved by my culture" mean the same thing.

Second Reason to Accept Moral Relativism.   It is well known that college students often tend to be moral relativists. Sometimes when students support the social form of moral relativism, they seem to be arguing in the following manner:

(1) The opposite of relativism (objectivism) implies that my society is right and other societies are wrong.

(2) One should not be so arrogant as to suppose that one's own society is necessarily right and other societies are necessarily wrong.

(3) Therefore, one should reject objectivism and support relativism.

Reply to the Second Reason.   The problem with this argument is that the first premise is false. Objectivism says that there is a transcultural moral truth. It does not say that one's own society has found it. It is perfectly compatible with objectivism to say that one's own society is closer to the truth in some matters, another is closer to the truth in other matters, and that we do not know who is closer to the truth in still other matters. Objectivism simply commits one to the belief that there is a truth to be closer to or further away from.

Third Reason to Accept Moral Relativism.   Some college students also give the following sort of argument:

(1) If objectivism (the opposite of relativism) is true, then we can pass judgment on people in other societies who to the best of their ability are doing what they think is their duty.

(2) It is arrogant to assume that one can pass judgment on people in other societies who to the best of their ability are doing what they think is their duty.

(3)Therefore, one should reject objectivism and accept relativism.

Reply to the Third Reason.   To reply to this argument, one needs to make a distinction between an action's being subjectively wrong and an action's being objectively wrong. If objectivism is true, then some practices of some societies (e.g., slavery in ancient Greece) are objectively morally wrong whether the people of that society realize it or not. But this does not necessarily mean that the members of these societies are morally blameworthy. If people act on the basis of their consciences, using the best moral insight and thinking available to them at the time, then what they do is subjectively right, and they are not subject to blame. So objectivism does not necessarily imply that when we regard the moral beliefs of people in other societies as wrong we are passing judgment on the people themselves or blaming them for their actions.

Arguments against the Social Form of Moral Relativism

If a belief has unacceptable consequences, that is a good reason to reject that belief. Some consequences of the social form of relativism certainly seem unacceptable. Some of these consequences are as follows:

(a) Suppose the moral views held by one's society undergo a change. Presumably, moral criteria should help determine whether such changes are for the better or for the worse. If relativism were true, then moral criteria could not serve this purpose, and it would make no sense to ask whether those changes in moral beliefs are for the better or for the worse.

Since it certainly seems to make sense to ask such a question, relativism is implausible.

(b) The social form of moral relativism seems to imply that everyone in a Nazi society ought to accept Nazi values. This seems implausible to say the least. Are we to say that a member of a Nazi society who deviates from the values of that society is doing something morally wrong? Surely not! So relativism is implausible.

(c) Sometimes it is said that social relativism implies that we ought to be tolerant of the moral practices of people in other societies. But it also implies that we ought to abide by the morality of our own society. If our own society values intolerance, then moral relativism seems to imply that we should be both tolerant and intolerant at the same time. Contradictory results are certainly unacceptable.

(d) A fourth problem can be illustrated by the following example: Suppose that a young man is brought up in a Ukrainian neighborhood in the United States where alcohol is accepted and where vehement anticommunism is understandably strong. Because of a religious experience and a disagreement with the Ukrainian Orthodox Church, he becomes an active member of a Menonnite church that emphasizes sexual monogamy, abstinence from alcohol, indifference to material values and social climbing, and involvement in the peace and antinuclear movements. He then gets a job at a company where his fellow workers vie for status by telling tales of their many sexual conquests. He then goes to a college where most of the students are indifferent to social issues and concerned only with getting high-paying jobs as investment bankers. Suppose he ends up marrying a Norwegian Lutheran farm girl, and after living in a small town in Minnesota for a while and then in Greenwich Village for a while they go to work for the Peace Corps in Zambia. Suppose at every point in this sequence he identifies with several of these societies or groups. What is he to do with the claim that what is right is whatever his society approves of? What is his society? Presumably, moral considerations are supposed to provide individuals with guidance as to how they should live. This form of relativism provides this individual with no guidance. Therefore, this form of relativism is implausible. Furthermore, it seems quite absurd to say that there is no way for this individual to seek to determine which of the values held by communities of which he has been part are better or worse, and that there are no reasons to which he could appeal.

INDIVIDUAL RELATIVISM OR SUBJECTIVISM

Relativism of the Appraiser

The relativism we have been considering would seem to imply that if Barbara says it would be wrong for Hester to have an abortion and Nancy says it would not be wrong, we could decide who is right by taking a public opinion poll of members of Hester's society. One can also think of moral judgments being relative, not to the society of the person whose actions are being appraised, but to the society of the appraisers. On this view, Nancy and Barbara would both be right if they were representing the viewpoints of the societies to which they each belonged. But then why bring the societies to which they belong into it at all? Each person could just as well be regarded as a society of one, setting forth her own point of view, based on her own values. So we arrive at individualistic relativism or subjectivism. An advocate of this position, the English philosopher Thomas Hobbes (1588–1679), wrote:

> But whatever is the object of any man's appetite or desire, that is it which he for his part calleth *good*: and the object of his hate and aversion, *evil*; and of his contempt, *vile* and *inconsiderable*. For these words of good, evil and contemptible, are ever used with relation to the person that useth them: there being nothing simply and absolutely so.[5]

Hobbes is speaking about judgments concerning things we might desire to have or avoid, but the same subjectivist approach can be applied to judgments about whether actions are right or wrong. (Hobbes himself, as we shall see in chapter 5, takes a different approach to the issue of right and wrong actions.)

Noncognitivism: Emotivism and Prescriptivism

One argument against the view that moral judgments are completely relative to the values of the appraiser (whether a society or an individual) is that it is self-contradictory, since it implies in a case like this that it is both right and wrong for Hester to have an abortion. But if Nancy and Barbara are not making assertions, but only expressing their personal tastes, then they are not contradicting each other any more than if one expressed a favorable attitude toward chocolate ice cream and the other expressed an unfavorable attitude toward it.

Some philosophers have in fact maintained that when we say something like "Deliberately killing innocent people is wrong," we are not saying anything that could be true or false, but are only expressing a personal feeling or attitude about killing innocent people (a position called *emotivism*).[6] Others say that we are expressing such an attitude, making a commitment to act in accordance with it, and making a recommendation to other people to act on the same attitude (a position called *prescriptivism*).[7] These positions also go by the name of *noncognitivism*, since they claim that there are no true moral judgments that convey knowledge (cognition) and no false moral judgments that convey misinformation.

What seem to be moral judgments are only recommendations and expressions of feeling, taste, or attitude.

Arguments against Noncognitivism

But there are differences between moral judgments and matters of taste. When our tastes change, we do not think of our earlier tastes as wrong, but when our moral views change, we regard our former views as mistaken. Second, people do not use such terms as "good," "bad," "right," and "wrong" only to *express* tastes or attitudes. They also use these terms when they ask questions about what their moral views should be when they have not yet decided what attitude to adopt, or when they begin to question attitudes they have. Third, if moral views are matters of taste, then no one would have a good reason to reflect on whether they should be changed or not, since there would be no way to decide whether any changes would be for the better or for the worse. But this seems undesirable and implausible.[8]

Degrees of Individual Relativism/Subjectivism/Skepticism

Suppose the young man who has been part of many subcultures asks what his moral views should be. He tries to sort out the different moral views that he has come into contact with to arrive at some general principles by which he can judge specific cases. Perhaps he concludes that he has found a set of exceptionless principles which he believes to be demonstrably true and which could provide the right answer for any moral dilemma he or anyone else might face. This is an extreme position sometimes called *absolutism*. There is also the opposite extreme. Perhaps he concludes that there are no objectively true moral judgments; that if there were any, we would have no idea of what they were; and that if we did have any idea of what they were, we could not be confident enough of them to apply them to anyone other than ourselves. This reflects complete *skepticism* or *subjectivism*. Moral judgments would not have validity in terms of any objective standard beyond one's own subjective values.

There are also all sorts of intermediate positions between these two extremes.[9] The young man might conclude that there are exceptionless principles that can decide some cases, but not all, or that there are principles that are generally reliable, but not exceptionless, or that there are principles that are more plausible than any alternatives, but that could not be proved with certainty. It is not necessary for a position to be on the extreme absolutist end of the spectrum to avoid subjectivism or extreme relativism. If there are some moral judgments of which we can be reasonably sure, then the subjectivism or relativism of the appraiser as a general theory is false.

FURTHER PROBLEMS WITH SUBJECTIVISM

There are additional problems with subjectivism or individual relativism. Three of them are discussed here.

There are some moral judgments that we can be reasonably sure of, and the reasons to believe that those judgments are true are stronger than any reasons we could have to believe that relativism is true.

One argument against extreme relativism or subjectivism is given by Renford Bambrough.[10] We know that a six-year-old child who is to undergo an operation that would be very painful without an anesthetic should be given an anesthetic. It would be morally wrong not to give the child the anesthetic if it is available. Therefore, there is at least one moral judgment we know to be true. Suppose someone gives an argument for moral subjectivism that goes like this: If X is true, then subjectivism is true, and X is true, therefore subjectivism is true. That can be countered with another argument. If subjectivism is true, then the moral judgment about the child and the anesthetic is false. But that moral judgment is not false; therefore subjectivism must be false. Which argument is stronger? The soundness of the first argument depends on X's being true (whatever X is). The soundness of the second argument depends on our judgment about giving the child the anesthetic being true. But there is nothing that X could stand for that we could be more certain about than the judgment about giving the child the anesthetic. Therefore, the argument that subjectivism is false must be stronger than the argument that it is true.

Relativism may be the appropriate position to take about *some* issues, either because there is no correct position, or because we are incapable of deciding what it is. But the time to decide whether this is the case, and whether a particular matter is one of those issues, is after we have thought hard about it, not before.

No one really lives as if he or she believed relativism to be true.

A major problem with extreme relativism is that it is doubtful whether there is anyone who consistently believes in it. While some anthropologists may claim to, they often then argue that tolerance is an absolute value, which it obviously cannot be if there are no absolute values. College students may justify their adoption of values different from those of their parents by appealing to relativism. However, usually they have not faced up to the consequences of the claim that *all* values and standards are relative to the individual or the society that holds them. Such a consequence would be that trying to save a drowning child is no better than ignoring her, laughing at her, or throwing rocks at her. We would have to conclude that there is nothing to choose between the values and practices of the Hopi and those of the Dobu, between those of the Franciscans and those of the Mafia, or between those of Mother Teresa and those of Hitler's SS.

Individualistic relativism may be a cop-out.

It has been claimed by some that relativism, when expressed by most people, is nothing but a cop-out. According to these critics, it means the following: "Everybody should tolerate *my* opinions; nobody should criticize them no matter how self-serving or poorly thought out they might be." Perhaps another component meaning is, "If in exchange for this tolerance I have to tolerate everyone else's opinions, well, so be it." For such people, relativism is not a philosophical position, "but rather a defense mechanism for protection against having to maintain any position or make any serious critical (reflective) effort."[11] It is the lazy person's way out to appeal to relativism in order to defend his or her choices or values rather than bring forward reasons why they are preferable to those of the people with whom one is disagreeing.

OBJECTIVISM AND HYPOTHETICAL CONSENSUS

We in fact do not treat all moral judgments as equally acceptable. If we are discussing a moral issue and we know that one person is influenced by irrational prejudice or by a concern for his or her vested interests, then we tend to dismiss that person's views. We also tend to dismiss the claims of a person who lacks any knowledge or understanding of some of the facts, or of the feelings and interests of some of the people affected, or of the likely consequences of a certain course of action. When involved in a discussion, we say, "If you weren't so prejudiced, or so uninformed, or your interests weren't so affected, you would think otherwise." Since people have different prejudices, different vested interests, and different gaps in their knowledge, the more they are influenced by these factors, the more widely their judgments will diverge. Conversely, the less people are influenced by these factors, the more likely their judgments will converge.

Thus it has been suggested that when we say that an action is (objectively) wrong, we are appealing to a consensus—not any existing consensus, but a consensus that *would* exist if everyone managed to travel the road of divesting themselves of irrational prejudice, selfishness, and ignorance to its very end.[12] Some people, called *intuitionists*, would say that as people move in that direction they progressively rid themselves of impediments to seeing the property of wrongness that certain actions exhibit. According to others, to say that an act is wrong is simply to say that it would be disapproved of by people considering it from an ideal point of view from which prejudice, ignorance, and selfishness have been eliminated. This is sometimes called the *ideal observer theory* or the *impartial spectator theory*.[13]

A legitimate question is: At what point would people in fact reach a consensus in such an ideal situation? A believer in God might tend to think that people, since they all have the same basic God-given nature, would reach a consensus when the distorting effects of prejudice, selfishness, self-righteousness, and other forms of sin were removed. Other people might be less confident of such a hypothetical consensus on many matters. But this difference may be only a matter of degree. Even where we are now, far from having eliminated the influence of human ignorance, folly, and evil, we can reach almost universal consensus on some matters, for example, on the wrongness of depriving the young child who is being operated on of an available anesthetic.

We dealt earlier with the question of whether present agreement between societies is relevant to what is actually right or wrong. We suggested that agreement might be relevant. Now we see that this is because examples of actual consensus support the possibility of an ideal consensus to a greater degree than examples of actual disagreement undermine such a possibility. Whether people looking at the matter from some ideal point of view would agree on disapproving of something because it is wrong or bad, or whether its being wrong or bad is just a matter of being disapproved of when considered from an ideal point of view, is of theoretical interest but is not of crucial importance for refuting relativism. Perhaps the first is true when we are talking about states of affairs and say something like "pain is bad" (or "knowledge is good"). Perhaps the second is true when we are talking about actions and say, "This act which causes unnecessary pain is wrong."

There are most likely a variety of legitimate moral criteria. In cases in which all or most of the criteria point in the same direction, an ultimate consensus could be achieved, and in some cases a real consensus may already exist. We do not know whether any consensus would ultimately be achieved in cases in which some criteria favor one course of action and others favor a different one. But for morality to be objective, it does not have to come up with one right answer for every situation. We can still imagine human beings in an ideal situation reaching a consensus that some courses of action are beyond the range of the morally acceptable, that some goals are intrinsically desirable and others not, that some character traits are admirable, and so on.

ETHICAL EGOISM

Types of Ethical Egoism

Someone may say, "I do believe in some moral standard; I believe in looking out for Number One." This is the point of view of *ethical egoism*. Whether or not to have an abortion or tell a lie or aid the hungry would be decided purely in terms of how it affects oneself. A person acting from this point of view would probably tell the truth much of the time, since it is usually to one's advantage to be thought of as truthful. But when the potential gain is great enough, then the advantages of lying may far exceed the disadvantages resulting from the risk of disapproval by others or the risk of punishment. Egoism probably dictates to the businessman that he should usually give in to the temptation "to be just a little less moral (according to prevailing standards in business) than his competitors—not enough to be operating outside the business 'moral code,' but enough to secure a competitive edge."[14]

It is not necessarily obvious, however, just what the advocate of egoism is saying. There are several possibilities to which we can attach various names.

	Personal Egoism	Universal Egoism
Weak Version	(1) I recognize no duty to do anything other than what is in my own interest (and so possibly no duties at all).	(3) No one has any moral duty to do anything other than what is in his or her own interest (and so possibly no one has any duties at all).
Strong Version	(2) I recognize no duty to do anything other than what is in my own interest, and I do recognize a duty to do whatever is in my own interest.	(4) No one has any moral duty to do anything other than what is in his or her own interest, and everyone does have a duty to do whatever is in his or her own interest.

Version 1 is nothing but the refusal to think about moral issues. Version 3 is the extreme of ethical minimalism, where the minimum fades into nothing. It is not a moral position, but the rejection of morality. If you show people who claim to accept version 2 or 4 that what they are doing (e.g., getting more and more deeply dependent on drugs) is in fact self-destructive, they may retreat to version 1 or 3 and claim a right to do whatever they wish, whether it is in their own long-range interest or not. Or they may acknowledge that they are violating a duty, but cannot or do not wish to stop doing so.

Implications of Ethical Egoism

If egoists try to adhere to version 1 or 2, they can be asked whether they also accept 3 or 4, that is, whether they believe in egoism for everyone. If they say no, then they can be asked what special characteristics there are about themselves that make what is true for them different from what is true for everyone else. If they have no answer, then it would seem that they do not have any moral position at all. Ethical minimalism is reduced to zero. They are not in a position to give any moral advice to others that others would have any reason to take seriously, nor are they able to make any moral judgments about any situation that does not affect them personally. The only advice that those who adhere to version 2 can give to other people is not to worry about violating any duties, because they have none. Again we have ethical minimalism at its extreme. The only one of the four possibilities that allows a person to discuss someone's contemplated action is version 4.

Criticisms of Ethical Egoism

If minimalism is inadequate, then egoism must be inadequate as well. But it also has other problems. Since it is often to one person's advantage that other people fail to pursue their own interests, egoists would frequently be in the strange position of violating their own principle by arguing in favor of it. In addition, adherents of 1, 2, or 3 would be in the position of not being able to claim that their own would-be murderer is doing anything wrong, and adherents of 4 would be in the same position unless they could show the murderer that his action would be to his own disadvantage. Furthermore, it would certainly be strange to argue, as an advocate of 4 would have to do, that those who sacrifice their own interests to help others or to avoid harming others have not only done something unnecessary, but have actually violated a duty and have done something immoral. Every version of egoism, then, seems to face very difficult obstacles to its acceptability.

Furthermore, if the ideal observer theory is anywhere near the truth, then egoism must be rejected. The fourth version of egoism may be attractive to someone who contemplates the evils (e.g., drug addiction) that many weak and self-destructive people bring upon themselves by failing to pursue their own good. However, it could hardly be advocated by an impartial spectator who also considers the great evils brought about by powerful people who single-mindedly pursue only their own good at the expense of everything else, even the preservation of the earth itself. While egoism may be attractive to the rich and powerful, it is hard to see how it could be advocated by anyone in the position of an impartial spectator who has a full appreciation of the aspirations, needs, and feelings of all people, including the weak and powerless, and an appreciation of the obstacles such people face.

Further Considerations on Egoism and Minimalism

According to version 4 of our egoism outline, one has a duty to pursue one's own good. Pursuing one's own good can be understood as (A) satisfying one's own desires whatever they happen to be, or (B) maximizing one's pleasure and minimizing one's pain, or (C) achieving what is good by some other standard.

Suppose a person asks the question: "Insofar as my preferences are under my control, which preferences should I choose to strengthen and which to weaken?" Position A has no answer to this question. The pleasure-maximizing egoist of position B, however, can give an answer: "Satisfy those desires that will bring you the most pleasure and the least pain." Suppose a person then asks: "Insofar as it is within my power to train myself to find pleasure in one thing rather than another, which things should I train myself to find pleasure in?" Now position B has no answer, but position C can answer, "Train yourself to find pleasure in those things that are really good." If attaining what is really good or ultimately in one's interest is difficult, then the fourth version of egoism would not be a version of moral minimalism.

Another criticism of the first two versions of egoism is that trying to live according to them is self-defeating. In the use of drugs, an ever-increasing negative reaction follows a pleasurable experience and comes more and more to outweigh the pleasurable experience itself. The result is that one seeks the drug no longer primarily for pleasure, but rather to counteract the pain of the negative reaction. Thus addiction arises. But this phenomenon, known as "affective contrast," holds true not only for drug use, but for the quest for pleasurable experiences generally. So, as psychologist Barry Schwartz writes, "the pursuit of pleasure is a perpetual wild goose chase. It requires people to be always on the lookout for new things."[15]

Egoism, Social Responsibility, and the Social Good

If egoism means satisfying one's desires whatever they happen to be, then obviously there is a great deal of potential for conflict between one person's interests and another's, and between egoism and social responsibility. If one's good is thought of as pleasure, then there is still potential for conflict. But the degree to which there is a conflict between egoism and social responsibility will depend on what one finds pleasure in doing or having. If one's goal is to achieve what is really worthwhile, as defined in some other way, then it is not as obvious that there must be some chasm between self-interest and social responsibility, or some deep conflict between the good life for one person and the good life for another. It will depend on what is ultimately worthwhile for human beings. This question will be returned to later.

PSYCHOLOGICAL EGOISM

What Psychological Egoism Is

There is another position, also called egoism, which has to do not with what human beings should do, but with what they are able to do. This position, called *psychological egoism*, maintains that human psychology is so constructed that human beings automatically do whatever they think furthers their own interests, or, in some versions, maximizes their pleasure and minimizes their pain. It is a position that can be used to support ethical egoism and minimalism. If no human beings are psychologically capable of doing anything other than what they perceive to be in their own interest, then it is pointless to regard them as having any duty ever to sacrifice their own interest for the sake of others.

Psychological egoism is another position associated with the name of Thomas Hobbes. We can see some of its implications in Hobbes's political philosophy. If human beings are incurably egoistic, then it is pointless to try to make society safer and more stable by trying to change them or by urging them to be anything else. Rather, social arrangements should be such that what a person finds to be in his or her self-interest (e.g., not getting punished, and so obeying the law) is not destructive of society. We will see how Hobbes tried to promote such arrangements when we look at social contract ethics in chapter 5. Modern society, on the whole, still tends to accept those views of Hobbes's that are conducive to moral minimalism. Liberals try to reduce crime by improving job opportunities, thereby making alternatives to a life of crime more attractive to an egoist. Conservatives try to reduce crime by increasing punishments, so as to make a life of crime less attractive to an egoist. Both tend to neglect the possibility that crime is due in part to a failure of human moral development, and that it can be cured *in part* by producing less egoistic people.[16] And yet this cure is the one most compatible with the teachings of ancient philosophers, such as Plato and Aristotle (both of the fourth century B.C.), as well as with the teachings of most of the world's great religions. Indeed, it was the answer that Confucius gave when seeking to reform a society torn by conflict and disorder.

The Case against Psychological Egoism

There are many arguments against psychological egoism. There is, for example, the historical argument, which contends that there have been periods in history when conditions were such that a rise in crime would be expected, but did not occur—precisely because massive efforts at improving moral development were remarkably successful, contrary to Hobbes's assumptions.[17] Many other arguments against psychological egoism have been set forth, most notably by Bishop Joseph Butler (1692–1752).[18] Psychological egoism assumes that there are only two kinds of motives for action. Actions could be egoistic and motivated by a desire for one's own happiness, or they could be altruistic and aimed at the happiness of others. But, according to psychological egoism, since no actions in fact are of the second sort, all must be of the first sort.

However, as Butler pointed out, psychological egoism begins with an obvious oversimplification. There is no reason to believe that there are only two possibilities. Some people are self-destructive and want to kill themselves or injure themselves. Some people want to get revenge and to harm someone, even if they destroy their own lives in the process. In these cases, people's motives are neither egoistic nor altruistic. Thus, it is false that all actions fit into the category of actions motivated by a desire for one's own happiness. Since not all actions fit into the first category, they may in fact fit into many categories, including the second, the category of altruistic actions. Some people want to reward another person and to see that person happy. Some people want to see various political movements in distant countries succeed or fail even though they have no expectation that such success or failure will affect them personally.

Some supporters of psychological egoism claim that the person who wants to see a political movement succeed, or someone else harmed or benefited, is in fact motivated by a desire for his or her own happiness, that is, the happiness he or she will feel when the desired goal is achieved. But this defense of psychological egoism seems to be mistaken. If the person did not have a desire to see these things occur, independent of any desire for personal happiness, then seeing them occur would not have any effect on his or her happiness. Furthermore, people can have a desire for things to be accomplished after their own deaths. They will not see these things happen and thus will not receive any personal benefit or happiness from their happening. They may receive happiness from the thought of these things happening in the future. But unless they first wanted them to happen for their own sakes, the thought of their happening would not bring them happiness. Psychological egoism is, therefore, false and cannot legitimately be appealed to as a support for ethical egoism or any form of ethical minimalism.

QUESTIONS

1. Write down your definitions of moral relativism, the social form of moral relativism, subjectivism or the individualist form of moral relativism (making clear the similarities and differences), the impartial spectator or ideal observer theory, ethical egoism, and psychological egoism. See if what you have written conforms to the definitions given in the chapter.

2. Do you think that the fact that different cultures have different moral ideas does support the view that there is no transcultural truth in matters of right and wrong? Do you think the fact that there are similarities between cultures supports the opposite view?

3. Were Jesus, Gandhi, the people who crusaded against dueling when it was an accepted practice, and the people who crusaded against slavery when it was widely accepted immoral people because they violated the standards of the societies of which they were a part? Does the social form of moral relativism imply that they were? If they were not, does this discredit moral relativism?

4. Would the widespread acceptance of the individualistic form of moral relativism and/or subjectivism lead to moral chaos? Why or why not? Is it already leading to moral chaos, as some have claimed?

5. A few hundred years ago in Japan, it was important to a samurai warrior to test his new sword to see if it worked properly, that is, if it would slice through a human being from the shoulder to the opposite flank with one stroke. He would test it by trying it out on almost any passerby who was not another samurai. How might a samurai try to defend such a practice philosophically? How successful could he be?[19]

6. Does the social form of moral relativism imply that it is improper for us to criticize the practice mentioned in question 5? If so, does it also mean that we cannot criticize apartheid in South Africa? Does it also imply that people outside the mainstream of American culture, such as Native Americans and citizens of Third World countries, cannot legitimately criticize anything in American culture? Is this "moral isolationism" plausible?

7. Can you restate Renford Bambrough's argument against the individual form of relativism or subjectivism? If you believe subjectivism is correct, how would you reply to his argument? Even if relativism is not correct, how effective do you think Bambrough's argument is?

8. Do you think that the author is right in saying that in spite of what people claim, no one really consistently believes in moral subjectivism, or acts as if he or she believes in it?

9. Many people, going back to Plato in the fourth century B.C., have been disturbed by the often dogmatic relativism of college-age young people, although such relativism is said to be even more prevalent today. The writer referred to in the text, Stephen Satris, was thinking of such young people when he referred to those for whom relativism is a cop-out. Another writer, Robert Fullinwider, agrees with Satris that the relativism of students is usually not a well-thought-out position. Satris evaluates such relativism very negatively, claiming that it is nothing but "a defense mechanism for protection against having to maintain any position or make any serious critical (reflective) effort."[20] Fullinwider, on the other hand, evaluates it less negatively, believing that student remarks such as "Who's to say?" and "That's just your opinion" are not really expressions of relativism, but "clumsy ways of rejecting the idea that moral judgments derive their validity just from being said by authorities."[21] Young people, he says, "have moral responses to instances of authority abused or insensitively used," but because they don't know any other way to respond to such instances, they protest against them with vocabulary that sounds relativistic, though in fact they are not really relativists. The author of this text presents some additional reasons why students support the social form of relativism. Which of these authors, if any, do you believe is closer to the truth?

10. Are there any important practical differences between the various forms of ethical egoism on one hand and subjectivism or individualistic relativism on the other? What would they be?

11. What is the difference between psychological egoism and ethical egoism? If you accept psychological egoism, must you also accept ethical egoism? If you accept ethical egoism, must you also accept psychological egoism?

12. There is a story, probably apocryphal, that someone saw Thomas Hobbes giving money to a beggar and asked him whether this act of kindness didn't refute his theory of psychological egoism. Hobbes answered that he acted in his own interest because giving money to the beggar made him feel better. How successful a defense of psychological egoism did Hobbes make? What would the author of the text say about it?

FURTHER READING

Relativism is discussed in the following:

Ladd, John, ed. *Ethical Relativism*. Belmont, Calif.: Wadsworth, 1973.

Pojman, Louis. "A Critique of Ethical Relativism." In Louis Pojman, ed. *Ethical Theory: Classical and Contemporary Readings*. Belmont, Calif.: Wadsworth, 1989, 24–32.

Stace, W. T. *The Concept of Morals*. New York: Macmillan, 1937. See chaps. 1 and 2.

Subjectivist views are defended in:

Ayer, A. J. *Language, Truth, and Logic*. New York: Dover, 1946. See pp. 102–3, 107–9.
Mackie, J. L. *Ethics: Inventing Right and Wrong*. Baltimore: Penguin, 1977. See pp. 15–49.
Russell, Bertrand. *Religion and Science*. Oxford: Oxford University Press, 1935. See chap. 9.

Subjectivist views are discussed in:

Blanshard, Brand. "The New Subjectivism in Ethics." *Philosophy and Phenomenological Research* 9 (March 1949): 504–11.
Fishkin, James. *Beyond Subjective Morality*. New Haven: Yale University Press, 1984.
Warnock, G. J. *Contemporary Moral Philosophy*. New York: St. Martin's Press, 1967. See chaps. 3 and 4.
Warnock, Mary. *Ethics Since 1900*. New York: Oxford University Press, 1960. See chap. 4.

Ethical egoism is defended in:

Rand, Ayn. *The Virtue of Selfishness*. New York: New American Library, 1964.

For both ethical and psychological egoism, see:

Milo, Ronald D., ed. *Egoism and Altruism*. Belmont, Calif.: Wadsworth, 1973.

The self-defeating character of hedonistic and similar varieties of egoistic living are discussed in:

Schwartz, Barry. *The Battle for Human Nature: Science, Morality, and Modern Life*. New York: Norton, 1986. See pp. 162–66.
Solomon, R. L. "The Opponent Process Theory of Acquired Motivation." *American Psychologist* 35 (August 1980): 691–712.

NOTES

1. See Ruth Benedict, "Anthropology and the Abnormal," *Journal of General Psychology* 10 (1934): 59–80 (reprinted in numerous anthologies), and Benedict, *Patterns of Culture* (Boston: Houghton Mifflin, 1961), 233–40.
2. W. T. Stace, *The Concept of Morals* (New York: Macmillan, 1937), chaps. 1 and 2. See also Henry Veatch, *Rational Man* (Bloomington, Ind.: University of Indiana Press, 1962), 32–46.

3. See Ralph Linton, "The Problem of Universal Values," in *Method and Perspective Anthropology*, ed. Robert F. Spencer (Minneapolis: University of Minnesota Press, 1954), 145–68; Clyde Kluckhohn, "Ethical Relativity," *Journal of Philosophy* 52 (November 1955): 663–76; and Solomon Asch, *Social Psychology* (Englewood Cliffs, N.J.: Prentice-Hall, 1952), chaps. 12 and 13.

4. See Paul Taylor, "Social Science and Ethical Relativism," *Journal of Philosophy* 55 (January 2, 1958): 32–44.

5. Thomas Hobbes, *Leviathan* (1651), parts I and II, ed. Herbert W. Schneider (Indianapolis: Bobbs-Merrill, 1958), pt. I, chap. 6, p. 53.

6. Such a position was taken by A. J. Ayer in *Language, Truth, and Logic* (New York: Dover, 1946), 102–3, 107–9. See also Bertrand Russell, *Religion and Science* (Oxford: Oxford University Press, 1935), chap. 9, and C. L. Stevenson, *Ethics and Language* (New Haven: Yale University Press, 1944). For a discussion of such views, see G. J. Warnock, *Contemporary Moral Philosophy* (New York: St. Martin's Press, 1967), chaps. 3 and 4; and Mary Warnock, *Ethics Since 1900* (New York: Oxford University Press, 1960), chap. 4.

7. Such a position was argued for by R. M. Hare in *The Language of Morals* (New York: Oxford University Press, 1952) and *Freedom and Reason* (New York: Oxford University Press, 1963).

8. These and other criticisms are found in Richard Brandt, *Ethical Theory* (Englewood Cliffs, N.J.: Prentice-Hall, 1959), chap. 8; Kurt Baier, *The Moral Point of View* (Ithaca, N.Y.: Cornell University Press, 1958), chap. 1; and Brand Blanshard, "The New Subjectivism in Ethics," *Philosophy and Phenomenological Research* 9 (March 1949): 504–11.

9. See James Fishkin, *Beyond Subjective Morality* (New Haven: Yale University Press, 1984).

10. See Renford Bambrough, "A Proof of the Objectivity of Morals," in *Understanding Moral Philosophy*, ed. James Rachels (Belmont, Calif.: Dickenson, 1976), 45–53. The same argument is also in Bambrough, *Moral Skepticism and Moral Knowledge* (Atlantic Highlands, N.J.: Humanities Press, 1979).

11. Stephen Satris, "Student Relativism," *Teaching Philosophy* 9 (September 1986): 199. Other interpretations of "student relativism" can be found in Robert Fullinwider, "The Menace of Moral Relativism," *QQ: Report from the Center for Philosophy and Public Policy* 7 (Spring/Summer 1987): 12–14, and in Roger Paden, "The Student Relativist as Philosopher," *Teaching Philosophy* 10 (June 1987): 97–102.

12. See William Frankena, *Ethics*, 2nd ed. (Englewood Cliffs, N.J.: Prentice-Hall, 1973), 112.

13. See, for example, F. C. Sharp, "Hume's Ethical Theory and its Critics," *Mind* 30 (1921): 54.

14. Graham Briggs, quoted in Timothy Blodgett, "Showdown on Business Bluffing," in *Harvard Business Review* (May–June 1968); reprinted in *Ethical Issues in Business*, ed. Thomas Donaldson and Patricia H. Werhane (Englewood Cliffs, N.J.: Prentice-Hall, 1979), 57.

15. Barry Schwartz, *The Battle for Human Nature: Science, Morality, and Modern Life* (New York: Norton, 1986), 163.

16. See James Q. Wilson, "Crime and American Culture," *Public Interest* 70 (Winter 1983): 22–49.

17. Ibid.

18. See Bishop Joseph Butler, *Fifteen Sermons Preached at the Rolls Chapel*, London: Bell, 1726), preface, sermon I, sermon XI. These are also found in *Five Sermons Preached at Rolls Chapel*, ed. Steven Darwell (Indianapolis: Hackett, 1983). See also C. D. Broad, *Five Types of Ethical Theory* (London: Routledge and Kegan Paul, 1930; Totowa, N.J.: Littlefield, Adams, 1965), chap. 3.

19. The question comes from Christina Hoff Sommers in *Vice and Virtue in Everyday Life*, 2nd ed., ed. Christina Hoff Sommers and Fred Sommers (New York: Harcourt Brace Jovanovich, 1989), 168. The example of the samurai is from Mary Midgley, *Heart and Mind* (New York: St. Martin's Press, 1981). It is reprinted as "Trying Out One's New Sword," in Sommers, *Vice and Virtue*, 162–68.

20. Satris, "Student Relativism," 199.

21. Fullinwider, "Menace of Moral Relativism," 13.

3

Ethics and Religion

RELIGIOUS ETHICS IN THE NEAR EASTERN AND WESTERN TRADITIONS

In the lives of many people, religion and ethics are inseparable. For many Jews, Christians, and Muslims, what is morally wrong is simply what is contrary to the will of God. In this chapter, we will (1) look at the religious traditions that have most influenced moral thinking in the Western world, (2) consider the question of how religious and nonreligious sources for thinking about morality might best be related to each other, and (3) consider some of the moral teachings of the Asian religions. (chapters 4 and 10 also touch on these concerns.) We begin by looking at the Hebrew Scriptures (which Christians call the Old Testament).

THE COVENANT AND ETHICS OF THE HEBREW SCRIPTURES

The early Hebrews were a seminomadic people for whom treaties or covenants were of utmost importance and were considered sacred. In the Near East, there were treaties between kings and smaller tribes. If a powerful king chose to make a treaty, then he was regarded as bound to fulfill his promises. The people of Israel understood their relationship to God on the model of such a treaty. Their scriptures contain few explanations of why certain laws or commands were good ideas for the community; they are presented as simply commanded by God. When reasons are given, they usually refer to past events in history—for example, the Israelites should obey God's command to pursue justice because God is just and delivered them from unjust slavery in Egypt. The Ten Commandments (Exod. 20:1–17; Deut. 5:1–22), in particular, state the people's duties under the covenant or treaty. They exclude those kinds of actions, including intentions (the prohibition against coveting), that are not in keeping with the nature of the bond between Israel and God. Much of Jewish law is case law that grew out of the attempt to apply these commandments to changing situations.[1]

THE BASIC THEMES OF JEWISH ETHICS

A principal Jewish ideal is the sanctification of life, that is, making life holy. A Jewish author writes as follows:

> The Jewish conception of ethical or moral conduct implies the following of a standard of right action that is universally valid, for its source is God Himself, and every action is measured by the degree to which it approaches that standard.[2]

That standard is the Jewish law summarized in the two scriptural commands to love God and to love one's neighbor. Loving God means, first of all, imitating God.

> Man must endeavor to conduct himself in such a way that his conduct shall resemble, insofar as there can be a resemblance, God's action as it is conceived and manifested in the world and in life. This is the meaning of all the laws and commandments given in the Torah [the first five books of the Hebrew Scriptures].[3]

The second commandment was also all-pervasive. A great scholar of early Judaism wrote: "The ideal of the religion of Israel was society in which all the relations of men to their fellows were governed by the principle, 'You must love your neighbor as yourself.' "[4] This was expressed in a concern for social justice. Will Herberg writes, "The passion for social justice runs through Judaism from the earliest writings to the present day."[5] Isaiah 5:16 says, "The Lord of Hosts is exalted in justice." Amos 5:23 says, "Take away from me the noise of your songs, . . . but let justice roll down like waters, and righteousness like an ever-flowing stream." The command to seek justice not only was part of the regulations of the Jewish people's covenant with God, but was also regarded as part of the commandments that God had given to all mankind, and was even regarded as standing first among such commands.

Related to the idea of justice is the idea of equality. For the Greeks, justice was seeing that people got what they were entitled to, but what they were entitled to could depend on social position. They had no idea of universal human equality. Ancient Near Eastern law codes prescribed different penalties according to the social class of the victim. The Hebrews saw things differently. Hilary Putnam writes that "The value of equality is . . . a unique contribution of the Jewish religion to the culture of the West."[6] Such equal respect for human beings was to be put into practice by taking up the cause of the poor and oppressed. God showed his justice by taking up the cause of the oppressed, neglected, and forgotten (see Ps. 35:10, Ps. 140:2, Prov. 39:8), and justice was equally the duty of the community. Justice included the negative duty of not oppressing the vulnerable (Deut. 27:19, Prov. 14:31), the positive duty of helping those in need (Prov. 21:13, Isa. 58:7), and the positive duty of speaking "up for people who cannot speak for themselves" and protecting "the rights of all who are helpless" (Prov. 31:8–9). So a righteous person "knows the rights of the poor; a wicked man does not understand such knowledge" (Prov. 29:7). Isaiah 1:17 says: "Learn to do good; seek justice, correct oppression; defend the fatherless, plead for the widow."

The rulers of Israel especially had a duty, as elsewhere in the ancient Near East, to look out for the interests of the orphans and the widows, that is, those people in society who had the least political and economic power and were most vulnerable. Also there was an institutionalized social security system. It was a requirement, not just a matter of charity, to leave a certain amount of one's crops for the poor (Lev. 19:9). There was a concern that no one get so rich or powerful that he or she could use that power to exploit others. Every seventh year (the Sabbatical Year) all debts were to be canceled, and every forty-ninth year (the Year of Jubilee) all agricultural land that had changed hands was to be returned to its original owners. (We do not know to what extent these commands were, in fact, carried out in various periods of Israelite history.) There was a recognition that great inequalities of wealth bring inequalities of power, and that inequalities of power breed cruelty. In addition, there was the command to love and treat justly the individual foreigner who was living in one's land. In times of war, however, there was no mercy for enemy nations, and some duties did not apply to the treatment of foreigners.

POSTBIBLICAL JEWISH ETHICS

As in the Hebrew Scriptures, so in postbiblical Judaism, there is no distinction between religion and ethics. For Judaism, study of the sacred texts is basic, important because it leads to righteous action. "The ultimate imperative of Jewish ethics," according to Will Herberg, "is . . . the affirmation of the living God and the repudiation of idolatry," where idolatry is understood to mean "the absolutization of the relative."[7] Herberg adds: "The imitation of God may be taken as the operative formula of Jewish ethics,"[8] and he quotes the rabbinic dictum, "As he [God] is gracious and merciful, be thou gracious and merciful."[9]

In the midst of Hellenistic society, in which a beggar was regarded as having no rights, Jews continued to emphasize ethical themes from their scriptures, including justice for the poor. When a potential convert to Judaism asked for the shortest possible formulation of Jewish teaching, the eminent first-century rabbi Hillel replied with one version of what we know of as the Golden Rule: "Do not do unto others what thou wouldst not have done unto thee. This . . . contains the essence of the teachings of Judaism; the rest is commentary."[10]

One more element of Jewish thought that deserves mention is its concern for peace. Peace among nations and among large and small social units is a principal aspiration of Judaism, and the person who brings peace is highly regarded.

THE ETHICS OF JESUS AND THE CHRISTIAN SCRIPTURES

Christianity in the Greek and Roman world was one religious movement among others. It differed from many other cults, however, in that moral values were a central concern of Christianity.

Before Christianity became a distinct movement in the Greek and Roman world, it began as one of many subgroups within Judaism. The only scriptures for the early Christians were the Hebrew Scriptures. So Jewish concerns, such as faithfulness or loyalty to the covenant, are important for Christianity as well. Likewise, the Jewish concern for justice and for the poor are continued in Christian writings. A New Testament story, told precisely to illustrate what it means to get the point of Jesus' message, is about a man who responds to Jesus by saying, "Behold Lord, the half of my goods I give to the poor and if I have defrauded any one of anything, I restore it fourfold" (Luke 19:8).

Jesus worked within the ethical traditions of Israel as they had developed up to his time, choosing to emphasize some parts more than others. Jesus identified with and intensified that part of the Jewish tradition that made the command to love God and neighbor supreme and that interpreted all other commands in the light of these. The meaning of these two commands is set forth in Luke 10:25-42, where the actions of the Good Samaritan toward the Jew who had been attacked by thieves illustrate love for the neighbor, and where Mary's undivided attention to Jesus' teaching illustrates love for God. This passage, along with many others, also illustrates Jesus' disregard of divisions between ethnic and racial groups, and his elevation of the position of women (who were traditionally prohibited from being students of the Torah). Unfortunately, this latter advance was reversed by the later church, even as early as New Testament times, despite the Apostle Paul's teaching that in the Christian movement, "there is neither Jew nor Greek, there is neither slave nor free, there is neither male nor female; for you are all one in Christ Jesus" (Gal. 3:28).

As in Judaism, so in the New Testament, the imitation of God (or Christ) is seen as the fundamental basis of ethics. "And walk in love, as Christ loved us" (Eph. 5:2a); "As the Lord has forgiven you, so you must forgive" (Col. 3:13b); "Beloved, if God so loved us, we also ought to love one another" (1 John 4:11). According to the New Testament, the goal of human life is to become a child of God. A child of something or someone is a person who reflects the nature of that thing. A son of anger, in the biblical idiom, is a person who resembles anger itself. A son of God, then, is a person who resembles God. The basis for the ethic of loving one's neighbor as oneself is the imitation of God, as is seen in Matthew 5:43–48, which states that to love one's enemy is to reflect the nature of God, who sends rain on the just and on the unjust.

The emphasis on love for the enemy is one area in which Jesus' teaching may have stressed something in the Jewish tradition in a new way. Love for the enemy relates to the Jewish concern for peace, which is reflected in Jesus' Sermon on the Mount in the beatitude, "Blessed are the peacemakers, for they shall be called sons of God" (Matt. 5:9). Jesus rejected the political agenda of the militant Jewish group known as the Zealots, who favored violent revolution to free Israel from the control of the Roman Empire. Indeed, a Mennonite scholar of the New Testament, John Howard Yoder, has argued forcefully that another distinctively new element in the ethics of Jesus is the complete rejection of violence as a method of achieving anything good in the world.[11]

The themes in the teachings of Jesus are taken up by most of the New Testament writers. Love, which is "patient and kind," "not irritable or resentful," is greater than faith and hope (1 Cor. 13:4, 5, 13). Christians are to think of their abilities as given to them to use for the general good of the community, and not primarily for their own benefit (1 Cor. 12:4–26, Rom. 12:4–8). The Apostle Paul wrote: "Live in harmony with one another. . . . If possible, live peaceably with all. . . . Never avenge yourselves. . . . No, if your enemy is hungry, feed him; if he is thirsty, give him drink. . . . Do not be overcome by evil, but overcome evil with good" (Rom. 12:16–20). Get rid of "wrath, malice, slander, and loud abuse from your mouth. Do not lie to one another. . . . And above all these put on love, which binds everything together in perfect harmony" (Col. 3:8, 9, 14).

THE ETHICS OF ISLAM

Islam is the religion taught by the prophet Muhammad, who lived in Arabia in the sixth and seventh centuries A.D. *Islam* comes from the Arabic word *salam*, which means "peace," as well as "surrender" or "submission." Its sacred book is the Quran (Koran), and it draws on the traditions of both Judaism and Christianity. Huston Smith says that if one looks at Arabia before the advent of Islam, and then afterward, one sees an ethical advance hardly to be seen elsewhere in history.[12]

Before Islam, there was primitive polytheistic religion, barbarism, constant warfare, extreme differences of wealth and poverty, little concern for the poor, infanticide of newborn girls, and widespread drunkenness and gambling. Women were regarded only as possessions. There were no limits on men's sexual behavior. Muhammad taught belief in one God, Allah, who was the source of the Quran, which prescribed, in great detail, how moral reform was to occur. Charity was commanded, including yearly contributions to the poor of two-and-one-half percent of one's total wealth. Muhammad forbade infanticide, had daughters included (though not equally) in inheritance, tightened the wedding bond, limited sexual contact to marriage and the number of a man's marriages to four, and taught racial equality. Islam teaches that "No difference whatever between an Arab and a non-Arab, a black man and a white man, can exist except in righteousness."[13] All of these commands were presumably for the good of humanity, but the proper response was not one of analyzing their consequences, but of submitting to their authority. "In Islam, ethics is inseparable from religion and is built entirely upon it."[14] No act is really meritorious unless it is dedicated to Allah. Islam goes further than most representatives of Christianity in saying that what is right is right simply because God commands it. Islam differs from Christianity in putting less emphasis on God's grace and more emphasis on man's freedom to do good or evil. According to one non-Muslim commentator: "God is the Compassionate, the Merciful—but only to the Moslem, the man who submits unquestioningly and enthusiastically to his holy will."[15]

SCRIPTURAL INTERPRETATION IN
CONTEMPORARY ETHICS

Obviously, Jewish, Christian, and Islamic believers today live in a far different world than that of the writers whose works are preserved in their scriptures. There are various ways of relating those scriptures to today's world. One writer, Allen Verhey, identifies three basic approaches in modern Christianity. According to the fundamentalist view, what is in the

Bible comes from God in such a direct sense that "if a rule or command or any moral teaching is found in scripture, then an identical rule or command or moral teaching is normative for the church today . . . unless the rule or command or teaching is intended to be only a temporary obligation.[16] According to the liberal view,

> if a rule or command or moral teaching found in scripture is the Word of God rather than merely human words, then (and only then) is it binding today and one discovers which words are binding today [not by sorting out the different ideas of scripture but] by attending carefully to contemporary needs and problems, to the Spirit of God in the age.[17]

A third approach, somewhere between the other two, tends to look for the intention behind the biblical commands and to interpret those intentions for the modern world.[18] For example, in biblical times, divorced women were in an extremely precarious economic position, and the intention behind the Christian prohibition against divorce can be seen as a way of protecting the vulnerable—that is, women and children—from the arbitrariness of the powerful—that is, men. The abundant literature of contemporary Christian ethics is to a significant extent an attempt to grasp such intentions, to understand the social situation of the modern world, and to work out the implications of those intentions for that social situation. Contemporary Judaism has its own versions of the three different approaches. Contemporary Muslims, perhaps because they believe that God has issued detailed directives for personal and social life, have generally stayed close to the first of the three approaches in their attitudes to the Quran.

Every interpreter of divine revelation is also guided by tradition, whether he or she is aware of it or not. In Christianity, this includes both the general Christian tradition and specific traditions, such as the Catholic, Lutheran, Wesleyan, Orthodox, and Reformed. Tradition is valuable as a restraint on the possible arbitrariness of the interpretations of any one individual, generation, or movement. If adhered to too rigidly, however, it can also stand in the way of new insight and reform. Some groups, especially fundamentalist groups, seem to believe that they read the Christian Scriptures uninfluenced by such traditions, but this is, in fact, impossible. Not being aware of the fact that one is influenced by a tradition prevents one from being critical of that tradition.

OBEDIENCE TO RELIGIOUS COMMANDMENTS

Suppose God is thought of as commanding something. Why should I abide by that command? One possible answer is that "right" or "good" simply means, by definition, "in conformity with God's will or nature."

This answer is not very successful.[19] A second possible answer is that one should obey because it would be foolish to resist absolute power.[20] This approach has been criticized widely on moral grounds by both atheistic philosophers[21] and philosophers who are religious believers,[22] as well as by theologians. A prominent twentieth-century Protestant theologian, Karl Barth, writes:

> Of itself this [God's power] does not provide us with the basis of the divine claim and the basis of human obedience to this claim. . . . Man as man is still free in the face of power as power. He can sink under it; he can be annihilated by it. But he does not owe it obedience, and even the most preponderant power cannot as such compel him to obey. Power as power does not have any divine claim, no matter how imposing or effective it might be.[23]

Some philosophers give as a reason for believers to obey what they regard as God's commands the fact that God as Creator in a sense has property rights over them.[24] While this is a partial answer, it is not in itself adequate. Presumably your employer has a right to your obedience on company time, but only up to a point. There are various legitimate reasons for disregarding his or her command—for example, that it is immoral, or too dangerous. Perhaps the way to consider the question of why we should regard God's commands as authoritative is to reflect on why we should ever treat anyone as an authority. The most convincing account of authority given by a philosopher is that of Joseph Raz. Raz writes:

> The normal and primary way to establish that a person should be acknowledged to have authority over another person involves showing that the alleged subject is likely better to comply with reasons which apply to him (other than the alleged authoritative directives) if he accepts the directives of the alleged authority as authoritatively binding and tries to follow them, rather than by trying to follow the reasons which apply to him directly.[25]

When we wish to do what is morally right, there may be times when we are more likely to do so by following an authority (e.g., parents, an admired advisor) and times we should rely on our own judgment. We may have good reasons not to pursue the goals an authority wishes us to pursue: They may be evil; they may be unattainable; they may conflict with some other desirable goal. We may also reject such claims to authority on the grounds that the purported authority is no more knowledgeable about a situation, or no more morally sensitive, or no more likely to be free from the influences of vested interest and personal prejudice than we are, or on the grounds that the commands and the practice of the supposed authority are inconsistent. But none of these reasons for rejecting purported authorities applies to God, since God, as frequently thought of, is concerned with a comprehensive good, is capable of achieving all purposes, is omniscient (all-knowing), is not subject to temptations to achieve short-range advantage at the expense of long-range good, is not subject to prejudice or the influence of vested interests, and is not inconsistent in any way. The combination of beliefs about God's being our creator, and God's goodness, omniscience, consistency, and power, would seem to be sufficient to impose on believers duties they would not otherwise have reason to acknowledge.[26]

An objection to using the will of God as a criterion for action is as follows:

> Well, suppose you get what seems to be a command of God ordering you to murder your mother-in-law. You should use your own moral judgment, or the moral views of your society, to decide that God didn't really command that, or that if God did, then God is not good and should not be obeyed. But if you use your own moral judgment to decide whether God really issued a command, or whether God should be obeyed, then why not just use your own moral judgment and leave God out of the picture entirely?

In reply, we can say that in general the Christian moral tradition does not see the issue as a matter of choice between the two possibilities stated above—that is, (a) God's command agrees with independent human moral judgment, so God's command is redundant and can be dispensed with, and (b) God's command conflicts with our human moral judgment, so we have doubts about whether God should be obeyed. There is a third possibility,[27] which is (c) God's commands do not conflict with the best of human moral wisdom, but go beyond it. For example, in the Sermon on the Mount, Jesus says that the prevailing moral wisdom is that you should love your friends, but in fact God commands you to go beyond that and love your enemies as well. Similarly, Christians believe that God's command does not disagree with the prevailing wisdom that a person ought to abide by the minimal requirements of justice, but that it goes beyond these requirements to demand a willingness to sacrifice for the benefit of the poor.

RELIGIOUS BELIEF, RELIGIOUS AUTHORITY, AND HUMAN REASON

Many people today, especially Christian and Muslim fundamentalists, reject philosophy and reason as a basis for morality and use their scriptures (the Bible or the Quran) as their tradition interprets them, not only as the sole guide for personal ethics, but also as the sole basis for the advocacy of public policy positions (e.g., the opposition to abortion and the support of, or rejection of, capital punishment). There are a number of reasons for thinking that there is something wrong with this approach.

(1) One reason is that religious authorities, such as the Bible, often speak in generalities such as "love your neighbor as yourself," and when

practitioners of religious or theological ethics seek to apply these generalities to specific moral issues, their reasoning often becomes very similar to that of nonreligious people thinking about the same issue.

(2) A second reason is that the Western religious tradition generally did not see an absolute contradiction between its teaching and that of its culture. The moral teaching of the Hebrew Scriptures draws on the common traditions of the ancient Near East. The New Testament draws on the teachings of the Jewish and Greek traditions. This is justified in part by the idea that the same God who was known through the Hebrew Scriptures and through Jesus was also known to the pagans through the law of nature. We will look at the natural law tradition in the next chapter.

(3) A third reason is that in a democratic society it is often useful, and sometimes necessary, to reach a consensus on moral issues among people with different religious beliefs, as well as those with no beliefs. Religious injunctions to love one's neighbor and to be a peacemaker support such attempts. This would seem to require that people try to think about and discuss matters of morality in a way that does not appeal only to their different theological beliefs.

(4) A fourth reason is that the religious authority, or some particular way of interpreting a religious authority, might be wrong, and one of the ways of deciding whether it is wrong is using one's own reason, including one's reasoning about morality. Historically, many people accepted Judaism, Islam, or Christianity because they found one of these religions to be morally superior to that with which they had previously been familiar, and supporters of these religions have argued for them on moral grounds. Today Christians, Jews, Muslims, and unbelievers alike use moral arguments against other religious groups. They argue, for example, that the sacrifice of autonomy that some sects and cults require of their members is morally objectionable. They also argue that some religious and quasi-religious movements involve their members in a quest for personal religious or psychic experience at the expense of responsibility toward their families, the community, or the world at large, and they claim that this too is morally objectionable. These examples show that most religious believers, as well as unbelievers, do in fact think that it is a good thing to judge the claims of purported religious authorities on the basis of moral considerations. But if moral considerations are used to judge the validity of specific religious claims, then some moral considerations (though not necessarily all) must be regarded as valid apart from any specific religion. If those who make these judgments try to convince others of them, then they in fact presuppose that others can come to accept the cogency of their moral arguments without accepting their theological beliefs.

Of course, if it is possible and appropriate to judge the religious claims of others on the basis of independent moral criteria, then one has to face the possibility that such criteria will conflict with claims made about the will of God in one's own religious tradition. Suppose you are a believer, and according to your religious tradition (or part of it) God commands something which by other criteria seems unacceptable. What do you do? (1) You may cease to believe that God is good; (2) you may cease to believe that God exists; (3) you may reconsider your views as to what is morally acceptable; (4) you may decide that a certain view of how the will of God is known, although usually reliable, sometimes is not; or (5) you may decide that a certain view of how the will of God is known must be rejected, and make any other necessary adjustments in your system of beliefs. If you previously had a negative view of the idea of divine forgiveness, for example, you may choose the third approach if and when you are convinced that God both grants and demands forgiveness.

Many Christians have chosen the fifth approach and rejected a literalist view that says that if the Bible says something, then it must be true. They have done so on the grounds that it is not possible to believe both that God is good and that God commanded the slaughter of the Canaanites, as different parts of the Hebrew Scriptures claim. Today many Catholics have chosen the same option in deciding that the Church does not speak for God in the matter of the use of contraceptives.[28] A person who regards his or her faith as a commitment to an unmodifiable system of beliefs is doing something that is probably both intellectually and morally objectionable.

ETHICS IN THE ASIAN RELIGIOUS TRADITIONS

To do justice to the variety of Asian religious traditions would be impossible in such a book as this, and the following are very sketchy outlines.

The Religious Traditions of China

The philosopher and political theorist Confucius (551–479 B.C.) was the founder of a tradition that, like Islam, was intended to bring order to a disordered society. Veneration for the proper way of doing things is basic to that order: "Being fond of System is better than merely knowing it. Taking one's delight in it is better than merely being fond of it."[29] Four important ideas of Confucian teaching are the love of one's fellow human beings, loyalty and reliability, reciprocity, and propriety.[30] Propriety means cherishing the rules of the system and playing one's proper role in it. Reciprocity means living by the golden rule, "Do not do unto others what you would not desire yourself."[31] The specific applications of the rule of reciprocity are that one should fulfill the roles of father, son, ruler, subject, older brother, younger brother, and friend as you would wish your father, son, ruler, subject, older brother, younger brother, or friend to fulfill it.[32] Of course it is assumed that you will have the same expectations of your son as your father has of you, and so on, since you will both also have respect for the traditional system. If the proper attitudes prevail, propriety will prevail. Something like the idea of the imitation of God is found in Confucianism with respect to the duties of superiors to inferiors, especially rulers to subjects. "Heaven loves the people, and the sovereign should reverently carry out the mind of heaven."[33]

Another religious tradition of China, Taoism, makes the same point with respect to rulers. It is the love of the people that fits one for being a ruler.[34] But for Taoism the way to rule with love for the people is generally to leave them alone, for the natural person is good. Indeed ethics is primarily a matter of "cherishing that which is within you,"[35] which is the natural goodness of human beings. Desire for gain and for knowledge corrupts that innate goodness. "The perfect man ignores self; the divine man ignores achievement, the true Sage ignores reputation."[36] Since Taoism is concerned primarily with inner attitudes, and not with external duties, we will leave it aside here.

The Religious Traditions of India

Gautama Buddha (*Buddha* means "enlightened") lived in the sixth century B.C. and taught a way of salvation from suffering, misery, and pain. Pain and grief come from failing to attain, or losing, what one desires or is attached to. Happiness, or *nirvana*, is the extinction of passion, desire, greed, and so on, which brings with it the extinction of grief, fear, and sorrow. One seeks to be delivered from this world even while in it. The perspective of Hinduism, from which Buddhism sprang, is similar. According to one writer, if we asked a philosophical Hindu and Gautama Buddha the question, "What must *I* do to be saved?" the answer would be the same: "Salvation veritably consists in overcoming the illusion that any such ego 'I' exists, and the way to this salvation would be described as the overcoming of craving."[37] Edward Conze writes that "the chief purpose of Buddhism is the extinction of separate individuality, which is brought about when we cease to identify anything with ourselves."[38] So a person who has attained the Buddhist goal has in a sense already died to the world.

Much of Buddhism shares the traditional Indian belief in the transmigration of souls and rebirth into another life. How one lives in this life determines the condition of one's soul in the next (the law of *karma*). To be reborn into this world for another life is to face suffering. So one seeks to be delivered from the cycle of death and rebirth in the perpetually recycling world. Whether deliverance from rebirth means extinction or immortality is not always clear. Deliverance depends on a person's realization that he or she is not really an individual being at all. In Hinduism, the individual is actually identical with the ultimate reality of Brahman, the ground of all being. "Brahman alone is—nothing else is. He who sees the manifold universe and not the one reality goes evermore from death to death,"[39] says one Hindu text. Another says, "Where there is consciousness of Atman [that is, Brahman], individuality is no more."[40] When one realizes this truth through concentration, one has achieved wisdom.

Truthfulness, self-restraint, and kindness were valued in early Hindu scriptures and were also developed by such modern Hindus as Gandhi. The Hindu way of life went through many phases and generated many differing forms. Intellectual Hinduism expressed itself in numerous very different philosophical schools. There are sources in the tradition that can give the impression that emphasis on the quest for liberation leaves little to be said about everyday morality and the proper relationship between human beings.[41] But the idea of the cosmic oneness and sacredness of all things ["Brahman alone is—nothing else is"] can be seen as the foundation for certain moral ideals, such as "respect for all forms of life and the duty to do good to all creatures."[42]

Many external actions, insofar as they are matters of moral duty, have to do with fulfilling one's station in life. Family duties were stressed in India, especially obedience by children. Buddhist teachings set out the duties of husband and wife, children and parents, pupils and teachers, friends, masters and servants, and laymen and monks. In Hinduism, moral duty was generally defined as abiding by the rules of one's caste. "Indeed until a century or so ago the acceptance of the caste system was considered by the orthodox to be the sole effective criterion of whether one was or was not a Hindu."[43] Buddhism rejected the caste system and so ended up dying out in India but flourishing elsewhere.

In Buddhism, the Middle Way or Eightfold Path helps one along the way of detachment, meditation, concentration, and personal salvation, with the aim of the ultimate elimination of lust, hatred, and delusion. This is the way of right view, right thought, right speech, right action, right livelihood, right effort, right mindfulness, and right concentration. The parts of this that have to do with external action require the avoidance of untruthful, slanderous, harsh, or frivolous speech; the avoidance of violence, theft, and sexual misconduct; and the avoidance of any occupation that might result in harmful social consequences. It is not possible to follow the way of mental concentration while ignoring morality.[44] Buddhist morality for the layman is also expressed in five commandments that were derived from earlier Hindu sources:

1. To abstain from taking life.
2. To abstain from taking what is not given.
3. To abstain from going wrong about sensuous pleasure.
4. To abstain from false speech.
5. To abstain from intoxicants as tending to cloud the mind.[45]

Since other aspects of the Middle Way have to do with eliminating evil dispositions and developing desirable ones, including compassion, we will return to Buddhism when discussing virtue and vice. Although a person is to behave in certain ways largely because of the way such behavior affects his or her own soul, Buddhists would claim that their approach is not egoistic. "The enlightened person intends the well-being of all, not only of himself. . . . For, in the long run, there is no opposition between what conduces to one's own well-being and the well-being of others."[46]

Asian Religion, Western Religion, and Philosophical Problems

We see that to a certain extent there are differences of emphasis in Asian religions and Western religions. In Islam, Judaism, and Christianity, the evil from which one must be delivered is basically moral evil, and what stands in the way of this deliverance is primarily a moral defect of the will. In Asian religions, there is more emphasis on deliverance from the evil of suffering, misery, and pain, and what stands in the way of such deliverance is a defect in knowledge or awareness, that is, the illusion that one exists as a separate individual self. In Judaism, Christianity, and Islam, there is concern for sanctifying life in this world. The world exists for the sake of being a stage on which righteousness can come to prevail and good deeds can be done.[47] In Asian religions, to varying degrees, there may be more emphasis on escaping this world. For some versions of Buddhism, the existence of contemplative monks on the way to achieving *nirvana* is the justification for the world's existence.[48] In Judaism, Christianity, and Islam, the ultimate goal is the triumph of righteousness. In some versions of Asian religion, "The highest state is one which lies beyond good and evil."[49] In the Western religions, loving one's neighbor must be expressed in relieving physical need. In Buddhism, the positive expression of loving one's neighbor is mostly a matter of teaching the way of deliverance.

The relationship of religion to philosophy in the Hindu and Buddhist traditions is quite different than it is in the theistic religions. The Western religions depend on accepting a controversial belief, namely that God exists and is revealed more in one place than another. Hindu and Buddhist ways of life, however, do not depend on whether one believes in one God, no god, or many gods.[50] So there is nothing like the question of accepting God's command as morally authoritative and relating this to one's own moral insight and reason. Nor did the idea of sin against a personal God appear in India until after it was influenced by Christianity.[51] However, Hinduism and much of Buddhism depend on different controversial beliefs, namely, the transmigration of souls and the law of *karma*.

RELIGION, MORALITY, AND PUBLIC ISSUES

Earlier, it was claimed that moral argument independent of religious presupposition has an important place in ethics, even if moral argument based on religious presupposition can also have an important place for believers, especially for guiding their personal lives. It was also argued that in a pluralistic democracy there are good reasons for seeking to carry out the discussion of public policy issues by appealing to criteria that everyone can accept or at least can see the point of.[52] However, when facing such issues as abortion, the environment, and the treatment of animals, it may not be possible to reach conclusions on the basis of "public" criteria.[53] To decide where to stand on these issues, people have to draw on their personal ideals, values, and experiences, and thus often on their religious beliefs.

> If all people must draw from their personal experiences and commitments of value to some degree, people whose experience leads them to religious convictions should not have to disregard what they consider the critical insights about value that their convictions provide.[54]

Furthermore, it is often impossible to sort out religious and non-religious strands in one's moral ideals. However, the Golden Rule, which is part of most religious traditions, should impose caution when religious beliefs influence public policy decisions. If Hindus became a major political force in the United States, the rest of the population would not want to submit to laws prohibiting the eating of beef, passed for reasons that they would find unacceptable and perhaps incomprehensible.

In the rest of this book we shall focus primarily on philosophical approaches to ethics. This is not to deny, however, that religious teachings of various traditions may have important contributions to make to the moral lives of believers in those traditions and to the communities of which they are a part. In chapter 10 we will discuss the contribution of religious ethics to the subject of virtue and vice.

QUESTIONS

1. If you are an adherent of any of the religions discussed in this chapter, or were brought up in one, compare the author's account of the ethics of that

in this chapter and in the chapter on virtue and vice) with the views with
ou are familiar. Are they similar? Are there any major differences? If so,
wha... e they?

2. If you are Jewish, Christian, or Muslim, give your assessment of the alternative ways of relating the Bible or Koran to contemporary moral concerns. Can you think of any other possibilities?

3. Chapter 1 described the case of Fred, who refused to give five dollars to a needy classmate (page 7). Would it make any difference if Fred claimed to be a Christian, Jew, Muslim, or Buddhist? If you are unsure about your answer, read the biblical passages referred to in the next question. Note that a distinction is sometimes made between subjective duty and objective duty. Subjective duty is what a person reasonably could conclude to be his or her duty, given what he or she was aware of at the time. Objective duty is what an impartial spectator might conclude that a person ought to do. In the ancient world, it probably would have been right for slaveowners to free their slaves, but unreasonable to have expected them to perceive that that was their duty.

4. Refer to chapter 1, question 2 (in the Questions section). Most likely the majority of the students referred to in question 2 were members of Christian churches. A few may have been Jewish. If you are Jewish, read Deuteronomy 22:4, Leviticus 19:9, and Proverbs 21:13. If you are Christian, read some of the following as well: Matthew 25:31–46, Luke 10:29–37, James 1:27, and (especially) 1 John 3:15–17. In the light of these passages, can there be any doubt about what the Jewish and Christian positions are on this question? If not, how was it possible for Christian and Jewish students to take the positions they did?

5. Refer again to chapter 1, question 2. If you consider yourself a believer and never thought of these or similar biblical passages when answering this question, what does that say about the impact of religion on the lives of people in our society? If you consider yourself to be Christian or Jewish and agreed with these other students about there being no duty to give the five dollars, how would you justify your position? How would you respond if someone claimed that you were a hypocrite? Is this the sort of issue on which you can differ with the scriptures of your religion, as you might about whether God really commanded the Israelites to slaughter the Canaanites, or about whether the Apostle Paul's instruction that women should keep their heads covered in church is applicable today?

6. Is the author saying that the religious believer should not be intimidated by the secular outlook of today's society into regarding religion as irrelevant to ethics? If so, do you agree?

7. What are the author's arguments in favor of the idea that neither the nonbeliever nor the religious believer should try to do without nonreligious moral arguments and considerations? If you disagree with the author's arguments, what objections do you have?

8. To what extent is nonviolence an ideal in the various religious traditions considered in this chapter? Is it a realistic ideal? If so, why has there been so much violence throughout history in countries where these religions were prominent?

9. In light of the contemporary ecological crisis, some people have claimed that non-Western religions, such as Hinduism (and perhaps Native American and indigenous African religions), with their emphasis on humanity's oneness with all life and all things, are more appropriate for our times than are Judaism, Chris-

tianity, and Islam. Discuss this claim. Do the Western religions have the resources on which to base a strong ecological ethic?

FURTHER READING

A useful work on the moral traditions of various religions is:

Crawford, S. Cromwell, ed. *World Religions and Global Ethics*. New York: Paragon House, 1989.

Expositions of Jewish approaches to ethics can be found in:

Fox, Marvin, ed. *Modern Jewish Ethics*. Columbus, Ohio: Ohio State University Press, 1975.
Herberg, Will. *Judaism and Modern Man*. New York: Jewish Publication Society of America, 1951; New York: Harper and Row, 1965. See chaps. 9, 10, 13, and 14.
Kasher, Asa. "Jewish Ethics: An Orthodox View." In Crawford, *World Religions*.
Shapiro, Rami M. "Blessing and Curse: Toward a Liberal Jewish Ethic." In Crawford, *World Religions*.
Waxman, Meyer. *Judaism: Religion and Ethics*. New York: Thomas Yoseloff, 1958. See pp. 170–185, 203–390.

Passages from the Hebrew Scriptures that should be read include Exodus 20, Leviticus 19, Deuteronomy 5, and those referred to in the text. Relevant passages from the New Testament include Matthew 5:1–28, Matthew 25:31–46, Luke 11:25–42, Romans 12, 1 Corinthians 12–13, Ephesians 4:25–5:33, Colossians 3:1–4:5, 1 John 4:7–21, and James 1:19–2:13.

Some accounts of Christian ethics from various traditions and ages in history can be found in the following:

The Heidelberg Catechism (1563), questions 104–112. In *The Heidelberg Catechism with Commentary, 400th Anniversary Edition*, with commentary by Andre Pery, 170–93. Philadelphia and Boston: United Church Press, 1962.
Luther, Martin. *Treatise on Good Works*. Translated by W. A. Lambert. In *Luther's Works*, vol. 44, *The Christian in Society*, edited by James Atkinson, 80–114. Philadelphia: Fortress Press, 1966.
Wesley, John. *A Plain Account of Genuine Christianity*, sect. 1, para. 1–15, and "The Use of Money." In *John Wesley*, edited by Albert Outler, 183–88, 238–50. New York: Oxford University Press, 1964.

The deep similarity between Christian and Jewish views is stressed in:

Lapide, Pinchas E. *The Sermon on the Mount: Utopia or Program for Action*. Translated by Arlene Swidler. Maryknoll, N.Y.: Orbis Books, 1986.

_____. "What Did Jesus Ask?: The Sermon on the Mount: A Jewish Reading." *Christianity and Crisis* (May 24, 1982): 139–42.

Books on Christian ethics, from many different perspectives and at many degrees of difficulty, are innumerable. Some of these are:

Collins, Raymond F. *Christian Morality*. Notre Dame, Ind.: University of Notre Dame Press, 1988.
The Common Catechism. New York: Seabury Press, 1975. See pp. 433–527.
Guroian, Vigen. *Incarnate Love: Essays in Orthodox Ethics*. Notre Dame, Ind.: University of Notre Dame Press, 1988.
Hallett, Garth L. *Christian Moral Reasoning: An Analytic Guide*. Notre Dame, Ind.: University of Notre Dame Press, 1983.
Hauerwas, Stanley. *The Peaceable Kingdom: A Primer in Christian Ethics*. Notre Dame, Ind.: University of Notre Dame Press, 1983.
Kotsonis, Jerome. "Fundamental Principles of Orthodox Morality." In *The Orthodox Ethos*, edited by A. J. Philippou, 229–48. Oxford: Holywell Press, 1984.
Manson, T. W. *Ethics and the Gospel*. London: SCM Press, 1960.
Ramsey, Paul. *Basic Christian Ethics*. New York: Scribner's, 1950.
Smedes, Lewis. *Mere Morality*. Grand Rapids, Mich.: Eerdmans, 1983.
Verhey, Allen. *The Great Reversal: Ethics and the New Testament*. Grand Rapids, Mich.: Eerdmans, 1984.
Yoder, John Howard. *The Priestly Kingdom: Social Ethics as Gospel*. Notre Dame, Ind.: University of Notre Dame Press, 1984.

Additional examples of essays on specific moral issues by Christian writers can be found in:

Jersild, Paul T., and Dale A. Johnston, eds. *Moral Issues and Christian Response*. New York: Holt, Rinehart and Winston, 1971, 1976, 1983, 1987.

An account of Islamic ethics can be found in the following:

Al Faruqi, Isma'il R. "Islamic Ethics." In Crawford, *World Religions*.

Discussions of the relationship between religion and ethics can be found in:

Drane, James F. *Religion and Ethics*. New York: Paulist Press, 1976.
Lucas, J. R. *Freedom and Grace*. Grand Rapids, Mich.: Eerdmans, 1976. See chaps. 11 and 12.
Mitchell, Basil. *Morality: Religious and Secular*. Oxford: Oxford University Press, 1980.
Outka, Gene, and John P. Reeder, eds. *Religion and Morality*. Garden City, N.Y.: Anchor Press/Doubleday, 1973.

"Religion and Morality," *QQ: Report from the Center for Philosophy and Public Policy* 6 (Spring 1986): 1–5.
Thomas, George F. *Christian Ethics and Moral Philosophy*. New York: Scribner's, 1955.
Van Wyk, Robert N. "Autonomy Theses Revisited." *Faith and Philosophy* 3 (October 1986): 372–82.

Many of the writings of the Asian religions can be found in:

Yutang, Lin, ed. *The Wisdom of China and India*. New York: Random House, 1942.

For discussions of various Asian religions, see Crawford, *World Religions*. The following are three works on Buddhism:

Coomaraswamy, Ananda K. *Buddha and the Gospel of Buddhism*. London: Harrap, 1916; New York: Harper and Row, 1964.
Little, David, and Summner B. Twiss. *Comparative Religious Ethics: A New Method*. San Francisco: Harper and Row, 1978. See chap. 8, "Religion and Morality in Theravada Buddhism."
Saddhatissa, H. *Buddhist Ethics*. New York: Braziller, 1970.

NOTES

1. This is based on Walter Harrelson, "Law in the Old Testament," *Interpreter's Dictionary of the Bible*, vol. 4 (Nashville: Abingdon Press, 1962), 77–89.
2. Meyer Waxman, *Judaism: Religion and Ethics* (New York: Thomas Yoseloff, 1958), 230.
3. Ibid., 239.
4. G. F. Moore, *Judaism*, vol. 2 (Cambridge, Mass.: Harvard University Press, 1927), 56; quoted in *Judaism and Modern Man*, ed. Will Herberg (New York: Jewish Publication Society of America, 1951; New York: Harper and Row, 1965), 148.
5. Herberg, 158.
6. Hilary Putnam, *The Many Faces of Realism* (LaSalle, Ill.: Open Court, 1987), 44.
7. Herberg, 96, 95.
8. Ibid., 97.
9. Abba Saul, quoted in Herberg, 98.
10. Waxman, 246.
11. John Howard Yoder, *The Politics of Jesus* (Grand Rapids, Mich.: Eerdman, 1972).
12. Huston Smith, *The Religions of Man* (New York: Harper and Bros., 1958), 242.
13. Muhammad H. Haykal, *The Life of Muhammad*, trans. I. R. alFaruqi (Indianapolis: American Trust Publications, 1977), 487; quoted in Isma'il R. alFaruqi, "Islamic Ethics," in *World Religions and Global Ethics*, ed. S. Cromwell Crawford (New York: Paragon House, 1989), 218.
14. Al Faruqi, 212.
15. John B. Moss, *Man's Religions* (New York: Macmillan, 1956), 700.
16. Allen Verhey, *The Great Reversal: Ethics and the New Testament* (Grand Rapids, Mich.: Eerdmans, 1984), 170. Of course there are endless disagreements about what is supposed to be a temporary obligation.

17. Ibid., 170–71.

18. Ibid., 172–74.

19. Suppose we define "God" as "that being who is worthy of worship." If so, then we need to refer to moral criteria to decide whether any being is worthy of worship, for an evil being, even if he were an all-powerful creator, would not be worthy of worship and so would not be properly called "God." Suppose, on the other hand, that we define "God" as "the eternal being who creates all else." Why should we adopt a definition of "good" in terms of obedience to such a being?

20. Supported, for example, by P. T. Geach, *God and the Soul* (London: Routledge and Kegan Paul, 1969), 126–27.

21. Such as Kai Nielsen, "God and the Good," *Theology Today* 21 (January 1964): 50.

22. Such as A. C. Ewing, "The Autonomy of Ethics," in *Prospect for Metaphysics*, ed. Ian T. Ramsey (London: George Allen and Unwin, 1961), 40.

23. Karl Barth, *Church Dogmatics*, vol. 2, *The Doctrine of God* (Edinburgh: Clark, 1957), 552–53.

24. See Baruch Brody, "Morality and Religion Reconsidered," in *Readings in the Philosophy of Religion*, ed. Baruch Brody (Englewood Cliffs, N.J.: Prentice-Hall, 1974). See also R. G. Swinburne, "Duty and the Will of God," *Canadian Journal of Philosophy* 4 (December 1974): 213–17; reprinted in *Divine Commands and Morality*, ed. Paul Helm (New York: Oxford University Press, 1981), 120–34.

25. Joseph Raz, "Authority, Law and Morality," *Monist* 68 (July 1985): 299; also Raz, *The Morality of Freedom* (New York: Oxford University Press, 1986), 46–59.

26. These views are expanded on in Robert N. Van Wyk, "Autonomy Theses Revisited," *Faith and Philosophy* 3 (October 1986): 372–82.

27. An example of the argument against religious ethics that overlooks the third possibility is found in James Rachels, *Elements of Moral Philosophy* (New York: Random House, 1986), 44.

28. See Van Wyk, "Autonomy Theses Revisited," 378–80.

29. *Lun Yu*, trans. by James Ware as *The Sayings of Confucius* (New York: New American Library, 1955), 3:3, 29.

30. *Lun Yu*, 2:22, 4:15, 9:25, 12:2.

31. *Lun Yu*, 12:2; also 5:12.

32. *The Golden Mean of Tsesze*, in *The Wisdom of China and India*, ed. Lin Yutang (New York: Random House, 1942), sects. 13–20; pp. 848–49, 853.

33. *Shu Ching (Book of History)* "Book of Chou, I, Ancient Script," sect. 1; trans. James Legge, in Yutang, *Wisdom*, 733.

34. See *Chuangtse*, in Lao Tzu, *The Way of Life: Tao Te Ching*, trans. R. B. Blakney (New York: New American Library, 1953), 13.

35. *Chuanqtse*, in Yutang, *Wisdom*, 679.

36. Ibid., 631.

37. Ananda K. Coomaraswamy, *Buddha and the Gospel of Buddhism* (London: Harrap, 1916; New York: Harper, 1964), 214.

38. Edward Conze, *Buddhism: Its Essence and Development* (Oxford: Cassirer, 1951; New York: Harper Torchbook, 1959), 106.

39. "Katha Upanishad," in *The Upanishads*, trans. Swami Prabhavananda and Frederick Manchester (Hollywood, Calif.: Vedanta Press, 1948; New York: Mentor Books, 1957), 21.

40. "Brihadaranyaka Upanishad," ibid., 88.

41. R. C. Zaehner, *Hinduism* (London: Oxford University Press, 1962), 14.

42. S. Cromwell Crawford, "Hindu Ethics for Modern Life," in Crawford, *World Religions*, 16.

43. Zaehner, *Hinduism*, 1.

44. H. Saddhatissa, *Buddhist Ethics* (New York: Braziller, 1970), 68.

45. Coomaraswamy, *Buddha and Gospel*, 130; Conze, *Buddhism*, 86.

46. P. D. Premasiri, "Ethics of the Theravada Buddhist Tradition," in Crawford, *World Religions*, 51.

47. Waxman, *Judaism*, 241.

48. Saddhatissa, *Buddhist Ethics*, 56.

49. Ibid., 18.

50. Zaehner, *Hinduism*, 1–2.

51. Ibid., 182.

52. See "Religion in Public Life," *QQ: Report from the Center for Philosophy and Public Policy* 7 (Spring/Summer 1987): 1–5; David Lyons, *Ethics and the Rule of Law* (Cambridge: Cambridge University Press, 1984), 191–92; Thomas Nagel, "Moral Conflict and Political Legitimacy," *Philosophy and Public Affairs* 16 (Summer 1987): 215–40.

53. As is shown by Kent Greenawalt, *Religious Convictions and Political Choice* (New York: Oxford University Press, 1988).

54. Ibid., 145. See also Robert N. Van Wyk, "Liberalism, Religion and Politics," *Public Affairs Quarterly* 1 (July 1987): 59–76, and Michael Perry, *Morality, Politics, and Law* (New York: Oxford University Press, 1988).

4

Natural Law Theory
and Its Antecedents

NATURAL LAW THEORY IN THE BROAD SENSE

Natural Law in History

There is a long tradition in Western society of reference to *natural law*. Belief in natural law in one sense is simply belief in a moral standard that does not depend on the customs or laws of any particular society. Nature is contrasted to custom. The Greek writer Cicero (106–43 B.C.) wrote of natural law as

> right reason in agreement with nature, of universal application, unchanging and everlasting. . . . There will not be a different law at Rome and at Athens, and different law now and in the future, but one eternal and unchangeable law for all nations and for all times.[1]

The concern for having a standard other than the customs and laws of a particular society was an important motivation for the idea of natural law. The person with whom the term "natural law" is most closely associated is the Medieval theologian and philosopher St. Thomas Aquinas (c. 1224–1274). One of his interpreters writes that

> Aquinas wanted to establish some rational standard by which social and political institutions could be judged, a court of appeal as it were, for the rejection of unjust laws. His natural law theory served importantly as a safeguard against government abuses, against the tyrannical assertion that human law was the pure command of the ruler.[2]

When the American civil rights leader Martin Luther King (1939–1968) was in a city jail in Birmingham, Mississippi, in 1963, he wrote a letter responding to those who asked how he could justify calling for obedience to some laws and disobedience to others. Quoting Augustine, he claimed that an unjust law was no law at all, and he defined an unjust law as one that "is not rooted in eternal law and natural law."[3]

Similar ideas are also found in the non-Western world. In the Confucian system that grew up in China, there is the idea of a natural harmonious order of things to which human beings should conform. Conforming to the natural system brings peace and harmony. Deviating from it brings disorder and chaos. A Japanese Buddhist writer who was influenced by Confucianism warned against the introduction into Japan of Western individualism with its "free play of human selfishness." He spoke of principles that are based on "the natural and immutable relations between sovereign and subject, parent and child, with all their corresponding rights and duties."[4]

Natural Law and Revealed Law

As the traditions of the Greek and Roman world came into contact with religions that appealed to the law of God as revealed in their scriptures, "natural law" came to refer to those moral standards that people of various religions should all be able to see as true and binding through the use of reason and "the light of nature" without reference to church teaching or any source of divine revelation. So natural law was contrasted not only with customary law, but also with the revealed law of God, though it was thought to overlap with both. In this sense, the only people who would not be believers in natural law would be moral subjectivists and relativists who believe in no moral truth, or none beyond the traditions of one's particular society, and those religious fundamentalists who believe that human beings are incapable of knowing any moral truth apart from the special revelation of God through their scriptures.

"NATURAL" AND "UNNATURAL" IN NATURAL LAW THEORY

There are other senses of the expression "natural law" as well. To the question, "How do human beings know this natural law?" some natural law theorists appeal to a distinction between what is natural and what is unnatural. Capitalists, for example, claim that since competition and the survival of the fittest is natural, it is therefore good. Some people claim that sexual acts can be divided between those that are natural, and thus sometimes morally permissible, and those that are unnatural, and thus never permissible. In the encyclical *Casti Connubi*, Pope Pius IX wrote that what is intrinsically against nature cannot be morally good. St. Thomas Aquinas claimed that divorce is wrong for a man because it is natural that a father's care for his son should endure to the end of his life, and wrong for a woman because a woman is naturally subject to the man's authority.[5] He also said that suicide is wrong because it is contrary to the inclinations of human nature.[6]

On the face of it, all such arguments seem to be extremely weak. Many things that few people would think are morally wrong are in one sense or another unnatural, such as vaccination, anesthesia, shaving, and civilization; while many things that are in some sense natural seem to be wrong in one way or another, such as revenge, prejudice, or rubbing one's eye when there is something in it. For this type of natural law theory to be at all plausible, there must be a way of specifying precisely what sense of "natural" or "unnatural" is relevant to determining whether an act is right or wrong and why it is relevant.

HUMAN NATURE AND HUMAN FLOURISHING

One answer is that what is morally good for human beings is what is appropriate for a being with the particular kind of nature that human beings have. Natural law is regarded by its supporters as transcending custom and the laws of particular societies because some aspects of human nature are the same for all human beings. The British philosopher David Hume (1711–1776), an advocate of a purely secular natural-law position, based his views on the natural inclination of human beings to serve their own interest, along with their natural, though limited, sympathy for other human beings.[7] Various arguments for capitalism are based on a view of human nature as purely self-seeking.

Why does the fact that human beings have a certain nature support some moral views rather than others? Some of those who refer to "what is natural" probably have no answer. Others answer that because human beings have a certain nature, they will live well or flourish, or find fulfillment or happiness, only if they live in certain ways. According to this view, natural law is the set of principles prohibiting those kinds of actions that interfere with human fulfillment and requiring those that promote it. Rules that protect human life and health, for example, would be rules demanded by natural law. Such rules would be flexible and revisable as knowledge of what protects and promotes health grows and changes.

THE FUNCTION OF HUMAN NATURE
AND HUMAN INCLINATIONS

Aristotle and the Function of a Human Being

One way of relating natural law to human nature is to say that what promotes human flourishing is what is in accordance with the function of human nature. This approach was adopted by St. Thomas from the Greek philosopher Aristotle (384–322 B.C.). Aristotle began his *Nicomachean Ethics* in this way: "Every art and every kind of inquiry, and likewise every act and purpose, seems to aim at some good; and so it has been well said that the good is that at which everything aims."[8]

These various human endeavors, such as military strategy, engineering, or medicine, each with its own goals, are all only parts of life. Is there some other superior goal to which these goals are in some sense subordinate? If there is, this would seem to be the highest good and the purpose of life. Sometimes people spend their lives pursuing certain goals and end up disappointed and unhappy. Perhaps they thought that the goal was worth pursuing for its own sake, and it turned out that it was not. Perhaps the goal was one they thought would be a means to some other goal, and it turned out not to be. We could avoid those tragic disappointments if we begin by aiming toward some goal that would not disappoint us. Aristotle writes:

> If then in what we do there be some end which we wish for on its own account, choosing all the others as means to this . . . , this evidently will be the good or the best of all things. And surely from a practical point of view it much concerns us to know this good; for then, like archers shooting at a definite mark, we shall be more likely to attain what we want.[9]

Is there something that can be identified as a goal or good for all human beings? Aristotle thinks it likely that there is because people, both common people and educated people, generally agree that there is such a good. It is called, in Greek, *eudaimonia*.[10] *Eudaimonia* is often translated "happiness," but a better translation would be something like "human flourishing." Aristotle says that *eudaimonia* consists of doing well and faring well.[11] Faring well means having enough of the good things in life that are not always under one's own control, such as health, possessions, freedom, and friends.[12] But what does doing well consist of? To know whether a carpenter is doing carpentry well, we have to know the goal or function of a carpenter. So, Aristotle believes, in order to know whether a human being is doing well—is flourishing—we have to know what the goal or function of human life is.[13]

The Moral Use of the Idea of Proper Functioning

Later we will deal at more length with the claim that the good is pleasure and the absence of pain, and the opposing claim that the good is fulfilling one's desires or preferences, whatever they are. If we look at a question about medical care, we can see some problems with these answers. Suppose a society tried to distribute medical care in terms of fulfilling desires or preferences. One possibility would be to weigh desires in terms of their number and intensity, perhaps by giving priority to people who were willing to pay the most or stand in line the longest, or who complained the loudest. In such a society, the poorest and sickest could be neglected while face-lifts and tummy tucks were provided to the wealthy. The second possibility would be to try to fulfill all desires, perhaps through the public financing of all medical care. But this could create an ever-expanding, potentially unlimited drain on the resources of society. It would seem to be important, therefore, to give priority to medical services that fulfill needs over those that are merely nice to have. This requires that "need" be defined.

In order to do this, philosophers have had to refer to the normal functioning of an organism. Norman Daniels, for example, defines "health-care needs" as "those things we need in order to maintain, restore, or provide functional equivalents (where possible) to normal species functioning."[14] According to natural law theory, then, if we fail to restore the natural functioning of the human organism by fixing a broken arm or correcting a dietary deficiency, then the natural law is violated. If we fail to provide for hair transplants, however, even to those who feel that they will be miserable without them, we do not violate the natural law.

The Function of a Human Being
and Human Flourishing

Now if we extend the idea of functioning well beyond the physical, so that it refers to functioning well as a total human being, then we could say that those laws that promote normal functioning are in accordance with the natural law and whatever stands in the way of normal functioning violates nature. For Aristotle, normal human functioning, as opposed to normal chipmunk functioning, for example, had to do with a life lived with full use of the distinctively human capacity of reason. When a believer in God speaks of the function of a human being, she or he means the function that human beings were created to fulfill, just as the function of a screwdriver is the function it was designed and manufactured to fulfill. The god Aristotle believed in, however, was not the Creator of the world, since both God and the world always existed, and in fact God paid no attention to the world. Aristotle thought that we can speak meaningfully of the function of a human being, even without belief in a Creator, because we can speak of the function of parts of a human being (liver, arms), and we can speak of the functions of types of human beings in society (carpenters, musicians).

Although Aristotle is probably wrong about this, it is still possible to ask about what is distinctively human. What is distinctively human according to Aristotle is the activity of using the faculty of reason, and the way in which human beings pursue their goals through the use of conscious, purposeful, rational activity. So human flourishing is, at least in part, not some specific activity, but all human activity done well—that is, according to rational principles. Aristotle regards the *eudaimonistic* person as "one who exercises his faculties in accordance with perfect excellence, being duly furnished with external goods, not for any chance time, but for a full term of years."[15]

Human Functioning and Natural Law in Aquinas

Aristotle's position is a version of naturalism but not a version of natural law theory. But suppose one adds to the above considerations the Christian belief that nature reflects the creative power of God. Whatever stands in the way of human flourishing or the normal functioning of human nature would then be regarded as violating the natural law, which is the law of God as known through nature. This would seem to be what Martin Luther King had in mind when he wrote in his letter from a Birmingham jail that "Any law that uplifts human personality is just. Any law that degrades human personality is unjust. All segregation statutes are unjust because segregation distorts the soul and damages the personality."[16]

Distorting the soul would seem to be the same as preventing human flourishing or the full functioning of humanity. This was the view of St. Thomas, to whom King referred in the letter. It is more difficult, however, to decide what the normal function of the human person as a whole is than it is to decide what the normal functioning of the human body is. Natural law theorists have generally said that we can discover the function of human nature, and thus the good for human beings, by looking at the inclinations of human nature.[17]

St. Thomas speaks of three categories of inclinations of human nature. The first category includes those that belong to all beings, such as the inclination to preserve itself in existence.[18] Aristotle wrote: "Life is in itself good and pleasant. We can see that from the very fact that everyone desires it."[19] The second category includes those inclinations that human beings share with animals, such as the inclination to engage in sexual relations and to care for offspring.[20] St. Thomas would certainly say that a tyrannical government that forced people to commit suicide, or that prohibited marriage and sexual relations for all or part of its society, or that took children from their parents to be indoctrinated in state ideology, would violate the natural law as known through these two categories of inclination. (Some of his other, more specific arguments are more dubious. He would, for example, seem to be inconsistent in interpreting the first category of inclination to prohibit voluntary suicide, while not interpreting the second category of inclination to prohibit voluntary celibacy.)

The third category of inclination includes those that are unique to human nature. One of these is the inclination to live in society, or as one writer puts it, "to order life cooperatively."[21] There should be stringent rules against actions, such as lying in court, that tend to undermine the associations and institutions of society that make cooperative life possible.[22] Another is the inclination to know God,[23] or, to put it in a theologically neutral way, the inclination to ask philosophical and religious questions about the meaning of one's life and of the cosmos as a whole. Presumably no animals have this inclination. Aldous Huxley's novel *Brave New World* (1932) describes a society that tries to control heredity and environment in such a way as to produce beings who live pleasure-filled lives but who do not ask religious and philosophical questions. Such a practice would seek to make human beings something other than human, and thus would radically violate natural law.

OBSERVATIONS CONCERNING
NATURAL LAW THEORY

Some people would say that human beings from different times and places differ too much for one to speak meaningfully of "human nature." Some modern proponents of natural law theory attempt to restate the theory with more awareness of human variety by making generalizations about human nature based on the study of various cultures past and present.[24] They would no doubt discard some of the arguments of older natural law theory while retaining others. Other people would reject the whole approach, saying that even if there is such a thing as human nature, why not try to improve on it and replace it with something better? It is, however, hard to see what criteria of being better might get any sort of support from human beings who have the nature they now have. Why should human beings who ask religious and philosophical questions accept any criteria, for example, by which human nature as reconstructed in *Brave New World* could be regarded as better? Religious versions of natural law theory would also say that the nature human beings now have, but with its corruptions removed, is human nature as God intended it to be, so attempts to change human nature, as in *Brave New World*, would violate God's will.

In general, it seems that natural law considerations of this sort may have a worthwhile contribution to make to moral reasoning, especially for those who accept its theological foundations. Some have also defended a minimal natural law theory on purely secular grounds. The position that will be developed later, in chapter 8, can be regarded as a development of natural law theory.

SPECIFIC CONCLUSIONS
CONCERNING MORAL ISSUES

Natural law theory as here developed may lead to very emphatic positions on a few matters. For the most part, however, it is quite unspecific. Christopher Mooney writes:

> Those directives which Aquinas believed were known clearly to everyone are of such a general character as seldom to give specific guidance regarding concrete decisions. . . . [They in effect say] something should be done to preserve life, to organize the family, to stabilize society. In the concrete this "somehow" and this "something" had to be derived from experience and enquiry by way of conclusion from these general principles. "What pertains to moral science," said Aquinas, "is known mostly through experience."[25]

So it would seem that there would be a great deal of difficulty in saying what *the* natural law position on many specific moral issues is. Such positions would depend on arguments concerning what does or does not advance human fulfillment or flourishing. St. Thomas himself acknowledged this element of relativism when he wrote that "in the practical order there is not the same truth or practical rightness for everybody, as far as detail is concerned, but only in general principles."[26] So with respect to personal ethics, natural law theorists might generally recommend that one abide by the moral laws and customs of one's own society, except where these can be shown to be subversive of human fulfillment or flourishing.

Natural law approaches have inspired a wide range of political positions, but, according to the Aquinas scholar Paul Sigmund, they generally have a moderating influence and cannot be legitimately used to support positions of either the extreme right or the extreme left.[27]

NATURAL LAW THEORY
AND THE FUNCTIONS OF HUMAN ACTS

In spite of what was claimed in the last section about the generality of natural law, *some* proponents of natural law theory have derived certain extremely concrete directives from it, including the absolute opposition to most means of contraception. Yet nothing dealt with in the preceding sections would seem to have the slightest relevance to the subject. That is because there is also another version of natural law theory that can be found both in Thomas Aquinas and in some of his modern followers, a version that began to be reemphasized in the nineteenth century. This version refers not only to the normal functioning of human nature in general, but also to the normal functioning of specific human activities, and to what "nature" intends in those activities. The argument is found in the left-hand column below.

A.

1. The obvious primary purpose of the sexual system and its use in sexual activity is to produce children.

2. There are secondary purposes, such as expressing intimacy and providing pleasure to oneself and one's partner.

3. If I choose to realize the secondary purpose but not the primary purpose, and therefore I use contraceptives, I am frustrating the primary purpose and thus acting against nature (while also employing something artificial).

4. Therefore using contraceptives is a sin against nature and thus also against God.

B.

1. The obvious primary purpose of the digestive system and its use in eating is to bring nourishment to the body.

2. There are secondary purposes, such as providing pleasure to the eater.

3. If I choose to realize the secondary purpose but not the primary purpose, and therefore I use nonnutritive substances, I am frustrating the primary purpose and thus acting against nature (while also employing something artificial).

4. Therefore eating food containing nonnutritive substances, like artificial sweeteners, is a sin against nature and thus also against God.

The weakness of the argument against contraception can be easily discovered by creating the argument found in the right-hand column above. These arguments seem to be parallel. Most people would regard the second argument as unsound. Thus the first would also seem to be unsound.[28] In the light of world population problems, there are many reasons to reject the conclusion of the first argument. This natural law argument clearly fails, and the burden of proof is on those who would maintain any other natural law arguments of a similar type on other issues.

HIERARCHY AND NATURAL LAW

Natural law theory refers to human beings reaching the fulfillment that is natural for them. But in the past, it was often thought that not all human beings had the same potential for fulfillment. Aristotle believed that slavery was a bad thing when those who were not natural slaves were enslaved; nevertheless, some people were natural slaves, and there was nothing wrong with their being enslaved. St. Thomas, following Aristotle, believed that women were physically, mentally, and spiritually inferior to men. Such views tend to favor the idea of a natural hierarchy. In the Confucian tradition, the natural and correct order of things is that ruler guides subject, father guides son, and husband guides wife. Women were expected to obey their fathers before marriage, their husbands during marriage, and their sons after the death of their husbands. We find a similar view of hierarchy in St. Thomas Aquinas:

> Therefore just as in the order of nature established by God lower elements in nature must be subject to higher ones, so in human affairs inferiors are bound to obey their superiors according to the order contained in the natural and divine law. [29]

Most thinking people today are likely to say that the tendency to regard hierarchies as natural is due to the tendency of the powerful to rationalize their oppression of the weak, and the inability of many people to envision things as being different from the way they are in their own society. While some people may be superior to others in terms of one characteristic or another (e.g., physical strength), it is hard to see what relevance this has to the subordination of some people to others. In chapter 3 we rejected the idea that human subordination to God could be argued for on the basis of divine power. How much less could the subordination of one group (e.g., women) to another (e.g., men) be argued for on the basis of differences in physical strength? A may have good reasons to accept the authority of B in some cases. B might have equally good reasons to accept the authority of A in other cases, and neither may have any reason to accept the authority of anyone else in still other cases. So there does not seem to be any good reason for believing in some pervasive natural hierarchy. Nor does there seem to be any reason why natural law theory cannot be separated from belief in natural hierarchies. We can learn from these errors to be cautious about concluding that what exists in our own society, or even in many societies, is somehow natural. [30]

NATURAL LAW THEORY
AND NATURAL RIGHTS THEORY

People speak not only of natural law, but of natural rights. The Declaration of Independence states that human beings are "endowed by their Creator" with the rights to "life, liberty and the pursuit of happiness." Even as traditional natural law theory inferred certain duties from the way the intention of the Creator was thought to be mirrored in the natural order, so one development of that tradition inferred natural rights in the same manner. The English philosopher John Locke (1632–1704) refers to the natural right to life as the other side of the natural law duty to preserve one's own life and to respect the lives of others. He also emphasizes natural rights to liberty and to property.[31]

For Locke, the right to life prohibits suicide as well as murder. While his emphasis is on what the right prohibits, by implication it follows that each person ought to do what he or she can do, within limits, to preserve the lives of others.[32] Locke further argues that liberty, or freedom from arbitrary power, is a natural right, since it is necessary to protect the right to life and since there is nothing in the natural order by which one could infer that some men were intended to rule arbitrarily over others.[33] So with Locke we have a version of natural law theory that has rejected the idea of natural hierarchies, even if it has not yet consistently applied that rejection to the relationship between men and women. Locke also argues that when individuals mixed their labor with previously unclaimed natural resources, they created a right to property.[34] The theory of natural rights has an important place in the history of political philosophy because it was used to justify the idea of limited government and resistance against arbitrary and autocratic rule.

Some modern authors seek to detach the theory of natural rights both from any idea of natural law and from the theological foundations that it had in Locke. In chapter 11 we will consider the natural rights theory of justice set forth by a contemporary philosopher, Robert Nozick. The appeal to rights is even more common outside of academic circles. As noted in chapter 1, in our day many individuals and groups argue that they have certain rights. In some cases, respecting the rights claimed by some would be incompatible with respecting the rights claimed by others. Some have claimed that we now, in fact, have a "population explosion of rights-claims."[35]

One practical criticism of the natural rights approach points out that if each person thinks that having a certain right is like having a trump card that settles a moral argument in his or her favor without any further discussion, then moral argument is cut off and there is little hope of finding compromise solutions to moral problems.[36] A second, more theoretical criticism of this approach focuses on the idea that rights are themselves basic in a moral theory and not derived from other moral considerations, such as what furthers a good life for human beings. If this idea is correct, it is hard to see what nonarbitrary criteria could be used to determine which rights claims should be accepted and which not, and which natural facts should be regarded as the grounds of rights and which not. So L. W. Summer writes:

> We are beings capable of choice—do we therefore have a right to be free? We are also beings with subsistence—do we therefore have a right to the necessaries of life? If we have both rights, how does our nature determine which is to take precedence when they conflict? How in general can we distinguish between the relevant and the irrelevant aspects of our nature without presupposing a particular outcome for the argument? The problem here is not that no arguments are possible from natural facts to rights. The problem is that too many such arguments are possible and that there seems no way to arbitrate among them by further appeals to the facts. But if this is so, then nature underdetermines selection of a set of basic rights and thus provides an ineffectual control over the proliferation of rights-principles.[37]

We will say something more about the place that the idea of rights should have in ethics in chapter 8.

QUESTIONS

1. Have you heard other people argue for or against something on the grounds that it was natural or unnatural, or have you argued that way yourself? What problems do you see in the argument that you heard?

2. What relevance does the discussion of anthropological views of relativism in chapter 3 have to the question of whether a natural law ethic is plausible?

3. Although Aristotle does not always base his arguments on the function of human nature, he sometimes does. We usually speak of functions in connection with things that were made for a purpose (e.g., screwdrivers, hammers). Do you think that it makes sense for a person (such as Aristotle himself) who does not believe that human beings were created for a purpose to talk about human nature as having a function? Are there problems with it even for those who do believe this?

4. Some who have thought about these issues might see some of the aspects of the human good that St. Thomas refers to as particular aspects of the more general good of human self-development. William Galston, for example, writes:

> We exist as beings of a certain kind, endowed with organs of sense, practical abilities, and intellectual capacities. These facts carry with them an evaluative force: in general we believe that it is preferable to develop and exercise these powers and that their full development constitutes the norm through which partial realizations are judged. This belief is not merely imposed on our existence. Children have a natural impulse to develop themselves by

sharpening their senses, gaining physical dexterity, and satisfying their curiosity.[38]

What might St. Thomas have said about developing the human capacities to lie and deceive (useful for spies, but also used by con men) and to kill (useful to soldiers fighting in a just cause, but also used by murderers). What, if anything, does this say about human self-development as an intrinsic good?

5. The section in this chapter entitled "Natural Law Theory and the Functions of Human Acts" discusses a view of natural law that differs essentially from the views described in the previous three sections. What is this essential difference? Do you agree with the author's differing assessments of each or not? Do you agree that the arguments the author sets forth regarding normal functioning of human activities, and using the reproductive and digestive systems as examples, are in fact completely parallel and do discredit the natural law argument concerning contraception? If not, why not?

6. We usually think of something that interferes with someone's normal biological functioning—for example, an injury or a disease—as an evil to be combated, and we would think of a person who inflicted such an interference on another person as an enemy who should be resisted. Could it make sense to regard normal biological functioning as itself an evil? *A few* feminist writers regard normal female biology and its functioning as the enemy that prevents women from being free from domination by men.[39] These writers wish to obliterate natural gender distinctions and work toward the day when biological functions are changed so that "one woman could inseminate another, so that men and nonparturitive women could lactate and so that fertilized ova could be transplanted into women's or even men's bodies."[40] Can normal biological functioning be considered an evil or an enemy in the same way as a disease?

7. There are perhaps many ways to argue against proposals for the widespread use of artificial means of reproduction (see the previous question), not the least of which is that their enactment would not likely achieve the goals that the people who advocate them desire. As Elaine Storkey writes, "If men are powerful and evil enough to exploit women because they bear children, how will it change when they have the future of the human race at the bottom of a test tube?"[41] Can one argue persuasively against proposals to reconstruct human biology and human reproduction simply on the grounds that what they propose is unnatural? Argue for your answer. Precisely what sense of "unnatural" is involved? Does an argument that such proposals are wrong because they are unnatural have to appeal to theological beliefs, or can it be made on purely secular grounds?

FURTHER READING

Relevant writings of St. Thomas Aquinas can be found in the following volumes. The Sigmund work also contains many relevant selections from modern writers.

Baumgarth, W. P., and R. J. Regan, S. J., eds. *Aquinas on Law, Morality and Politics*. Indianapolis: Hackett, 1988.

Sigmund, Paul, trans. and ed. *St. Thomas Aquinas on Politics and Ethics: A New Translation, Backgrounds, Interpretations*. New York: Norton, 1988.

Other works relevant to this chapter:

Donagan, Alan. "The Scholastic Theory of Moral Law in the Modern World." In *Proceedings of the American Catholic Philosophical Association*, 1966. Reprinted in *Aquinas: A Collection of Critical Essays*, edited by Anthony Kenny, 325–39. Garden City, N.Y.: Doubleday, 1969.
Grisez, Germain G., and Russell B. Shaw. *Beyond the New Morality: The Responsibilities of Freedom*. Contains a different interpretation of natural law theory.
King, Martin Luther. "A Letter from a Birmingham City Jail." *Why We Can't Wait*. New York: Harper and Row, 1963.
Locke, John. *Second Treatise of Civil Government*. 1690. Edited by C. B. MacPherson. Indianapolis: Hackett, 1980. Chap. 2 is especially relevant.
Maritain, Jacques. *Man and the State*. Chicago:University of Chicago Press, 1951. See especially pp. 84–97.
McInerny, Ralph. *Ethica Thomistica: The Moral Philosophy of Thomas Aquinas*. Washington, D.C.: Catholic University Press, 1982. Offers a traditional interpretation.
Mooney, Christopher. *Public Virtue*. Notre Dame, Ind.: University of Notre Dame Press, 1986.
O'Connor, D. J. *Aquinas and Natural Law*. New York: St.Martin's Press, 1967. A critical evaluation.
Regan, Richard J. *The Moral Dimensions of Politics*. New York: Oxford University Press, 1986. A Thomistic approach to political morality.
von Leyden, W. "John Locke and Natural Law." *Philosophy* 21 (1956): 23–35. Reprinted in *Life, Liberty, and Property: Essays on Locke's Political Ideas*, edited by Gordon J. Schochet, 12–79. Belmont, Calif.: Wadsworth, 1971.

For works on Aristotle, see chapter 10, on virtue and vice.

NOTES

1. Cicero, *De Republica*, trans. and ed. C. W. Keyes (London: Loeb Classical Library, 1928), 3.33.
2. Christopher F. Mooney, *Public Virtue* (Notre Dame, Ind.: University of Notre Dame Press, 1986), 142.
3. Martin Luther King, "A Letter from a Birmingham City Jail," *Why We Can't Wait* (New York: Harper and Row, 1963), 78.
4. Viscount Torio, quoted in Ananda K. Coomaraswamy, *Buddha and the Gospel of Buddhism* (London: Harrap, 1916), 135.
5. Thomas Aquinas, *Summa Contra Gentiles* (New York: Benzinger, 1924–28), vol. 3, pt. 2, chaps. 123–124.
6. Thomas Aquinas, *Summa Theologiae*, in *St. Thomas Aquinas on Politics and Ethics*, trans. and ed. Paul Sigmund (New York: Norton, 1988), 2–2 (the second part of part 2), qu. 64, art. 5, p. 70.

7. Hume as a natural law theorist is discussed by Duncan Forbes in *Hume's Philosophical Politics* (New York: Cambridge University Press, 1975), chap. 2.

8. Aristotle, *Nicomachean Ethics* 1, 1:1094a1–3. Unless otherwise designated, quotations from Aristotle are from the translation by F. H. Peters, 8th ed. (1901).

9. Ibid. 1, 2:1094a20–24.

10. Ibid. 1, 7:1097b14–15.

11. Ibid. 1, 8:1098b20–22.

12. Ibid. 1, 7.

13. Ibid. 1, 7:1097b21–1098a3.

14. Norman Daniels, "Health-Care Needs and Distributive Justice," *Philosophy and Public Affairs* 10 (Spring 1981), 159.

15. Aristotle, *Nicomachean Ethics* 1, 8:1098a7–9.

16. King, *Why We Can't Wait*, 78.

17. See for example, Jacques Maritain, *Man and the State* (Chicago: University of Chicago Press, 1951).

18. Aquinas, *Summa Theologiae* 2–2, qu. 94, art. 2, pp. 49–50.

19. Aristotle, *Nicomachean Ethics* 9, 9:1170a25–26.

20. Aquinas, *Summa Theologiae* 2–2, qu. 94, art. 2, p. 50.

21. David Little, "Calvin and the Prospects for Christian Theory of Natural Law, " in *Norm and Context in Christian Ethics*, ed. Gene Outka and Paul Ramsey (New York: Scribners, 1968), 188.

22. See the approach taken by Arthur J. Dyck in *On Human Care: An Introduction to Ethics* (Nashville: Abingdon Press, 1977), 92–105.

23. *Summa Theologiae* 2–2, qu. 94, art. 2.

24. This is what David Little attempts to do. See note 21.

25. Mooney, *Public Virtue*, 142–43. Quote from Aquinas is from *In decem libros Ethicorum expositio* 1.3.38. See also *Summa Theologiae* 1–2, qu. 94, arts. 2 and 6.

26. Aquinas, *Summa Theologiae* 1–2, qu. 94, art. 4.

27. See Paul Sigmund, "Thomistic Natural Law and Social Theory," in *St. Thomas Aquinas on Politics and Ethics*, ed. Sigmund, 180–88.

28. P. T. Geach, a supporter of the anticontraception position, recognizes the worthlessness of the traditional natural law arguments. See Geach's *The Virtues* (Cambridge: Cambridge University Press, 1977), 137–41.

29. Aquinas *Summa Theologiae* 2–2, qu. 104, p. 75.

30. There is another version of natural law theory proposed by a group of Catholic writers including John Finnis, Joseph Boyle, and Germain Grisez, that will be looked at later.

31. John Locke, *Second Treatise of Civil Government* (Indianapolis: Hackett, 1980), chap. 2, para. 6, p. 9.

32. Ibid.

33. Ibid., chap. 4, para. 23, p. 17

34. Ibid., chap. 5, para. 27, p. 19.

35. L. W. Summer, "Rights Denaturalized," in *Utility and Rights*, ed. R. G. Fey (Minneapolis: University of Minnesota Press, 1984), 37.

36. See chapter 1 of this book.

37. Summer, "Rights Denaturalized," 38–39.

38. William Galston, *Justice and the Human Good* (Chicago: University of Chicago Press, 1980), 61.

39. See Shulamith Firestone, *The Dialectic of Sex: The Case for Feminist Revolution* (New York: Morrow, 1970), 223–24, 270–271.

40. Allison Jagger, "Human Biology in Feminist Theory: Sexual Equality Reconsidered," in *Beyond Domination*, ed. Carol Gould (Totowa, N.J.: Rowman and Allenheld, 1983), 41.

41. Elaine Storkey, *What's Right with Feminism* (Grand Rapids, Mich.: Eerdmans, 1985), 100.

5

Social Contract Ethics:
Moral Law as a Human
Creation

THOMAS HOBBES AND THE SOCIAL
CONTRACT

In the modern world many people do not believe in God, and those who do have different views of God and God's will. Furthermore, many people have doubts that human nature is similar enough in all people so that it can be used as the basis of a universal natural law. What is left on which to base the moral law or moral rules?

One answer is that human agreement could be the source of a moral law. The English philosopher Thomas Hobbes (1588–1679), whose views on relativism and egoism have already been noted, imagined a situation in which government did not exist, a situation he called the state of nature. In such a situation there would be no binding moral law; it would make no sense to refrain from killing or stealing (in fact, property could not even be said to exist), or from doing whatever you thought might protect your own life and interests, because you would have no reason to believe that other people would refrain from these things. It would be dangerous not to protect yourself in such a situation. But under such conditions, life, as Hobbes put it, would be "nasty, poor, brutish, and short,"[1] so human beings, even complete egoists, would have every reason to try to come to a mutual agreement on a set of rules by which they would restrain their passions in exchange for others' doing so as well. Such an agreement is called the *social contract*. (In fact, social contract views are frequently set forth by those who wish to justify morality to egoists.)

In Hobbes' view, the social contract is something like this: We will set up a government, and I will agree to abide by the laws of the government, which prevent me, on pain of punishment, from harming you or failing to keep my contract with you. In return, you also pledge to abide by the laws of the government, which prevent you, on pain of punishment, from harming me. This government will set up laws that define these harms.

Philosophers who take this approach may leave the government out of the picture when talking about moral rules that may not be embodied in law. Social norms can be enforced in other ways as well—for example, by family members, social pressure, fear of disapproval or ostracism, professional organizations, and so on. The basic idea is that moral rules are rules that the people of a society tacitly agree to obey because they are better off if everyone obeys the rules than if no one does. Gilbert Harman writes that "morality arises when a group of people reach an implicit agreement or come to a tacit understanding about their relations with one another."[2]

DUTIES UNDER THE SOCIAL CONTRACT

Do we have a duty to obey all the rules a society regards as moral rules? That is one possible view, but there is another. Since the purpose of the social contract is to deal with situations in which the interests of people conflict, perhaps only rules that deal with conflicting interests are legitimate. So, for example, there could be no duties of self-improvement. The emphasis would be on prohibitions or negative duties. I accept a rule not to kill because I can conceive of myself being either a perpetrator or a victim or both. I am willing to forfeit the liberty to act on any possible desire to initiate violence against another in return for others giving up their liberty to initiate violence against me.

Since I can conceive of myself being in a position of needing help, I *might* also be willing to contract to abide by a rule to help others within rather narrow limits, perhaps through my taxes. However, I may be in an advantageous position and unable to see any possibility of ever being in a certain kind of disadvantageous position. I may be rich and relatively sure that I will never be poor. I may be a male in a patriarchal society and absolutely certain that I will never be a female. Under those conditions, I may not find any reason to accept a rule that protects or furthers the interests of people in the disadvantageous position.

Could there be any duties to help distant people? Here there is a question as to what extent people of different nations belong to the same social contract and, to the extent they do, to what degree this would include positive duties as well as negative ones. Where there is no likelihood of its people ever being in danger of hunger, for example, it is hard to see what reason a country would have for accepting a rule to relieve the hunger of others. From the social contract point of view, there would not seem to be any duties to those with whom we have not entered into any kind of agreement for reciprocal advantage, or at least with whom we have the potential for doing so.

Since we cannot enter into agreements with future generations for any mutual advantage, or with ourselves, or with fetuses, there would seem to be no duties to future generations, or to ourselves (e.g., duties of self-perfection), or to the unborn. With the general lack of emphasis on positive duties, with doubts about duties to distant people, especially positive duties, and with little place for valuing heroism that goes beyond duty, it would seem that social contract approaches to ethics would tend toward a minimalist view.

THE SOCIAL CONTRACT AND RELATIVISM

A social contract view of ethics would establish a duty not to kill any member of society unjustly, or, to put it another way, it would regard as part of the terms of the contract that people have such claim-rights as a right not to be killed unjustly. One could hardly imagine anyone having any reason to abide by a social contract unless it established such a right by which he or she could be protected. Is there also a duty not to cause harm to others in a certain way, say by smoking in small seminar rooms, or by dumping garbage in the local stream, or by overgrazing public land? I have a duty if and only if a prohibition of such behavior exists as part of the generally agreed-upon moral code of the society in which I find myself. This is a kind of relativism, since different societies and different groups could have different rules, or since, as Harman puts it, "an action may be wrong in relation to one agreement but not in relation to another."[3]

But with respect to most rules, changes in people's attitudes can in effect change the social contract and its rules—for example, about smoking and polluting. We can renegotiate the social contract or make a new social contract to abide by a new set of rules. We have an interest in trying to change the rules in a way that better protects our interests—for instance, by protecting us from cigarette smoke or toxic chemicals. But in a view of ethics that is based completely on the social contract, there is no moral duty to try to improve the rules, perhaps to make them better serve the common good. This is because there is no moral standard outside the rules themselves by which they could be evaluated. Such a view avoids personal relativism or subjectivism by adopting the social form of moral relativism. Going back to the example in chapter 2 of the young man who partici-pated in many societies and groups, the social contract view would presumably tell him to live according to the rules recognized by whatever group he was interacting with.

A number of years ago, an article appeared in the *Harvard Business Review* describing the deceptions that the author claimed were widespread in business. He justified such practices on the grounds that business and private life are games played by different rules. Members of the business community are part of a different social contract when engaged in business than they are when leading their private lives.[4] Deception in business is justified because, according to the social contract in force among business people, the truth is not expected.

THE SOCIAL CONTRACT VIEW: ADVANTAGES, IMPLICATIONS, AND PROBLEMS

The conventionalist or contractual approach to ethics that has its historical roots in the writings of Thomas Hobbes is helpful in dealing with some moral issues, especially many in which the moral question has to do with fairness. Consider duties to deal fairly with competitors or with enemies, or to pay one's dues to an organization or taxes to the government, or to fight for the defense of one's country, or to limit one's take of fish or game. It makes sense to regard duties to abide by these practices as binding if and only if a sufficient number of other people generally abide by the same practices, or can be made to do so (either from a sense of duty or because of coercion). If other people are not willing to do their part and are not being compelled to do so, then the sacrifices that one individual makes are likely to be pointless, since they will be for the sake of some goal that will not be achieved anyway. The social contract idea also has value as a way of arguing against certain practices on the grounds that they are violations of the society's social contract.

But there are also consequences of this point of view that would appear to many to be defects.

(1) Hobbes imagines a society in which there is basically one social contract. But we in fact live in a pluralistic society that could be thought of as made up of many social contracts. Suppose the person who belongs to many groups tries to live by the terms of the various social contracts. What does this effort eventually do to that person's character? A letter in response to the article on deception in business pointed out that a person cannot separate the ethics of his business life from that of his home life. The author of the original article responded in this way:

> Over the long run, that is probably true. What happens is that, in too many instances, the ethical outlook of business comes to dominate in the home as

well. Perhaps that accounts for the notorious instability of the middle-class home in our society. . . . It may also explain why the wives of businessmen have, like their husbands, been conscience-washed into undiscriminating acceptance of corporation policies.[5]

Many regard what happens to a person's character as the central topic of moral philosophy. We have already noted that the social contract approach seems to have no place for duties of moral self-development. Does it in fact unwittingly favor moral self-destruction? Suppose one social contract a person lives under is very lenient about truthfulness. What happens to such a person? As Sissela Bok writes: "Psychological barriers wear down; lies seem more necessary, less reprehensible; the ability to make moral distinctions can coarsen; the liar's perception of his chances of being caught may warp."[6]

(2) Imagine that the standards of truthfulness in business, insofar as they are not precisely written into the law, depend on a kind of informal contract in the business community. The requirements of the contract will not be precise, so each person will tend to interpret the requirements as leniently as possible when applying them to himself or herself. As one businessman wrote in a reply to the *Harvard Business Review* article, "Every businessman is tempted to be just a little less moral than his competitors."[7] As this process goes on over time, however, the standards will get more and more lax until the social contract self-destructs and anarchy prevails. The social contract would thus seem to be in danger of collapsing unless a significant number of people also recognize a separate duty to sacrifice their own advantage to raise the standards of the social contract. As one of the commentators on the article wrote, "The only guard against a gradual decline in [business] morals is the ideals of each businessman."[8] But a purely social contract approach to ethics has no room for a duty based on such ideals.

(3) Suppose that we are in a situation in which no contract yet exists. Gilbert Harman sees the degree to which people have rights to economic benefits as the product of the moral negotiation between the rich and the poor, the outcome of which depends on their relative numbers and power.[9] Suppose a powerful group of people can coerce the less powerful to accept a set of rules that is very beneficial to the powerful at the expense of others. The social contract view would imply that there are no moral standards by which one could say that the contract was unjust, nor could any proposed set of rules be said to be more just than another. This is certainly implausible.

(4) As already indicated, the purely social contract view of morality would seem to imply that there are no duties to others with whom we have not entered into some mutually beneficial relationship, so that we could have no moral duties regarding the treatment of animals, infants, fetuses, or future generations. Presumably, according to this view, if a member of

one tribe met a member of another tribe with which there had not been previous contact, it would be morally indifferent whether he sought to establish friendly contact with this other person, or whether he avoided being seen and went on his way, or whether he simply killed the other person in cold blood. But this seems implausible.

(5) Hobbes, living in a time of civil war, saw a world in which the danger of aggression had to be checked. This seems to be a characteristic way for men to see the world.[10] Therefore for Hobbes, and for many men, the rules that arbitrate disputes and prevent aggression are important. Women, however, tend to see aggression as a result of a breakdown in human relationships. Instead of limiting aggression, what is more important is strengthening human relationships so that aggression is prevented.[11] As Carol Gilligan writes, women are more likely to see "life as dependent on connection, as sustained by activities of care, as based on a bond of attachment rather than on a contract or agreement."[12] Women tend to see themselves and others as having duties to care for other human beings simply because they are fellow human beings. So the question can be raised as to whether the social contract view is inadequate in that it seems to ignore the way that half of the human race tends to look at morality.

(6) Furthermore, to the degree that the social contract view is a version of moral minimalism, many questions one might have about the general trend to moral minimalism would apply to the social contract approach as well.

PARTIAL AND HYPOTHETICAL SOCIAL CONTRACT VIEWS

In the last chapter, we noted that the directives of the principal theory of natural law, in the words of writer Christopher Mooney, "are of such a general character as seldom to give specific guidance regarding concrete decisions," so that they in effect say that "something should be done to preserve life, to organize the family, to stabilize society."[13] Many of the specifics concerning the protection of life, the duties parents and children have to each other, and the rules designed to stabilize society can still be based on a social contract approach. This view of the social contract differs from Hobbes's view in that on this view the purpose of the social contract is not just to reconcile conflicting interests, but to further the common good. A second difference is that on this view there are objective criteria for deciding what the common good is.

Sometimes the social contract is not thought of as giving an account of all morality, but only of social and political morality or justice. Michael Walzer defines the social contract as "an agreement to redistribute the resources of the members in accordance with some shared understanding of their needs, subject to ongoing political determination in detail."[14] This is understood to have results quite different from those of minimalism. Walzer writes: "When all the members share in the business of interpreting the social contract, the result will be a more or less extensive system of communal provision."[15] He uses this concept to criticize certain practices of American society, such as the inadequacies in the distribution of medical care, because these practices violate the basic principles that Americans generally recognize as defining their social contract. We will return to these views in chapter 11, on social justice.

There is another position in philosophical ethics that is called a *contract view*. It differs from what has been discussed in this chapter in that it does not depend on any tacit or explicit mutual understanding between the members of a society. Rather, the contract it appeals to is the contract that rational people *would* agree to *if* they were temporarily ignorant of such things as what sort of power or wealth they would have, perhaps what generation they would be in, and so on. We will consider this approach in the chapter on social justice in the context of discussing the views of John Rawls.

QUESTIONS

1. Suppose two countries are at war.
    (a) Suppose the countries promise each other not to use some particular weapon, such as poison gas. Suppose one country breaks its promise. Is the other country released from its promise?
    (b) Suppose one country begins to torture prisoners of war. Does that give the second country moral permission to do the same thing?
    (c) If your answers to these two questions are different, what is the difference between the two cases?

2. Is it possible to argue on the basis of a social contract point of view that we have moral duties to people in distant countries? How might such an argument go?

3. In a very pluralistic society, is the social contract view destructive of character? Can this be avoided?

4. How do you respond to Carol Gilligan's observations about the differences between the way men and women look at morality?

FURTHER READING

Relevant works by Thomas Hobbes are as follows:

De Cive or the Citizens. New York: Appleton-Century-Crofts, 1949.
Leviathan, parts 1 and 2, edited by Herbert W. Schneider. Indianapolis: Bobbs-Merrill, 1958. Originally published in 1651.

Discussions of Thomas Hobbes's views can be found in various histories of philosophy, histories of ethics, and histories of political thought. A few relevant works are:

Copleston, Frederick, S.J. *A History of Philosophy.* 8 vols. Garden City, N.Y.: Doubleday/Image, 1962–77. See vol. 5, pt. 1, pp. 41–60.
Kavka, Gregory. *Hobbesian Moral and Political Philosophy.* Princeton, N.J.: Princeton University Press, 1986.
Lessnoff, Michael. *Social Contract.* Atlantic Highlands, N.J.: Humanities Press, 1986. See pp. 42–58.
Peters, R. S. *Thomas Hobbes.* Baltimore: Penguin, 1956. See chap. 7.

There are a number of rather abstract and difficult contemporary works written from a social contract point of view. Gilbert Harman's works probably provide the most accessible contemporary version of contract ethics. They include the following:

"Libertarianism and Morality." In *The Libertarian Reader*, edited by Tibor R. Machan, 231–34. Totowa, N.J.: Rowman and Littlefield, 1982.
The Nature of Morality: An Introduction to Ethics. New York: Oxford University Press, 1977.
"Moral Relativism Defended." *Philosophical Review* 84 (1975): 3; reprinted in *Relativism: Cognitive and Moral*, edited by Michael Kraus and Jack W. Meiland, 189. Notre Dame, Ind.: University of Notre Dame Press, 1982.
"Relativistic Ethics: Morality as Politics." In *Midwest Studies in Philosophy*, vol. 3, *Studies in Ethical Theory*, edited by Peter A. French, Theodore E. Uehling, Jr., and Harold K. Wettstein, 109–22. Minneapolis: University of Minnesota Press, 1978.

Social contract approaches are criticized in two essays included in a single collection:

Baier, Annette C. "The Need for More than Justice." In *Science, Morality and Feminist Theory, Canadian Journal of Philosophy*, Supplementary volume 13, edited by Marsha Hanen and Kai Nielsen, 41–58. Calgary: University of Calgary Press, 1987.
Held, Virginia. "Non-Contractual Society." In *Science, Morality and Feminist Theory*, 111–38.

NOTES

1. Thomas Hobbes. *Leviathan* (London, 1651), ed. Herbert W. Schneider (Indianapolis: Bobbs-Merrill, 1958), pt. 1, chap. 13, p. 107.
2. Gilbert Harman, "Moral Relativism Defended," *Philosophical Review* 84 (January 1975): 3; reprinted in *Relativism: Cognitive and Moral*, ed. Michael Kraus and Jack W. Meiland (Notre Dame, Indiana: University of Notre Dame Press, 1982), 189.

3. Ibid.

4. Albert Carr, "Is Business Bluffing Ethical?" *Harvard Business Review* 46 (January–February 1968): 143–53.

5. Albert Carr, "Mr. Carr Comments," *Harvard Business Review* 46 (May–June, 1968): 168–70.

6. Sissela Bok, *Lying* (New York: Random House, 1978), 27.

7. Graham Briggs, quoted in Timothy Blodgett, "Showdown on Business Bluffing," *Harvard Business Review* 46 (May–June 1968): 187.

8. Ibid.

9. Harman, "Libertarianism and Morality," in *The Libertarian Reader*, ed. Tibor R. Machen (Totowa, N.J.: Rowman and Littlefield, 1982), 231–34.

10. Carol Gilligan, *In a Different Voice* (Cambridge, Mass.: Harvard University Press, 1982), 43.

11. Ibid.

12. Ibid., 57.

13. Christopher F. Mooney, *Public Virtue* (Notre Dame, Ind.: University of Notre Dame Press, 1986), 142.

14. Michael Walzer, *Spheres of Justice* (New York: Basic Books, 1983), 82.

15. Ibid., 83.

6

Duty-Based Ethics: The Moral Philosophy of Immanuel Kant

THE GOOD WILL

The German philosopher Immanuel Kant (1724–1804) began by assuming that the moral tradition of the Western world as influenced by Christianity was basically correct. For Kant, the fundamental moral problem facing the individual is not so much deciding what one's duty is; rather, it is doing one's duty when it conflicts with natural inclinations. To do that, one needs what Kant calls a *good will*. Kant begins his *Fundamental Principles of the Metaphysics of Morals* with these words:

> Nothing can possibly be conceived in the world, or even out of it, which can be called good, without qualification, except a Good Will. Intelligence, wit, judgment, and the other talents of the mind, however they be named, or courage, resoluteness, and perseverance as qualities of the temperament, are undoubtedly good and desirable in many respects, but these gifts of nature may also become extremely bad and mischievous if the will which is to make use of them, and which, therefore constitutes what is called character, is not good.[1]

It is important to remember that when Kant uses the expression "the good will," he does not necessarily mean the same thing as other people might mean by the same term. (For some people, having a good will might mean being generous.) For Kant, the good will is the will to do one's duty, and the person with a good will is the person who is conscientious about morality. Intelligence, courage, and similar qualities can be used for evil by an evil person, but the good will cannot. The good will is of supreme value in itself, not because of its desirable consequences. The person who sets out to do his or her duty, but whose efforts are frustrated, is not morally inferior to the person who succeeds in his or her endeavors. It is not enough to do what duty demands. I may do the right thing because I am naturally kind or because I am seeking the approval of others. In either case, however, my action would lack moral worth because it sprang from natural inclinations which were products of my heredity and early environment, over which I have no control. The good will is the will to do one's duty for its own sake, simply because it is one's duty. The first basic proposition concerning duty is that an action only has moral worth if I do it because I know it is my duty, no matter what my natural inclinations might be. In practice, however, it is impossible to know whether my act has moral worth, since I cannot be certain whether I would still have done what was right (because it was my duty) regardless of what my inclinations may have been.

THE PRINCIPLE OF UNIVERSALIZABILITY

Respect for the Moral Law

I may do something or refrain from doing it because of some goal I have or purpose I want to achieve (e.g., good health). I may also do something (or refrain from doing it) because otherwise I would be acting on a policy that would conflict with some principle. If that principle is derived from the moral law, then I would be acting, or refraining from acting, out of respect for the moral law. According to Kant, the moral worth of an action is not derived from the purposes it seeks to achieve, but from its being in accordance with a policy—or, to use Kant's term, a *maxim*—that respects the moral law.

Hypothetical Imperatives and Categorical Imperatives

What, then, is the content of this moral law the commands of which I am to respect? Although Kant does not wish to come up with new moral conclusions, he does wish to put a new philosophical foundation under traditional morality. He also wishes to support a view of the moral law that applies to all human beings, regardless of what society they belong to (or even to all rational beings if there are rational beings other than human beings), without making it depend on any particular religious beliefs.

He proceeds in the following way. Some commands or imperatives are of this sort: "Study hard while you are in school." Someone might ask, "Why?" The answer might be, "Because otherwise you will not get good enough grades to graduate (or to get a good job, or to get into graduate school)." But if a person does not care about any of these goals, then the appeal loses all force. In effect it means: "Study hard if you want . . . " Kant calls this a hypothetical imperative. If morality is to be the same for everyone, it cannot be based on this sort of command. Since what comes after the "if" would refer to different goals for different people, different injunctions would precede the "if" for different people.

One way to avoid this problem is to claim that there is something that can follow the "if" that applies to everyone, for example, "if you want to attain happiness." So then we have: "You should do such and such if you want to attain happiness, and human nature being the same in everyone, everyone does want this, and the way to attain it is the same for everyone." This is, according to some interpretations, the approach taken by St. Thomas Aquinas, but Kant finds it unsatisfactory. He calls such impera- tives *assertorial imperatives*, and he regards them as having to do with prudence and not with morality. For one thing, such principles as could be derived from this method would not apply to all rational beings, if there are any, whose basic nature is different from that of human beings, and Kant's professed purpose in *The Fundamental Principles* is to deal with the principles derived from the concepts of rationality and rational being. In the application of his basic principles, however, Kant does appeal to human nature.

The Categorical Imperative

So what would the content of the moral law be, if it makes no reference to the purposes human beings happen to have? There is some- thing we can know about the moral law simply because it is a law, without further inquiry—namely, that all actions are to conform to it. From this notion of the nature of law itself Kant hopes to generate all our duties. If I am considering performing some action, then I must ask myself, "Is there some law or principle to which this action conforms, to which all other actions can also conform?" As Kant puts it, "I am never to act otherwise than *so that I could also will that my maxim should become a universal law*."[2] Kant calls this the *Categorical Imperative*. Kant twice gives the following example. A person may be considering borrowing money, mak- ing a promise to pay it back, when in fact he knows that he will not be able to do so. That person should ask himself: "Can I will that everyone act on the maxim (or policy): 'When I can get out of a difficulty by making a lying promise I should do so'?" If the situation existed in which when people used the words "I promise" they were no more likely to do what followed those words than under any other circumstances, then the words "I promise" would be treated by others as not signifying anything at all. Under those circumstances nothing would be treated as a promise, so no one could make a promise, so also no one could make a lying promise. There could not be, therefore, a society in which false promises are made whenever it is convenient. Thus to will that the practice of making false promises be universal is to will the impossible, and so to act against reason. But if it is against reason to will that everyone make false promises, then it is against the concept of law for me to grant to myself the permission to do what it is impossible for everyone to do. If I make false promises, I am acting on a policy which I know it is impossible for everyone to act on, and so I am making an exception in my own favor. Most people would agree with Kant in seeing this as sufficient to show that I am acting unfairly, and thus immorally. But whether Kant has shown that acting immorally is irrational, as he ultimately wishes to do, is much more questionable.

One problem with which Kant did not adequately deal is that an action can be described in different ways and thus can be seen as conforming to different policies. I can describe the same behavior as conforming to the policy "I will eat supper at 6 P.M.," or as conforming to the policy "I will eat supper whenever I choose to do so providing that doing so does not interfere with any other responsibilities." In our industrialized society it would be impossible for everyone (including police officers, airline pilots, etc.) to conform to the first policy, but there is no problem in conforming to the second. If I describe what I am proposing to do by referring to the first policy, it would seem that my act would violate the Categorical Imperative, but if I describe what I am proposing to do by referring to the second policy, there is no violation. Nevertheless, the act is the same in either case.

The Categorical Imperative and Exceptions

Kant says the Categorical Imperative is the fundamental principle of morality to which other principles must conform. He takes the position that these principles must be exceptionless. Would this not, however, have the strange consequence of ruling out the most plausible policy concerning eating supper, since it has an "except" in it? Such rules as "One should never steal except when it is necessary to save someone from starvation or severe malnourishment" have almost always been recognized as morally correct in Western society. What is really important is that a person not unfairly make himself or herself an exception *to* the rule that he or she believes everyone else should abide by, not that there not be any exceptions *in* the rule that do not unfairly benefit any specific person or group. The problem is that while it may not be difficult to see when the spirit of Kant's Categorical Imperative is being violated, it is difficult to specify precisely a way of allowing exceptions that do not unfairly benefit certain people or groups of people, while ruling out exceptions that do (e.g., "One should never lie except when one is at such and such a longitude and such and such a latitude, and one is a certain number of years old"—all describing the situation in which one finds oneself when one wants to lie).

Further Applications of the Categorical Imperative

Kant considers the example of someone asking whether or not to act on the maxim: "While not harming others I will do nothing to help them when they are in need."[3] This differs from the false-promise example in that it is perfectly possible to imagine a world in which everyone acts according to this policy. But, Kant says, it is impossible for me to will or to want everyone to act on this policy because at some time I may need and want the help of others. Thus if I choose not to help others, I am making an exception in my own favor to a rule I want other people to follow. Again, most people would agree with Kant that this inconsistency is sufficient to show that a person who adopts such a viewpoint is acting immorally. According to some scholars, Kant's fundamental contribution to moral philosophy was to point out that no action or policy or behavior that does not conform to this general principle of universalizability could possibly be considered morally right, and furthermore, that no code that fails to recognize this principle could be called a code of morality.

The Principle of Universalizability and the Golden Rule

When applied in this manner, the Categorical Imperative sounds similar to the Golden Rule (or what can be called the reversibility principle): "Do unto others as you would have them do unto you." The Categorical Imperative includes the Golden Rule, but it is more general. The Golden Rule applies to one-to-one situations: "Do not lie to X if you would not want X to lie to you." Suppose, however, I am considering engaging in a major act of civil disobedience against the laws of the state (for instance, parking my car in the middle of a freeway and causing a major traffic jam because my property taxes are five dollars more than my neighbor's). Here the reversibility or Golden Rule argument does not fit. The state cannot commit acts of civil disobedience against the individual. But the universalizability argument does apply: "Do not violate the laws of the state by committing major disruptive acts of civil disobedience to protest an insignificant injustice unless you would be willing to have everyone who is a victim of some insignificant injustice commit major disruptive acts of civil disobedience.

Further Problems with the Universalizability Principle

But, critics of Kant contend, the universalizability principle is just a formal principle, and little or no specific moral guidance can be derived from it. Suppose that a person takes a moral minimalist point of view and says that he is not making an exception in his own favor when he acts on the policy of never helping other people, since he is perfectly willing to have no one help him in time of need if he in turn doesn't have to help anyone else. This, in fact, seems to be in our day an increasingly popular position, advocated by representatives of various sorts of libertarian and right-wing points of view. The existence of such people, along with the rest of our discussion up until now, raises three problems for Kant's point of view.

(1) Kant says that morality does not depend on consequences, and yet it seems that acting on a certain policy or maxim is morally wrong when we find that the consequences of everyone's acting on it are unacceptable to us.

(2) If Kant were to judge that the ideas of the above-mentioned people were not immoral because they in fact are making no exception in their own favor when they refuse to help other people, then he would contradict his conviction that the moral law is the same for all people.

(3) If we, along with Kant, believe that the ideas of these people are morally unacceptable, then we would have to conclude that while any act that violates Kant's Categorical Imperative may be morally wrong, the Categorical Imperative is not in itself sufficient to weed out all immoral policies or acts. This is probably true, but it contradicts Kant's claim that the Categorical Imperative is *the* fundamental principle of morality. Insofar as Kant wants not only to set forth a plausible morality but wants to derive it from one basic principle, he probably does not succeed.[4]

HUMAN NATURE AS AN END IN ITSELF

Kant, as we see, does not want morality to depend on goals that people just happen to have, and so on human preferences and inclinations. (One reason for this is his belief that actions that spring solely from our inclinations are not the product of free will.) We can say that an end is something for whose sake we act. One kind of end we act for the sake of is a goal. We can also, however, refrain from acting, not for the sake of something we wish to accomplish or bring about, but for the sake of something that already exists. We can, as we have seen, act or refrain from acting for the sake of respecting a moral principle. Similarly, we can act or refrain from acting for the sake of a person, as in cases of showing gratitude or courtesy or respect. So it is possible to regard human beings as ends in themselves.

Treating something as an end can be contrasted to treating it as a means. If I pick up a brick and use it for building a house that will make my life more comfortable, I use it as a means to an end. If I force another human being to become my slave in order to make my life more comfortable, I use him or her as a means to an end. I am treating a human being no differently from a brick (or a robot). Unlike bricks, human beings have purposes and plans of their own and the ability to formulate and act on such purposes and plans, but I am not allowing that fact to interfere with my pursuit of my own ends. To do that, however, is to violate what Kant regards as a second formulation of the Categorical Imperative: "So act as to treat humanity, whether in your own person, or in that of any other, in every case as an end withal, never as a means only."[5] Kant regards this principle as being derivable from the first, since human beings think of themselves as being ends in themselves—that is, as existing not for the purposes of other people, but for the sake of their own choices and plans. They cannot will, therefore, that all human beings refrain from treating others, including themselves, as ends as well as means.

What is valuable in human nature, unique among the creatures of earth, and worthy of respect, according to the Kantian point of view, is

> a kind of freedom which lower animals lack—ability to foresee future consequences, adopt long-range goals, resist immediate temptation, and even to commit oneself to ends for which one has no sensuous desire [as well as] the capacity and disposition to act on principles [including both principles] of prudence and efficiency (hypothetical imperatives) and "unconditional rules of conduct" (categorical imperatives, i.e., the moral law).[6]

This puts the individual human being above all these other ends. As a contemporary philosopher, Alan Donagan, puts it:

> For by the very fact that there is no producible end, not even his own happiness, which a man cannot rationally choose to relinquish, it follows that he stands to all producible ends, even to those which are natural to him, in the position of what St. Augustine called "a judge." Having this power to judge his producible ends, which as such, is a higher kind of power than brute animals possess, human beings, as rational, are of a higher kind than any others they have yet encountered in nature. Nor can there be any creature higher in kind, although there may be some higher in degree.[7]

Since this rational nature of human beings is superior to any possible end or purpose a human being might be pursuing, it is "that which must never be acted against in the pursuit of any of these other ends or purposes, and so never be treated purely as a means."[8]

Numerous contemporary philosophers have adopted Kant's principle, or something very close to it, as fundamental to their own positions, each expressing it in his or her own way. Alan Donagan formulates it this way:

"It is impermissible not to respect every human being, oneself or any other, as a rational creature."[9] Charles Fried writes:

> What we may not do to each other, the things which are wrong, are precisely those forms of personal interaction which deny to our victim the status of a freely choosing, rationally valuing, specially efficacious person, the special status of a moral personality. . . . Thus what constitutes doing wrong to another may also be regarded as a denial of the respect owed to another's moral personality.[10]

Donagan regards such a principle as being at the foundation of what he calls "the common morality" of the Western world with its Jewish-Christian heritage. In contemporary philosophical discussion, positions based on this formulation of Kant's Categorical Imperative, or something like it, often present the principal alternative to utilitarianism, and provide one foundation for the belief that individuals have certain basic human rights that are not to be sacrificed for the sake of the general welfare.

Why might we accept Kant's principle? One reason is that we might find the whole line of reasoning by which Kant himself arrives at it in some sense intellectually compelling, though this is not the reason why most of its contemporary adherents accept it. Perhaps it simply intuitively appears to be true. Daniel Maguire claims that we "experience" persons as valuable, and that "if we do not accept the fundamental role of our perception of the value of persons and their environment" we are untrue to our own experience, and we also (to give another reason) undermine the possibility of moral discourse.[11] Perhaps we just think that a moral theory that gives this principle an important place survives critical evaluation better than any competitors.

PERFECT DUTIES TO OTHERS

Lying and Deception

Kant applies the second formulation of the Categorical Imperative to the same examples to which he applied the first. When I borrow money by means of a false promise, I am using the other person only as a means and am not respecting the fact that as a free and rational person he or she could not possibly agree to my actions. One could adduce many other examples of deceit to illustrate violation of the principle of treating people not merely as means, but as ends in themselves. A man obviously violates the principle if he intentionally misleads a woman into believing that he intends to marry her in order to obtain sexual favors that he would not otherwise be granted. A woman obviously violates the principle if she leads a man to believe that she is more interested in him than she really is so that he will continue to spend money on her until somebody she is more interested in comes along. Charles Fried writes, in a Kantian spirit:

> Lying is wrong because when I lie I set up a relation which is essentially exploitative. It violates the principle of respect, for I must affirm that the mind of another person is available to me in a way in which I cannot agree my mind would be available to him—for if I do so agree, then I would not expect my lie to be believed.[12]

Are There Exceptions?

Approaching the matter from this point of view, what kind of exceptions might there be to the rule against lying? We previously discussed the view that deception is morally permissible in many business contexts because it is like bluffing in a poker game, part of the strategy of the business game understood and accepted by all the players.[13] Kant discusses the case of an assassin asking a person about the location of his intended victim.[14] Although Kant himself says that even here it is wrong to lie, this, in fact, may be a case in which the game analogy does justify deception. The assassin and the person he questions both know that he has no right to information about the location of his intended victim, and they both know that the other knows this, so we are in a game-playing situation in which "falsehood ceases to be falsehood . . . [because] it is understood on all sides that the truth is not expected to be spoken."[15] The assassin, furthermore, has forced the person he is questioning into the situation by not giving that person the option of refusing to answer without risking personal harm. It would seem that the person questioned, therefore, has the right to lie and can do so without violating either version of the Categorical Imperative.[16]

A German theologian, Dietrich Bonhoeffer, discusses the case of a teacher confronting a child, in front of the class, with the question of whether it is true that his father often comes home drunk.[17] Bonhoeffer says that the child has the right to lie if he does not have the maturity to figure out some other way of extricating himself from the situation without revealing family secrets to an outsider. The same argument could be used here. The teacher and the child both know that the teacher has no right to obtain this information from the child, at least in this manner, or to risk humiliating the child in front of the class, and so both should know that the truth cannot be expected in this situation. (If one does not know whether the teacher or assassin knows this, it is at least reasonable to believe that he or she does know it.) Another justification would be in terms of self-defense, parallel to the justification for killing in self-defense, in which the lie is simply a method of preventing the liar from being used purely as a means to someone else's ends.[18]

Other Perfect Duties

The prohibition of lying, as well as of the lying promise, is called a *perfect duty*, one that requires a specific course of action that must be taken or avoided with respect to a particular person, the violation of which is not only bad but wrong. If the perfect duty is to another person, that person can be said to have a corresponding right. The person to whom a promise is made has a right to its being carried out. Alan Donagan derives the following perfect duties to others from the principle of respect for persons:

> It is impermissible for anybody at will to use force upon another. . . . Three precepts are readily derivable from the general prohibition of the use of force: that no man may at will kill another; that no man may at will inflict bodily injury or hurt on another; and that no man may hold another in slavery.[19] [Only the third of these is unqualified.] . . . It is impermissible for anybody to break a freely made promise to do something in itself morally permissible.[20] [There is usually a common understanding that there could be numerous conditions that would annul this obligation.] . . . Sexual acts which are life denying in their imaginative significance (e.g., sado-masochistic acts, or acts of prostitution), or are exploitative (e.g., casual seduction) are impermissible.[21]

We can add to these that it is impermissible for anyone to use power over others to humiliate or degrade them.[22] In addition, there are other duties, such as those that forbid stealing, or that deal with one's relationship to government, that depend on the political and economic institutions of a particular society.

One of the most blatant and most widespread violations of respect of persons is obviously rape. "Rape is first and foremost a crime of violence against the body, and only secondarily (although importantly) a sex crime."[23] One can imagine a desperate person engaging in other acts of violence, such as mugging someone or even killing someone, but it is hard to imagine any such thing as raping out of desperation. Rape would seem to be a greater evil, therefore, because it is a crime without excuse, to which extenuating circumstances are irrelevant. It would also seem to be a greater evil than many other crimes, since it more directly violates the principle of respect for persons. According to Carolyn Shafer and Marilyn Frye,

> rape is an act which belies respect, and it is often an act actually intended to communicate the fact of disrespect. Whether it is the rapist's intention or not, being raped conveys for the woman the message that she is a being without respect, that she is not a person.[24]

Rape does not have worse consequences than murder, but from a Kantian point of view moral worth has to do with intention, not with consequences. The murderer may not intend disrespect, but the rapist does. Shafer and Frye continue:

> Looked at microscopically, an individual rape on the street, as it were, done by a stranger . . . is bad in the way assault in general is, but its wickedness is compounded by the fact that it is a use of a person, not just the injury of a person, and a use of a person in pursuit of ends not its own and/or contrary to its own. That is profoundly disrespectful and a clear case of failing to treat a person as a person. It is also a use of a person which involves tampering with parts of its self which are for most people centrally rather than peripherally involved in their personal identity.

> Looked at macroscopically, rape is the point of application of a monstrous device of social control in which insult and injury are heaped upon one another in such complex abundance that one can scarcely keep the accounts of it.[25]

While homosexual rape is not unknown, especially in prisons, obviously most rapes are acts of violence by men against women. Feminists ask society to consider how rape may be encouraged by the prevalence of messages indicating that women are nonpersons in society—for example, by the popularity of violent pornography; by rape victims not being respected and taken seriously by police departments; by complaints of sexual harassment not being taken with full seriousness by men; by language (used by men) that refers to women using names of things that are not persons (such as "doll," "fox," "chick," derisive terms for parts of the female anatomy, etc.[26]). Although Kant himself shared the prejudices of his time with respect to women, Kant's principle calls on us to be sensitive to all ways in which women are treated as nonpersons.

IMPERFECT DUTIES TO OTHERS

The principle of respect for human nature is first of all the source of *negative duties*, that is, duties not to do certain things. Kant writes: "This principle, that humanity and generally every rational nature is *an end in itself* . . . is the supreme limiting condition of every man's freedom of action."[27] While some modern admirers of Kant claim there are no positive duties at all to benefit one's neighbor, Kant himself claims that we do have such duties. "For the ends of any subject which is an end in himself, ought as far as possible [also] to be *my* ends, if that conception [of an end in itself] is to have its *full* effect on me."[28]

Kant may not be consistent. At one point he indicates that failing to aid others may be bad, but strictly speaking not wrong.[29] Part of the problem may lie in Kant's failure to distinguish between promoting the happiness of others (which may be optional) and helping others in distress.[30] Many contemporary philosophers with a Kantian orientation are unambiguous on this question. Alan Donagan writes: "It is impermissible not to promote the well-being of others by actions, in themselves permissible, inasmuch as one can do so without proportionate inconvenience."[31]

"Respect for persons" has been seen as equivalent to the Christian teaching of *agape* (love),[32] Donagan sees Kant's position as a philosophical underpinning of the common morality of the Western world that springs from Judaism and Christianity.[33] But these religions certainly regard failure to help as often being as serious as direct harm.

Respect for others as rational and self-determining implies that when we seek to further the happiness of other people, we should try to further their happiness as they choose it, not as we would choose it. We may decline to help if we judge that their choices are too wide of the mark (or else we would allow ourselves to be just the means to the ends of others).[34] These qualifications would not detract from a duty to aid a person lacking the basic necessities of life, since such a lack is an obstacle to being self-determining and to attaining happiness according to anyone's conception of happiness. Some people who would agree with the principle of respect for persons in general think that Kant and some Kantians overemphasize concern with other people's freedom or autonomy at the expense of concern for all of their interests.

There are certain limitations that the Kantian approach would likely set on the duty of beneficence. Kant says that a person should "not push the expenditure of his means in beneficence . . . to the point where he would finally need the beneficence of others."[35] Second, help should not be given in a manner or to an extent that reduces the ability of the person (or group) that is helped to be self-reliant and self-determining. Third, every effort must be made to "carefully avoid any appearance of intending to obligate the other person, lest he (the giver) not render a true benefit, inasmuch as by his act he expresses that he wants to lay an obligation upon the receiver."[36]

Fourth, it would seem that the giver could refuse to give if a recipient had agreed to use past contributions to improve his or her ability to be self-sufficient and had failed to do so, on the grounds that the giver was just being used as a means to an end. The relevance of these points to government welfare programs and foreign-aid programs should be obvious.

IMPERFECT AND PERFECT DUTIES TO ONESELF

Duties to Oneself

Social contract approaches to ethics, as well as some other types of "liberal" ethics, insist that morality has to do only with conflicts between the interests, desires, or rights of different people, so that it makes no sense to say that we have moral duties to ourselves. Advertisers, perhaps for the sake of overcoming any guilt we might have about buying luxuries for ourselves while the needs of others are so great, sometimes suggest that we have a duty—perhaps because we have worked hard all week or all year— to benefit ourselves by buying their beer or their vacation trips. Kant disagrees radically both with the view that we have no duties to ourselves and with this particular idea of duties to oneself.

> Not self-favor but self-esteem should be the principle of our duties towards ourselves. This means that our actions must be in keeping with the worth of man. . . . Man must not appear unworthy in his own eyes; his actions must be in keeping with humanity itself if he is to appear in his own eyes worthy of inner respect.[37] . . . Whoever acts in such a way that he cannot be an end, uses himself as a means and treats his person as a thing.[38]

Imperfect Duties to Oneself

One self-regarding duty that Kant discusses is the duty to develop one's talents. It is an imperfect duty because it does not specify which talents and to which degree. Kant says that the individual may not live by the policy of neglecting all of his talents because "he cannot possibly *will* that this should be a universal law of nature or be implanted in us as such by a natural instinct,"[39] and because

> there are in humanity capacities of greater perfection which belong to the end which nature has in view in regard to humanity in ourselves . . . . To neglect these might perhaps be consistent with the *maintenance* of humanity as an end in itself, but not with the advancement of this end.[40]

Developing my potential increases my ability to set goals and to attain them, and so to be a rational, self-determining being. The policy of not doing so contradicts an aspect of human nature—a rational being's tendency to employ its reason and develop its faculties. Alan Donagan puts it this way: "Common morality demands of every human being that he adopt some coherent plan of life according to which, by morally permissible actions, his mental and physical powers may be developed."[41]

Perfect Duties to Oneself

The remaining kind of duty is a perfect duty to oneself. One example Kant uses is the prohibition of suicide, because to commit suicide in order to avoid suffering is to use oneself purely as a means to another end. Others have argued, however, that there are other justifications for suicide that would not involve a failure to treat oneself as a rational, self-determining being. Kant's own reasoning concerning some duties to oneself is very dubious.[42] This does not mean, however, that no duties to oneself can legitimately be derived from the Kantian basic principles. Alan Donagan writes:

> Since a man is a rational creature who is a rational animal, respect for man as the rational creature he is implies respect for the integrity and health of his body. Hence it is impermissible . . . for anybody to mutilate himself at will, or to do at will anything that will impair his health. . . . It is contrary to the precept forbidding the impairment of health so to use drugs as to incapacitate oneself for the ordinary business of life. And, perhaps more importantly, it is impermissible to allow the use of a drug to become the main point of life. For anybody to place any kind of drug-induced enjoyment before the full use of his capacities as a rational creature is a plain case of failure to respect himself as the kind of being he is. The objection is not to the enjoyment itself, but to the inordinate value set upon it.[43]

It has also been effectively argued that a person can violate a duty to himself or herself by being deficient in self-respect. This duty is violated by allowing oneself to be abused, manipulated, controlled, emotionally blackmailed, humiliated, or taken advantage of by another person, where there is any possibility at all of getting out of the situation in which any of these things happen.[44] Kant writes:

> We are not indifferent to cringing servility; man should not cringe and fawn; by so doing he degrades his person and loses his manhood. . . . Moreover, if a man gives up his freedom and barters it away for money, he violates his manhood. . . . It is absurd that a reasonable being, an end for the sake of which all else is means, should use himself as a means. It is true that a person can serve as a means for others (e.g., by his work), but only in a way whereby he does not cease to be a person and an end. Whoever acts in such a way that he cannot be an end, uses himself as a means and treats his person as a thing.[45]

KANT AND AUTONOMY

Kant's emphasis on duty has sometimes been blamed for the alleged German tendency toward slavish obedience to authority. But to obey laws that are imposed on a person by others is precisely what Kant rejects. To do something because someone else (even God) commands one to do it is to be *heteronomous* (from the Greek *heter*, "other" and *nomos*, "law"). But the moral person must be *autonomous* (from *autos*, "self,"and *nomos*, "law"). The individual person must act in such a way that she or he can regard herself or himself as being the author of the moral law.[46] Blindly accepting the orders of one's superiors is to violate the principle of autonomy. "The touchstone of everything that can be concluded as a law for a people lies in the question whether the people could have imposed such a law upon itself."[47]

This does not mean that each person can invent his or her own morality. Other people are rational beings who must be treated as ends in themselves. Therefore, the moral law of which each individual is the author must be of such a nature that it could be the universal law for all rational beings. Since reason is the same in all of us, we will be the authors of the same laws, and subject to the same laws. The form of the moral law is the principle of universalizability. The content of the moral law is the demand to treat all rational beings as ends in themselves. The moral ideal is a community in which all live in harmony as moral equals, since each person is a ruler and each person is a subject. Each person is to live by the rules which each person's reason sees to be generated by the Categorical Imperative. Kant calls this the kingdom (or realm) of ends.[48]

BEYOND THE BASIC PRINCIPLES

We have looked at the content of Kant's moral philosophy and at the implications of its basic principles, especially the principle of respect for persons. Much of what he has to say seems reasonable, perhaps because it is nothing other than the working out of the implications of the common moral tradition of the Western world that we and Kant share. But Kant did not only want to set forth a plausible moral philosophy, he also wanted to show that reason supports that morality by showing that to be immoral is, in some sense, to violate standards of reason. For Kant, violating the principle of respect for persons necessarily involves violating the universalizability principle, which necessarily involves violating rationality itself. Most philosophers believe that there are gaps in his arguments that cannot be filled, so that he did not succeed in that effort.

As far as the content of Kant's moral philosophy is concerned, there are three other things to take note of. One is that Kant has interesting things to say about virtue and vice, so we will deal again with Kant in the chapter on that subject. The second is that while the principles of universalizability and respect for persons provide insight into our duties to other human beings in general, they seem to be rather far removed from some of the specific duties we have to each other as husband and wife, parent and child, employer and employee, and so on. More will be said about these duties in later chapters. The third is that Kant does not have much to say about ideals that would give positive guidance for people's lives. Any ideals that violate the Categorical Imperative are obviously excluded. But we might also like to know, within the realm of the permitted, which ways of life are more ideal and which less.[49]

QUESTIONS

1. Can you state precisely what Kant means by the "good will"? Can you explain the difference between hypothetical and categorical imperatives? Can you state the two versions of the Categorical Imperative that are discussed in this text?

2. In your opinion, is the good will, or the will to do one's duty for its own sake, the only ingredient that makes up the morally praiseworthy person? Is it an ingredient at all?

3. Racist positions in general would seem to fail to pass the universalizability or reversibility (Golden Rule) tests. Do people who hold such views think that they are morally justified in doing so? If so, do they think that they pass such a test, or do they not accept the ideas of universal applicability and reversibility? How can they possibly think their views are morally justified?

4. Can you think of any actions, attitudes, or policies that would be disqualified by the universalizability test, but that you would still wish to maintain were morally permissible? How would you argue for them? Can you think of any actions, attitudes, or policies that you think would pass the universalizability test, but that you think would nevertheless be immoral? How would you argue?

5. If you do not accept the validity of Kant's formulation of the moral principle concerning treating people as ends in themselves, how would you argue against it?

6. Discuss the meaning and correctness of the statement: "Rape is the exposure of the public lie that women are respected persons."[50] Is the author of this text correct that (at least from a Kantian point of view) rape is usually more evil and is less excusable then robbery or even murder?

7. According to one survey, 70 percent of teenage males think that it is permissible to lie to a girl about their true feelings toward her in order to get her to agree to sexual relations. This would appear to be an obvious violation of Kant's principle forbidding treating people purely as means to one's own ends. Can you think of any possible way of arguing that it is not such a violation? Can you think of any way of defending these views? Is there any imaginable way that these 70 percent could defend their behavior to themselves? Is this statistic evidence that we live in a society that has rejected the "common morality" of the Western world of which Kant was a spokesman? Is this further evidence that many men think of women as nonpersons?

8. It is common for people who take drugs or drink too much to say, "I'm not doing anything wrong since I'm not hurting anybody other than myself." What are some ways that Kant or other Kantians would respond to that? If you disagree with Kant, how would you reply?

9. What is the difference between the Kantian view of duties to oneself and the view that, in the face of a request to contribute to charity, responds, "I've worked hard for my money and I have a duty to myself to spend it on something I want"? Which is more adequate? Under what conditions might Kant use a duty to oneself as a reason for turning down a request for help?

10. Would you agree that servility is morally wrong? For example, is the abused wife who does not take any opportunity to break away from her abusive

husband violating such a duty to herself? If not, how would you reply to the Kantian point of view? If servility is not violating a duty to oneself, what, in your opinion, would be violating a duty to oneself? According to some surveys, most girls in their early teens who have sexual relations do not really enjoy them, or really want to have them, but just give in to pressure. Are they, thus, violating a duty not to be servile?

FURTHER READING

Kant's works on ethics that are used in this chapter are:

Fundamental Principles of the Metaphysic of Morals, from *Kant's Critique of Practical Reason and Other Works on the Theory of Ethics.* Translated by Thomas Kingsmill Abbott. 2nd ed. London: Longmans, Green, 1879. There are other translations with different titles.
Lectures on Ethics. Translated by Louis Infield. New York: Harper and Row, 1963.
The Metaphysical Principles of Virtue. Translated by James Ellington. Indianapolis: Bobbs-Merrill, 1964.

Other works about Kant, or that take a Kantian approach, are:

Acton, H. B. *Kant's Moral Philosophy.* New York: St. Martin's Press, 1970.
Donagan, Alan. *The Theory of Morality.* Chicago: University of Chicago Press, 1977.
Downie, R. S., and Elizabeth Telfer. *Respect for Persons.* New York: Schocken, 1970.
Fried, Charles. *Right and Wrong.* Cambridge, Mass.: Harvard University Press, 1978.
Green, O. H., ed. *Respect for Persons.* Tulane Studies in Philosophy, vol. 30. New Orleans: Tulane University Press, 1982.
Hill, Thomas E., Jr. "Humanity as an End in Itself," *Ethics* 91 (October 1980): 84–99.
_____. "Servility and Self-Respect." *Monist* 57 (January 1973): 87–104.
Lo, Ping Cheung. "A Critical Reevaluation of the Alleged 'Empty Formalism' of Kantian Ethics." *Ethics* 91 (January 1981): 187–89.
Murphy, J. G. *Kant: The Philosophy of Right.* New York: St. Martin's Press, 1970.
Paton, H. J. *The Categorical Imperative: A Study of Kant's Moral Philosophy.* New York: Harper and Row, 1967.

NOTES

1. Immanuel Kant, *Fundamental Principles of the Metaphysic of Morals*, in *Kant's Critique of Practical Reason and Other Works on the Theory of Ethics*, trans. Thomas Kingsmill Abbott, 2nd ed. (London: Longmans, Green, 1879). The English has been slightly

modernized from the Abbott translation. Other translations of this work appear under several other titles, including *Groundwork for the Metaphysic of Morals*. Page references in these notes appear in parentheses and refer to the *Konigsliche Preussische Akademie der Wissenschaft* edition; these references appear in the margins of most English translations.

2. Ibid., section 1 (402). This is repeated with slightly different words in section 2 (421).

3. Ibid., section 2 (424, 430).

4. Kant does in fact have an answer to these reservations or objections. Kant says, "Act as if the maxim of your action were to become by your will a universal *law of nature* [ibid., section 2, (421)]" If we willed that the policy of not helping others should be a general law, that would mean that we will that no one help us. But that would be to will something that it is impossible for me to will or to want without contradicting something built into human nature and thus without violating the "law" of my own nature. The idea of a law suggests that one's maxims must be consistent with all other laws, including the laws of nature.

What Kant might mean here is that if I am claiming to want something (such as not being helped in a time of need) that it is impossible for my human nature actually to want, I am just allowing my present advantageous position to cloud my imagination and I am deceiving myself. (This may well be true.) Or Kant might be giving a natural law argument: If I do in fact want a world without mutual help, then my wants run contrary to human nature, as a whale's wanting to fly would run against its nature. In either case, it is not a matter of willing something that, if universalized, contradicts one's fluctuating desires or has undesirable consequences, but rather it is a matter of contradicting what is intrinsically part of the human nature of all people. But whether something is intrinsically part of the human nature of all people or not is debatable.

5. Ibid., section 2 (429). See also Kant's *Metaphysical Principles of Virtue*, trans. James Ellington (Indianapolis: Bobbs-Merrill, 1964), pt. 1 (424–426), 85–88, and his *Lectures on Ethics*, trans. Louis Infield (New York: Harper and Row, 1963), 168–71.

6. Thomas E. Hill, Jr., "Humanity as an End in Itself," *Ethics* 91 (October 1980): 86. See also R. S. Downie and Elizabeth Telfer, *Respect for Persons* (New York: Schocken, 1970), 20–21, and Ping Cheung Lo, "A Critical Reevaluation of the Alleged 'Empty Formalism' of Kantian Ethics," *Ethics* 91 (January 1981): 187–89.

7. Alan Donagan, *The Theory of Morality* (Chicago: University of Chicago Press, 1977), 232.

8. Ibid., 65.

9. Ibid., 66.

10. Charles Fried, *Right and Wrong* (Cambridge, Mass.: Harvard University Press, 1978), 29.

11. Daniel Maguire, *The Moral Choice* (Garden City, N.Y.: Doubleday, 1978), 84.

12. Fried, *Right and Wrong*, 67.

13. Allan Carr, "Is Business Bluffing Ethical?" *Harvard Business Review* (January–February 1968): 143–55.

14. Kant, "On the Supposed Right to Tell Lies from Benevolent Motives," in *Kant's Critique of Practical Reason and Other Works on the Theory of Ethics*, trans. Abbott.

15. Henry Taylor, quoted in Carr, "Business Bluffing," in Donaldson and Werhane, *Ethical Issues*, 46.

16. See the discussion in Fried, *Right and Wrong*, 69–78.

17. Dietrich Bonhoeffer, *Ethics* (New York: Macmillan, 1965), 363–72.

18. For a further discussion of this question, see Robert N. Van Wyk, "When Is Lying Morally Permissible?: Casuistical Reflections on the Game Analogy, Self-Defense, Social Contract Ethics, and Ideals," *Journal of Value Inquiry* 23 (1989); forthcoming.

19. Donagan, *Theory of Morality*, 82–83.

20. Ibid., 92–93.

21. Ibid., 107.

22. See Philip Hallie, "From Cruelty to Goodness," *Hastings Center Report* 11 (June 1981): 23–25.

23. Susan Rae Peterson, "Coercion and Rape: The State as a Male Protection Racket," in *Feminism and Philosophy*, ed. Mary Vetterling-Braggin, Frederick A. Elliston, and Jane English (Totowa, N.J.: Littlefield Adams, 1977), 364.

24. Carolyn Shafer and Marilyn Frye, "Rape and Respect," in Vetterling-Braggin et al, *Feminism and Philosophy*, 342.

25. Ibid., 345.

26. See Robert Baker, "'Pricks' and 'Chicks': a Plea for 'Persons,'" in *Today's Moral Problems*, ed. Richard Wasserstrom (New York: Macmillan, 1975), 152–70.

27. Kant, *Fundamental Principles*, section 2 (430).

28. Ibid.

29. See Kant, *Metaphysical Principles of Virtue*, introduction, 7 (390), 48.

30. See J. G. Murphy, *Kant: The Philosophy of Right* (New York: St. Martin's Press, 1970), 45–46.

31. Donagan, *Theory of Morality*, 85.

32. Downie and Telfer, *Respect for Persons*, 29.

33. Donagan, *Theory of Morality*, 26–31, 59–66.

34. See Kant, *Metaphysical Principles of Virtue*, introduction, 5, B (388), 46.

35. Ibid. 1 (454), 118.

36. Ibid. 1 (453), 118.

37. Kant, *Lectures on Ethics*, 124–25.

38. Ibid., 120.

39. Kant, *Fundamental Principles*, section 2 (423).

40. Ibid., 430; see also Kant, *Metaphysical Principles of Virtue*, pt. 1 (444–445), 108–9.

41. Donagan, *Theory of Morality*, 80.

42. See Donagan, *Theory of Morality*, 77–78. In general, concerning perfect duties to oneself, Kant says, in *Metaphysical Principles of Virtue* 1, pt. 1, (419), 79, that they "forbid man to act contrary to his natural end," in which he includes not only happiness and perfection, but also the intentions and goals of the instinct of self-love and of sexual activity. He ends up with the same contorted arguments, especially with respect to sexual matters, that we find in the most question-begging of the natural law arguments. See *Metaphysical Principles of Virtue* 1, pt. 1 (424–426), 85–87, subsection entitled "Concerning Wanton Self-Abuse." The absolute prohibition of lying is also based on a similar discussion of lying as a violation of a duty to oneself. Contemporary philosophers in the Kantian tradition have, rightfully, dropped this aspect of his moral philosophy. See Donagan, *Theory of Morality*, 105–6.

43. Donagan, *Theory of Morality*, 79–80.

44. See Thomas E. Hill, "Servility and Self-Respect," *Monist* 57 (January 1973): 87–104.

45. Kant, *Lectures on Ethics*, 118–19.

46. Kant, *Fundamental Principles*, section 3 (434).

47. Kant, "What is Enlightenment?" quoted in H. B. Acton, *Kant's Moral Philosophy* (New York: St. Martin's Press, 1970), 42.

48. Kant, *Fundamental Principles*, section 3 (436).

49. See Acton, *Kant's Moral Philosophy*, 63–64.

50. Shafer and Frye, "Rape and Respect," in Vetterling-Braggin et al., *Feminism and Philosophy*, 343.

7

Hedonism and Utilitarianism

THE UTILITARIAN IDEA

Perhaps moral and political rules cannot be based on a promise or a social contract because those who do not consent to such a contract would not be bound by them. Perhaps there are no such things as natural rights. Has anyone ever seen or touched or tasted one? Perhaps God does not exist, or if God does exist, perhaps there is no way of knowing God's will. On what, then, is morality to be based? David Hume, the English philosopher (1711–1776), answered that it is based partly on self-interest, as the social contract view maintains, but also partially on the sympathy human beings feel for other human beings, sharing to some extent their pains and pleasures. Self-interest guides us to support those rules, customs, and laws that produce beneficial results for ourselves. Sympathy guides us to support the same rules, customs, and laws because they have beneficial results for other people.[1] This approach, which emphasizes results, eventually came to be known as *utilitarianism*.

The rules, customs, and laws that prevail in any society are almost always beneficial in the sense that having them is better than doing without any rules, customs, or laws. For this reason, some utilitarians, or precursors of utilitarianism, such as Hume and William Paley (1743–1805), tended to be quite conservative, as they generally opposed anything that might undermine the existing rules. But these rules, customs, and laws might be much less beneficial for human beings than others that might replace them. The laws of England in the eighteenth century, for example, seemed to many at that time to be a hodgepodge of inconsistencies and absurdities that, because of their complexity, served to increase the power of judges and lawyers. Later utilitarians, such as Jeremy Bentham (1748–1832) and his eighteenth-century and nineteenth-century followers, were interested in reforming the laws. They proposed to do so in terms of comparing the consequences of those laws with the likely consequences of possible alternatives.

Utilitarianism is the theory that not only laws, but also actions, policies, and so on, ought to be evaluated in terms of which of the proposed alternatives will have the *best* overall consequences. An obvious candidate for a bad consequence is unhappiness, and an obvious candidate for a good consequence is happiness. Bentham defined utilitarianism in this way:

> By the principle of utility is meant that principle which approves or disapproves of every action whatsoever, according to the tendency which it appears to have to augment or diminish the happiness of the party whose interest is in question; or, what is the same thing in other words, to promote or to oppose that happiness.[2]

John Stuart Mill (1806–1873), the son of Bentham's younger associate, James Mill (1773–1836), and a defender of a modified version of utilitarianism, similarly wrote: "The creed which accepts as the foundation of morals 'utility' or the greatest happiness principle holds that actions are right in proportion as they tend to promote happiness; wrong as they tend to produce the reverse of happiness."[3] But if it is correct that the best consequences should be produced, then there must be some way of measuring the various consequences. Is happiness something that can be measured? Before trying to answer that question, we will approach the matter from another angle.

INTRINSIC GOODNESS

In order to evaluate actions or policies in terms of their results, we have to know which results are good and which bad. To say that something is good or bad can often be just a way of expressing one's favorable or unfavorable attitude toward it.[4] Children often use "good" and "bad" in this way. But as Hume pointed out, if we are to discuss matters of evaluation with other human beings, words such as these must be applied on the basis of public criteria and not purely on the basis of private considerations.[5] Sometimes when we say that something is good, we are saying that it rates high on a rating scale that uses criteria appropriate for rating that sort of thing.[6] So a good fishing pole is one that rates higher than most fishing poles according to recognized criteria for evaluating fishing poles. This is *goodness of a kind*. The criteria for goodness in fishing poles or toothbrushes depend on the function of each of these kinds of things. But those who dislike fishing would not consider the production of good fishing poles to be important.

We can also ask, however, what fishing poles or toothbrushes are good for. Philosophers sometimes speak of this sort of goodness as *instrumental* or *extrinsic goodness*. Toothbrushes are good for cleaning one's teeth, which in turn is good for avoiding tooth decay, which is good for avoiding pain, among other things. It doesn't seem to make much sense, however, to ask what the avoidance of pain is good for. It would seem to be good without being good *for* anything. So we say that the absence of pain is *intrinsically good* and that pain is *intrinsically bad*.

Unless there is at least one thing that is intrinsically good, or at least one thing that is intrinsically bad, then the instrumental goodness of something would not give us any good reason to want that sort of thing. Even if each rung of a ladder were good as a means to be used for reaching the top of the ladder, if there were nothing desirable in itself at the top, or nothing to be avoided at the bottom, or if the activity of climbing the ladder were not in itself intrinsically good, then the rungs, no matter how useful in getting to the top or away from the bottom, would not have any value. What then is it, philosophers have asked, that is intrinsically good, whether that be one thing or many, whether it be a goal to be reached or an activity?

HEDONISM AND HEDONISTIC UTILITARIANISM

If it is correct that the best consequences should be produced, then there must be some way of measuring the various consequences. For the most part, the various sciences began to make real progress when they began to deal quantitatively with phenomena. So it might seem plausible to argue that ethics can only be scientific and can only make real progress when it, too, deals with quantifiable phenomena that can be measured on the same scale of good or evil. If there are various kinds of things that are intrinsically good or evil that cannot be measured against each other on some common scale, then there is no way of determining what the best thing to do is. Is it possible that there is just one thing that is intrinsically good, and/or one thing that is intrinsically bad? The classical utilitarians, including Jeremy Bentham, claimed that pain is the one thing that is intrinsically bad and that pleasure is the one thing that is intrinsically good. Bentham also says that happiness is the one thing that is intrinsically good, but an individual's happiness is advanced by whatever "tends to add to the sum total of his pleasures; or, what comes to the same thing, to diminish the sum total of his pains."[7] The interests of the community are advanced by whatever adds to the total pleasures of the individuals that make it up.

The view that pleasure is the one thing that is intrinsically good and pain the one thing that is intrinsically bad was not something new to the modern world. Aristotle, in the fourth century B.C., found it necessary to reply to others who had taken this position. Epicurus (341–270 B.C.) is famous for advocating this point of view. Only those with a philosophical nature, however, have the wisdom to reject short-range pleasures that may lead to long-range suffering, and to accept short-term suffering that will lead to long-term pleasure. What is new with Bentham is the idea that what is right has to do with the distributing of pleasures and pains, and the idea that such a distribution could be implemented with mathematical precision. Pleasures and pains could be considered in terms of their sity, duration, certainty or uncertainty (the probability of their following from a certain act or policy), propinquity or remoteness, fecundity (the probability of their leading to additional pains or pleasures), purity (the probability of their "not being followed by sensations of the opposite kind, that is, pains, if it be a pleasure: pleasures, if it be a pain"), and extent ("the number of persons to whom it extends").

> Sum up all the value of all the pleasures on the one side, and those of all the pains on the other. The balance, if it be on the side of pleasure, will give the *good* tendency of the act upon the whole, with respect to the interests of that *individual* person; if on the side of pain, the bad tendency of it upon the whole. Take an account of the *number* of persons whose interests appear to be concerned; and repeat the above process with respect to each. . . . Take the *balance*; which, if on the side of *pleasure*, will give the general *good tendency* of the act, with respect to the total number of the community of individuals concerned; if on the side of pain, the general *evil tendency*, with respect to the same community.[8]

John Stuart Mill wrote:

> The ultimate end, with reference to and for the sake of which all other things are desirable—whether we are considering our own good or that of other people—is an existence exempt as far as possible from pain, and as rich as possible in enjoyments, both in point of quantity and quality.[9]

Not all utilitarians who wish to base ethics on a mathematical calculation wish to try to measure the intensity and duration of pains and pleasures. Sometimes they seek to measure the number and strength of people's desires or preferences. Often people's desires are a good indication of what they find pain or pleasure in, but perhaps it is possible for people to desire things other than pleasure. This approach will be considered below.

ADVANTAGES OF UTILITARIANISM

The classical utilitarian position has a number of things to recommend it.

1. It locates the basis of morality in something undeniably real and important, namely pain and pleasure. While people may not be able to reach agreement about the will of God, or natural rights, they can all agree that pain is real and that they wish to avoid it. They can also agree that they want their desires or preferences satisfied.

2. When opponents of utilitarianism appeal to such things as natural rights, or a social contract, or the will of God as revealed in nature, they can be accused of appealing to things the reality of which (in contrast to the reality of pleasure and pain) is open to doubt.

3. Utilitarianism has a plausible account of why people have some tendency to act morally and why they can be appealed to to act morally. This is the natural sympathy human beings have for one another, which allows them to identify with the pain and suffering, or pleasure and happiness, of others.

4. The moral point of view has to do with impartiality. Utilitarianism would seem to be the position that would be supported by a spectator who impartially experienced the pains and pleasures of everyone equally. Sometimes such an impartial spectator is identified with God, so that to maximize the balance of pleasure over pain is also to maximize the happiness of God.[10]

5. As already touched upon, utilitarianism would seem to give us a way that would in principle be capable of settling all moral disputes by an impartial and scientific method.

ACT-UTILITARIANISM

The Nature of Act-Utilitarianism

Whether or not we ought to ask if one set of results will be better than another in terms of the balance of pleasure over pain, or in some other way, there is still the question of what we ask that question about. Do we ask which individual action produces the best results, or do we ask which rule, or policy, or way of life produces the best results? We can imagine many situations in which there would be a difference. *Act-utilitarianism* is the view that a right action is an action that produces at least as good results as any other that an individual might choose. If we are faced with a person who is suffering from a terminal illness, should we sustain the life of that person, or should we perhaps hasten that person's death by disconnecting life-sustaining equipment, or should we perhaps end the person's suffering by killing him or her directly? The act-utilitarian answer is that we make a decision by weighing all the good and bad consequences of each alternative for all the people affected.

Criticism of Act-Utilitarianism

The criticisms of act-utilitarianism are numerous.

1. The first thing that might be noticed about act-utilitarianism is that when an individual decides what to do, only the future is taken into consideration, not the past. But this certainly seems to be questionable. Consider the following cases:

a. Suppose that John causes three hundred dollars' worth of damage to Bill's car. He is about to pay Bill the three hundred dollars when Tom appears on the scene. He finds out that Tom is more in need of three hundred dollars than Bill is and that the balance of happiness over unhappiness in the world will be greater if he gives the three hundred dollars to Tom instead of to Bill. It would seem, according to act-utilitarianism, that it is indeed John's duty to give the money to Tom.

b. Suppose Nancy estimates that she can provide ten units of benefit to Alice by spending an hour she has available in helping Alice prepare for a calculus test, or seven units of benefit to Mary by helping her prepare for the test, or five units of benefit to herself by doing neither. She has, however, promised to help Mary. She estimates that she would be doing two units of harm by breaking the promise because she would be making people less trustful of promises, especially hers. But she calculates that the balance of benefit over harm will still be greater if she helps Alice (eight units) rather than Mary (seven units), or if she spends the time doing something that would provide five units of benefit to herself. Is Nancy in fact freed from her duty to Mary? Furthermore, does she in fact have a duty to use the hour helping Alice?

c. Consider a case similar to the previous one except that Nancy has not made any promise. In the past, however, Mary has repeatedly helped Nancy with her chemistry. Does Nancy in fact have a duty to use the hour helping Alice, as act-utilitarianism would seem to imply, or should she spend the time helping Mary because of a duty of gratitude to her?

2. Utilitarianism seems to regard the only morally relevant relationship between human beings as that between possible benefactor and possible beneficiary. But this seems dubious. Suppose that I conclude that my neighbor's child would accomplish more good in the world if he or she goes to a prestigious college than my own child would. My neighbor, however, is unwilling or unable to pay for that education. If I can afford to pay for such an education for one person, do I really have a duty, as act-

utilitarianism suggests, to finance my neighbor's child's education while neglecting my own child's education?

3. Utilitarianism seems to ignore some important considerations. Some people would emphasize the distinction between what one does directly and what one only allows to happen. Others would emphasize the distinction between what one intends to do (or what one does intentionally) and what one brings about as a by-product of what one intends to do. Consider this imaginary case. Five people show up at the emergency room of a hospital, all of them needing the same drug, which happens to be in short supply. One, however, needs five times as much as the other four. Suppose that all else is equal, setting aside possible judgments about whose life is more valuable to society. The doctor uses all the medicine he has in order to save the lives of four of the people, with the result that the fifth person, who needed the larger dose, dies. But then consider a different imaginary case. Four people show up at the emergency room of the hospital all needing a certain serum that is not available, but that can be made from the blood of certain people. The doctor happens to know that such a person is present and kills him in order to make the serum for the other four, saving their lives. In these two cases, the results are the same: four people live and one dies. If the results are all that count, as act-utilitarianism claims, then the actions of the doctor in these two cases are morally equivalent. But that seems absurd.

4. Those who support act-utilitarianism presumably do so because they think that acting as an act-utilitarian will advance the utilitarian goal of increasing the balance of good over evil in the world. But this would seem to be false. Suppose that on election day I decide whether to vote or to stay home and watch TV. Since there is very little likelihood that my one vote will make any difference to the election, and therefore very little likelihood that it will produce any good in the world, and since there is every likelihood that I will get some pleasure from watching TV, it seems that I should watch TV. But if everyone acted as an act-utilitarian, the result would be disastrous for the democratic system.

5. The same problem arises when one considers cooperation between various parts of one person's life. Suppose that I figure that in order to go to medical school I need to get good grades, and that I therefore ought to study about sixty thousand hours while in college. When I come to one of the hours I intended to use for studying, I figure that the contribution that this one hour of study makes to my long-range plans is insignificant compared to the good I could do by visiting lonely people in a nursing home, or raising money for charity, or whatever. So as an act-utilitarian, I should do one of these other things and only study 59,999 hours. But, of course, the same thing is true about every other hour as well. So as an act-utilitarian, I may never get to study and so never achieve the desired goal.

6. Another objection to act-utilitarianism is that it is too demanding.

Am I ever permitted to take a nap or go see a movie when I could be using that time decreasing misery or increasing happiness in the world? Suppose I consider all the possible careers I might choose. Using act-utilitarian criteria, it is very likely that I would have to conclude that it was my duty to choose a position that would accomplish a great deal of good in the world but that no one else would likely be willing to take, such as being a poorly-paid physician in some dangerous, remote, and undesirable place. This would be my duty even if it made me miserable because I really wanted to be a musician. My own misery would be far outweighed by the good being done for others that would otherwise not be done. The good one can do in the world should probably count much more in career choices than it does for most people, but should it really count for everything?

PRIMA FACIE DUTIES AND INTUITIONISM

Most people would regard one or more of these considerations as fatal to act-utilitarianism. Some of these considerations were brought up by a British philosopher, W. D. Ross (1877–1968).[11] Ross's position, like Kant's, is called a *deontological* position (from the Greek *deon*, duty, and *logos*, reasoning). This term is used to refer to those points of view that say that the rightness or wrongness of actions is not based solely on their consequences (or, in Kant's case, not based on consequences at all). Ross concluded that we have duties which are based on our own past acts (duties to keep promises and to make reparations, as in cases 1a and 1b above) and on the past acts of others (duties of gratitude, as in case 1c above), as well as on the needs of others (duties of beneficence), and the existence of others (duties not to harm). He also included duties to advance one's own virtue and knowledge as well as a duty to correct injustice. Ross believed that we intuitively see that these are our duties. He called these *prima facie* or *conditional duties*, rather than *absolute duties*. This means that any one of these things tends to be our duty and is our duty unless it conflicts with some other *prima facie* duty. In cases of conflict, we just have to use our intelligence and intuition to try to decide which of these *prima facie* duties should prevail in any given circumstances. Presumably, we should see intuitively in case 4 above that the duty not to harm overrides the duty of beneficence, as it does in most cases of conflict between the two duties.

RULE-UTILITARIANISM

Utilitarians can agree that we do have the duties Ross says we have, or some similar list of duties, but they can argue that the reason we have such duties is that recognizing such duties in fact furthers the most good for the most people. So, for example, we should follow a rule that recognizes a duty to keep promises. Those who take this approach, such as Hume and Mill, are called *rule-utilitarians*.

One reason rules are important is that they contribute to the development of character. For Bentham, physical happiness is the goal of human conduct. Mill, however, qualifies his appeal to utility: "It must be utility in the largest sense, grounded on the permanent interests of man as a progressive being."[12] Part of this utility in the larger sense has to do with the development of character. For Bentham, the only virtue is being a good calculator of pleasures and pains and of the likelihood of their resulting from various courses of action. Benthamites consider rules against lying, for example, as prejudices. One should lie or not lie, depending on the good or bad consequences. In Mill's opinion, this is a case in which the Benthamites ignore the inner life. An individual act of lying might contribute to the happiness of the community. But the community's being made up of truthful and virtuous people would contribute far more to its total happiness in the long run.[13] General rules, such as the general rule against lying, are therefore important because they help to form character for oneself and others in a particular way, and people's characters ought to be so formed that they find pain in the very prospect of doing something vicious. That sort of present pain should weigh against the act, not just prospects of future pain. Here Mill sounds very much like Aristotle.

CRITICISM OF THE UTILITARIAN GOAL

The goal of providing the most good (pleasure, or satisfaction of preferences, or something else) for the most people is common to both act-utilitarianism and rule-utilitarianism. So the successful discrediting of that goal would discredit both versions of utilitarianism. And there would seem to be major problems with that goal.

1. In some cases, is it not legitimate to point out that one person deserves more than another? If a wealthy person is deciding how to distribute his wealth, utilitarian considerations, such as which of his children has the greatest financial needs, would certainly seem to be relevant, but so also might considerations of desert, such as that one child took care of him during his illness while others did not.

2. But suppose that merit is not relevant. Picture the Roman Colosseum, in which a handful of people will suffer harm, against their will, by being fed to the lions, while fifty thousand others will experience great pleasure, which they wish to experience. Whether we see the good in

terms of the balance of pleasure over pain, or in satisfaction of preferences in accordance with their number and intensity, we could still get the result that it is not only permissible to feed people to the lions in these circumstances, but also that one has a moral obligation to do so. But this is obviously absurd. Kantians would say that the utilitarian goal permits the treatment of some people purely as means to the ends of others. What is important for utilitarianism would seem to be pleasures and pains, or desires and preferences, rather than the individual human beings who experience the pleasures and pains, or who have the desires and preferences. As the contemporary ethicist John Rawls puts it, the question is whether the imposition of disadvantages on a few can be outweighed by a great sum of advantages enjoyed by others. Perhaps utilitarians think that the disadvantages of some could be outweighed by the advantages to others because they fail to "take seriously the distinction between persons,"[14] and so they think that "just as it is rational for one man to maximize the fulfillment of his system of desires, it is right for a society to maximize the net balance of satisfaction taken over all of its members."[15]

3. In the next sections, the theories of hedonism and preference-utilitarianism will be evaluated. If they both turn out to be implausible, then if utilitarianism were still to be supported, it would have to be a utilitarianism that said that we ought to promote what is good and discourage what is evil, while at the same time specifying that there are various things that are good and various things that are evil. But this would be to undermine the various selling points of utilitarianism. The connection between sympathy and moral action would become more tenuous. Utilitarianism would no longer be based on something that everyone regards as real, such as pain, and that everyone regards as an evil to be avoided. It would no longer be possible to settle moral issues with mathematical calculations.

THE EVALUATION OF HEDONISM

What Hedonism Entails

Hedonism as set out systematically by William K. Frankena, includes the following doctrines:[16]

1. Happiness equals the balance of pleasure over pain; unhappiness equals the balance of pain over pleasure.
2. All pleasures are intrinsically good; all pains are intrinsically bad.
3. Only pleasures are intrinsically good; only pains are intrinsically bad.

4. Pleasantness is the criterion of intrinsic goodness;
   pain is the criterion of intrinsic badness.
5. The intrinsic goodness of an activity or experience is proportional to the quantity of pleasure it contains, and the intrinsic badness of an activity or experience is proportional to the quantity of pain it contains.

Hedonism, Pleasure, and Intrinsic Goodness

Mill's predecessor, Jeremy Bentham, accepted all five of these propositions as true. Mill himself accepted the first four. He rejected the fifth on the grounds that qualitative as well as quantitative distinctions could be made between pleasures. He thus rejected Bentham's idea of turning ethics into a quantifiable science. (In fact, however, Bentham's calculus of pleasures and pains is already impossible apart from Mill's complications. How is intensity to be balanced against duration? How are pains to be weighed against pleasures?)

It seems certain that some of hedonism's doctrines are false, which ones depending on the precise meaning given to "pleasure." (It is quite possible that they are all false.) A number of writers have analyzed these claims in detail. These analyses become rather complex, partly because it is really not all that clear what is meant by "pleasure" and "pain."[17] A pleasure might be (1) an enjoyable experience taken as a whole (e.g., an enjoyable meal with friends). But we can also use the word "pleasure" to refer to one's subjective experience, which might also be broken down into two aspects: (2a) specific physical and psychological sensations that are part of the enjoyable experience, without which it would not be enjoyable (e.g., the taste of the food, the sense of exhilaration at making a witty remark), and (2b) something beyond this without which the sensations would not really be enjoyable, something that has been called the hedonic tone. (The hedonic tone would be what is missing if you experienced the same taste sensations at two different times, but at one time circumstances were such that the enjoyment was not there.)

We can refute the hedonist position if we can come up with an example that would show that any of the beliefs on Frankena's list is false (or at least any one of the first four). Aristotle considered the example of disreputable pleasures.[18] We might agree that a malicious pleasure would fit that category. Suppose a mob of people experience enough pleasure at seeing someone else beaten up that their pleasure exceeds the amount of suffering the victim experiences. Is the pleasure good? If we mean by "pleasure" the total experience, then the answer would be no, so the second proposition on the list is false. Suppose we mean just the subjective experience (the thrilling sensations along with the hedonic tone). Perhaps the hedonist would say that subjective pleasure is intrinsically good, but it is bad in this context. If it is bad, it must be because the good of the pleasure is outweighed by some other evil. It cannot be the evil of the suffering of the person beaten up because we have already weighed that in. Is it because of possible future bad effects? I think we would wish to say that this situation is bad in itself apart from future bad effects. Something else, such as the maliciousness itself, must be the ingredient that makes the total situation bad. But then the third proposition on the list is false, since something other than pain is intrinsically bad.

There is also an argument that the third proposition is false on the grounds that pleasure cannot be the only thing that is intrinsically good. If it were, we should be ready to sacrifice everything else for it. But consider this example. Suppose a scientist offers you the opportunity to spend the rest of your life strapped in a chair in a laboratory with pleasure-stimulating electrodes attached to your head.[19] Suppose you are convinced that you will be able to eliminate any pain and obtain any pleasant sensation you might want by pushing the appropriate button. Would you take him up on the offer? If you would not, it must be because you are convinced that pleasant sensations and hedonic tone are not all that is desirable in itself.

Aristotle makes the same point in a similar way. Think of some particular stage of your childhood when life was happy in the subjective sense, with much pleasure and little care, worry, or suffering. No matter how great the pleasures were at that stage of life, if it were possible for you to remain at that stage for the rest of your life, it is unlikely that you would choose to do so.[20] Furthermore, as Aristotle also points out, pleasure is often something that accompanies an activity and in a sense completes the activity. The pleasure, somehow detached from the activity, is not all we really want (e.g., we do not crave merely the sensations and hedonic tone that accompany a pleasant dinner and good conversation with friends, detached from the total event and activity). Or, as John Rawls puts it,

> it seems obvious that hedonism fails to define a reasonable dominant end. We need only to note that once pleasure is conceived as it must be, in a suffi- ciently definite way [as a subjective experience] so that its intensity and duration can enter into the agent's calculations, then it is no longer plausible that it should be taken as the sole rational aim.[21]

Furthermore, since there are different kinds of pleasures, as Aristotle maintains and as even Mill had to admit, that come from different ac- tivities, just being told that pleasure is the good gives little guidance for a person deciding what sort of life to pursue. If the question is, "What sort of activities should I develop my capacity to find pleasure in?" then hedonism offers no answer at all. Aristotle's conclusion is that those pleasures that accompany and encourage distinctively human flourishing are to be regarded as most desirable and those that interfere with it are to be regarded as undesirable.[22]

An additional way of discrediting the hedonist's position is by producing examples of other things we would regard as intrinsically good. This is one method Aristotle uses. He claims that the arguments that have been put forth to show that pleasure is *the* good really only show that it is *a* good, and that in fact pleasure cannot be *the* good because we would not consider a life of pleasure as desirable as a life of pleasure that also embodied some other characteristic, such as wisdom.[23] In the next chapter we will consider other additional characteristics of the good life.

Hedonism, Pleasure, and Happiness

Leaving aside the question of what is intrinsically good, we can look at the first proposition on Frankena's list of beliefs that go to make up the hedonist's position. Of what does happiness consist? Sometimes people who have access to all sorts of pleasures still kill themselves. That would seem to be conclusive evidence that they were not happy. Perhaps some kind of mental pain outweighed their pleasure, but if it was pain due to something missing in their lives, such as happiness, we can't say that happiness is the balance of pleasure over pain and then define the pain as due to a lack of happiness. That would be circular. Whatever such a person is missing would seem to be closely related to happiness, or to be happiness itself. Some people have defined happiness as the accomplishing of one's goals no matter what they are.[24] This view would be in line with preference-utilitarianism. But while the accomplishment of at least some of one's most important goals (or at least the appearance of doing so) may make an important contribution to happiness,[25] it is certainly not itself happiness, since there are people who have set out to achieve a certain goal and after attaining it have discovered that they were no happier than they were before.

What is missing in the life of the person who has a balance of pleasure over pain, or who has achieved his goals, and yet commits suicide is "satisfaction with one's life as a whole,"[26] or "comprehensive satisfaction."[27] Indeed, that is how "happiness" is more adequately defined.[28] The experience of pleasure may make a small contribution to satisfaction with one's life as a whole. The absence of pain and the accomplishing of one's goals would seem to make larger contributions, "provided that we are not threatened with the loss of what we have gotten or achieved, and provided that what appeared good when we sought it continues to appear good after it is attained."[29]

We will take up the discussion of happiness in the next chapter. At this point it is sufficient to note that the hedonistic view of happiness seems to be false. If happiness is satisfaction with one's life as a whole, then one cannot distribute it to people. People have to find it for themselves. What one can do for other people is remove obstacles to their finding it.

PREFERENCE-UTILITARIANISM AND ITS EVALUATION

Preference-Utilitarianism and Desire

If happiness is the balance of pleasure over pain, perhaps some psychologist can calculate what our duties are to everyone to increase that pleasure. If happiness is satisfaction with one's life, then we can ask people if they are more satisfied in one situation than they were in another, and whether they then think they might be more satisfied in a third. Presumably they desire that which they think will make them more satisfied. So we have the idea that what we owe to people is to try to satisfy their desires or preferences. *Preference-utilitarianism* is the doctrine that we ought to try to satisfy desires or preferences in terms of intensity, duration, and the number of people who have them. One problem with the hedonistic utilitarian idea is that no one has ever come up with a unit of measurement for all kinds of pleasures and pains. Those who wish to preserve Bentham's ideal of ethics as a quantifiable science have been attracted to preference-utilitarianism, since preferences can be measured in terms of how people vote, how they spend their money, how long they are willing to stand in line for something, and so on. Some people also favor this approach as a basis for government policy because it tolerantly takes into consideration each individual's own idea of what is good or what will bring satisfaction.

Happiness and the Fulfillment of Desire

Why should we seek to satisfy desires? One answer is because this produces happiness. But in fact neither the fulfillment of individual desires nor the fulfillment of a large number of desires is closely related to happiness. Advertisers produce desires in children and adults to have particular products. Often after a person purchases such a product and satisfies that particular desire, he or she is disappointed with it and no longer has any desire for it. Neither does the cumulative satisfaction of desire bring happiness. Between 1946 and 1970 the inflation-adjusted income of Americans rose an average of 62 percent. If in 1946 the members of an American family were asked whether they would be happier if they had a 62 percent increase in income to spend on whatever they wanted, they would probably have little doubt that they would be. In fact, however, Americans were no happier in 1970 than they were in 1946.[30]

Another answer is that satisfying preferences is a good thing whether or not it brings happiness. With such an approach no one need justify his or her preferences, since it is the existence and strength of a preference, not its justification, that is relevant. A child's desire to play in the middle of a busy highway must be weighed along with a parent's desire that the child not do this. The rapist's desire to rape must be weighed in the balance with the victim's desire not to be raped. On this view, preference-utilitarianism is not really neutral with respect to different conceptions of what is intrinsically good. Rather, it treats the satisfaction of preferences as itself intrinsically good, a position that does not seem very plausible. Is it intrinsically good that a child's desire to get a new product is satisfied when the child then discovers that the product is a total disappointment? Mark Sagoff writes:

> It cannot be argued that the satisfaction of preferences is a good thing in itself, for many preferences are sadistic, envious, racist, or unjust. Why should we regard the satisfaction of preferences that are addictive, boorish, criminal, deceived, external to the individual, foolish, grotesque, harmful, ignorant, jealous, . . . or zany to be a good thing in itself? . . . Ordinary consumer preferences . . . are usually regarded not as intrinsically good but as arbitrary from a moral point of view. People should be free to pursue these preferences, to be sure, but why should it be an intrinsically good thing that they succeed in satisfying them?[31]

Happiness and the Elimination of Desire

It would then seem to make sense to be concerned with satisfying desires only if doing so leads to happiness or to something else that was intrinsically desirable. On the view that unhappiness is an excess of pain over pleasure, the reduction of suffering is perhaps the major component of happiness. On the view that happiness is satisfaction with one's life, suffering is an obstacle to such satisfaction. Many people have argued that apart from outright physical pain, the chief sources of suffering are failing to attain what we desire and losing that to which we are emotionally attached. Everything that increases pleasure, thus, also has the potential for increasing pain. Perhaps, therefore, the best strategy is to decrease pain and the potential for pain. If our desires will always bring us more suffering than pleasure, then (contrary to preference-utilitarianism) perhaps eliminating desires rather than fulfilling them is the way that wisdom dictates. If attachments will usually bring us suffering in the long run, then instead of trying vainly to hold on to what we are attached to, perhaps we should reduce the level of emotional attachment. We can learn to do this for ourselves, and we can teach others the way of decreasing desires. This is the approach taken by Buddhism, as well as by the Greek and Roman philosophical school called Stoicism. Buddha said he taught about four matters: suffering, the origin of suffering, the destruction of suffering, and the path leading to the destruction of suffering.[32] Perhaps unfulfilled desires, and loss of what was desired, both of which bring suffering, will always outweigh the fulfillment of desire, which brings happiness. Thus, having desires will always increase unhappiness. So the Buddhist way to happiness is the way of eliminating suffering by eliminating desire and attachment, the causes of suffering. (Death might be another alternative, but for the Indian tradition, death leads to rebirth.) Buddhism's answer to preference-utilitarianism is that "from affection comes grief, from affection comes fear; he who is free from affection knows neither grief nor fear."[33] Buddhism's answer to hedonistic utilitarianism is that "from pleasure comes grief, from pleasure comes fear; he who is free from pleasure knows neither grief nor fear."[34] The primary way of reducing suffering in the world, then, is following and teaching the way of enlightenment.

Fulfilling Preferences People Would Have or Should Have

Buddhist and Stoic teachings certainly caution us against thinking that getting what we think we want is the obvious road to happiness. If, however, happiness is not primarily a matter of the balance of pleasure and pain, then eliminating desire because it is a cause of pain may not be the most important consideration. Furthermore, seeking to fulfill all desires or to eliminate them all are not the only options. Christianity, for example, does not tell us to eliminate desire, but to "hunger and thirst after righteousness" (Matt. 5:6). Aristotle tells us to train ourselves to desire what is ultimately worthwhile. John Stuart Mill believed that unenlightened preferences deserved less respect than enlightened ones. So a child's desire to get a certain product does not count if one knows that after the child gets it, he or she will be disappointed in it and will no longer want it. This is also true for adults.

Some preference-utilitarians say that only certain desires should count, or only the desires that people have for certain reasons, or only the desires that people would have if they were fully informed and fully rational. To take this approach, however, is to give up the idea of a utilitarian calculus, since there is no way of measuring desires that people would have under certain conditions but, in fact, do not now have. Nor is there any way of distinguishing desires people have for one kind of reason from those they have for some other kind of reason. There is also the problem of determining what desires people would have under different conditions. There will be some additional discussion of these issues in chapter 11. Perhaps whether desires should be respected has to do with whether they are for that which is really worthwhile. The next chapter begins with the question of what is worthwhile or intrinsically good.

CONCLUSION

Utilitarianism is certainly right in believing that consequences are important and that the production of human misery counts against any proposed action, rule, or policy. But the claim that consequences are always all that count and that they can be weighed in some scientific manner is more problematical. It would seem that however one defines the most good for the most people, there are major objections to any version of act-utilitarianism, some of which are equally applicable to rule-utilitarianism. The problems are only multiplied when one defines the good either in terms of the balance of pleasure over pain or in terms of the satisfaction of preferences or desires.

QUESTIONS

1. Should all pleasures, or all preferences, count the same, or are there criteria for determining which ones are more worthy of consideration?

2. A writer in Christian ethics, Joseph Fletcher, set forth a position he called situation ethics.[35] This position says that one should follow Jesus' command to love one's neighbor as oneself. This means that in any situation one should be willing to break any moral rule for the sake of doing the most loving thing to all people affected. Is there any difference between this position and act-utilitarianism?

3. Three accounts of happiness are included in this chapter: the balance of pleasure over pain, the achievement of one's goals, and satisfaction with one's life as a whole (which is developed in the next chapter). Can you think of any other alternatives? Which do you think is most adequate? Why?

4. Does it make sense to say that we ought to provide the most happiness for the most people? Can happiness be distributed to people as money, for example, could be?

5. Which arguments against act-utilitarianism would Kant support? What additional arguments are there? Do you think these arguments are decisive? Why or why not?

6. What is hedonism? Is it true for you that you would not give up everything else for the sake of pleasure? How is the answer to this question supposed to discredit hedonism? What other arguments against hedonism are there? (You

might wish to check the beginning of the following chapter as well.) Which of these arguments were used by Aristotle? Do you think that they are decisive?

FURTHER READING

The writings on utilitarianism are practically endless. Some that might be most useful to a student include the following:

Bentham, Jeremy. *An Introduction to Morals and Legislation*. London, 1789. Sections are reprinted in *Ethical Theories*, 2nd ed., edited by A. I. Melden. Englewood Cliffs, N.J.: Prentice-Hall, 1967.

Brock, Dan W. "Utilitarianism." In *And Justice for All: New Introductory Essays in Ethics and Public Policy*, edited by Tom Regan and Donald VanDeVeer. Totowa, N.J.: Rowman and Littlefield, 1982.

Hospers, John. *Human Conduct*. 2nd ed. New York: Harcourt Brace Jovanovich, 1982. See chaps. 4 and 6.

Mill, John Stuart. *Utilitarianism*. Indianapolis: Hackett, 1971.

John Plamenatz. *The English Utilitarians*. Oxford: Blackwell, 1958.

Quinton, Anthony. *Utilitarian Ethics*. 2nd ed. LaSalle, Ill.: Open Court, 1988.

Semmel, Bernard. *John Stuart Mill and the Pursuit of Virtue*. New Haven: Yale University Press, 1984.

Williams, Bernard, and J. J. C. Smart. *Utilitarianism: For and Against*. New York: Cambridge University Press, 1973.

On happiness, see:

Brandt, Richard. "Happiness." *Encyclopedia of Philosophy*. 3:413–14. New York: Macmillan, 1967.

Kekes, John. "Happiness." *Mind* 91 (July 1982), 358–76.

Tatarkiewicz, Wladyslaw. "Happiness and Time." *Philosophy and Phenomenological Research* 27 (September 1966), 1–10.

Telfer, Elizabeth. *Happiness*. London: Macmillan, 1980.

On pleasure and hedonism, see:

Aristotle. *Nicomachean Ethics*. Book 10. Many editions.

Brandt, Richard. "Hedonism." *Encyclopedia of Philosophy* 3:432–35. New York: Macmillan, 1967.

_____. *Ethical Theory*. Englewood Cliffs, N.J.: Prentice-Hall, 1959. See chap. 12.

Broad, C.D. *Five Types of Ethical Theory*. New York: Humanities Press, 1956. See chap. 6, 227–40.

Epicurus. "Letter to Menoeceus," trans. C. Bailey. In *Ethical Theories*, 2nd ed., edited by A. I. Melden, 143–46. Englewood Cliffs, N.J.: Prentice-Hall, 1967.

Hospers, John. *Human Conduct*. 2nd ed. New York: Harcourt Brace Jovanovich, 1982. See chap. 2.
Schwartz, Barry. *The Battle for Human Nature: Science, Morality and Modern Life*. New York: Norton, 1986. See pp. 162–66.

Discussions of preference-utilitarianism include:

Raz, Joseph. "Liberalism, Autonomy, and the Politics of Neutral Concern." In *Midwest Studies in Philosophy*, vol. 2, *Social and Political Philosophy*, edited by Peter A. French, Theodore E. Uehling, Jr., and Howard K.Wettstein, 89–120. Minneapolis: University of Minnesota Press, 1982. See section 4, 98–102.
Sagoff, Mark. *The Economy of the Earth*. New York: Cambridge University Press, 1988. See chap. 5 and elsewhere.

NOTES

1. David Hume, *Enquiry Concerning the Principles of Morals* ed. J. B. Schneewind (Indianapolis: Hackett, 1975), section 9, part 1; and *Treatise of Human Nature*, ed. L. A. Selby-Bigge (Oxford: Clarendon Press, 1988), book 3, part 1, chap. 2, p. 471, and part 3, chap. 1, pp. 581–84.

2. Jeremy Bentham, *An Introduction to the Principles of Morals and Legislation* (London, 1789, rev. ed. 1823), chap. 1, sect. 2. In *Ethical Theories*, 2nd ed., ed. A. I. Meldon, 369 (Englewood Cliffs, N.J.: Prentice-Hall, 1967).

3. John Stuart Mill, *Utilitarianism*, ed. George Sher (Indianapolis: Hackett, 1979) chap. 2, 7.

4. See, for example, A. J. Ayer, *Language, Truth, and Logic* (New York: Dover Publications, 1946), chap. 6.

5. Hume, *Enquiry*, section 9, part 1; and *Treatise*, 472 and 581–84.

6. See J. O. Urmson, "On Grading," *Mind* 59 (1950): 145–69.

7. Bentham, *Morals and Legislation*, chap. 1, section 5, 369.

8. Ibid., chap. 4, section 5, 386 (Italics are Bentham's.).

9. Mill, *Utilitarianism*, chap. 2, 11–12.

10. See Charles Hartshorne, *Man's Vision of God and the Logic of Theism* (New York: Harper, 1941).

11. W. D. Ross, *The Right and the Good* (New York: Oxford University Press, 1930), chap. 2.

12. Mill, *On Liberty*, ed. Elizabeth Rapaport (Indianapolis: Hackett, 1978), chap. 1, 10.

13. Mill, *Utilitarianism*, chap. 2.

14. John Rawls, *A Theory of Justice* (Cambridge, Mass.: Harvard University Press, 1971), 27.

15. Ibid., 26.

16. Adapted from William K. Frankena, *Ethics*, 2nd ed. (Englewood Cliffs, N.J.: Prentice-Hall, 1973), 84.

17. For a further discussion of these issues, see C. D. Broad, *Five Types of Ethical Theory* (New York: Humanities Press, 1956), chap. 6, 227–40; and Richard Brandt, *Ethical Theory* (Englewood Cliffs, N.J.: Prentice-Hall, 1959), chap. 12.

18. Aristotle, *Nicomachean Ethics*, 10, 4:1173b20–34.

19. This example comes from J. J. C. Smart, "An Outline of a System of Utilitarian Ethics," in J. J. C. Smart and Bernard Williams, *Utilitarianism: For and Against* (New York: Cambridge University Press, 1973), 18f. It is also used by Robert Nozick, *Anarchy, State and Utopia* (New York: Basic Books, 1974), 42–45.

20. Aristotle *Nicomachean Ethics*, 10, 3:1174a:1–8.

21. Rawls, *Theory of Justice*, 556–557.

22. Aristotle, *Nicomachean Ethics* 10, 4, and 10, 5.

23. Ibid. 10, 2:1172b28–35.

24. See W. F. Hardie, "The Final Good in Aristotle's *Ethics*," *Philosophy* 40 (1965): 277–95.

25. See John Kekes, "Happiness," *Mind* 91 (July 1982): 359–60.

26. Vladyslaw Tatarkiewicz, "Happiness and Time," *Philosophy and Phenomenological Research* 27 (September 1966): 1. See also Elizabeth Telfer, *Happiness* (London: Macmillan, 1980), 45.

27. William A. Galston, *Justice and the Human Good* (Chicago: University of Chicago Press, 1980), 69.

28. In 1737 (before Bentham), John Wesley wrote the following: "By happiness I mean, not a slight, trifling pleasure, that perhaps begins and ends in the same hour; but such a state of well being as contents the soul, and gives it a steady lasting satisfaction." From "On Love," sermon 149 in *The Works of John Wesley*, vol. 4, ed. Albert C. Outler (Nashville: Abingdon Press, 1987), 386. Wesley's words reflect the views of Richard Lucas, *Enquiry after Happiness*, 5th ed. (London, 1717), 1.26, 2.10.

29. These observations are made by Galston, *Justice*, 69.

30. T. Scitovsky, *The Joyless Economy* (Oxford: Oxford University Press, 1976), as reported in Barry Schwartz, *The Battle for Human Nature* (New York: Norton, 1986), 164.

31. Mark Sagoff, *The Economy of the Earth* (New York: Cambridge University Press, 1988), 102. See also Sagoff, "Values and Preferences," *Ethics* 96 (January 1986): 302–3.

32. "The Sermon at Benares," trans. Samuel Beal, in *The Wisdom of China and India* ed. Lin Yutang (New York: Random House, 1942), 360–62.

33. *The Dhammapada*, trans. F. M. Mueller, in Yutang, *Wisdom*, 341.

34. Ibid.

35. Joseph Fletcher, *Situation Ethics* (Philadelphia: Westminster Press, 1964).

8

Toward an Adequate Moral Theory: Pursuing the Good and Protecting the Vulnerable

ETHICS AND HUMAN WELL-BEING

Many people might say that much of what Kant and his modern admirers have to say is insightful, but after all is said and done, ethics has more to do with promoting human well-being than he allows. And while ethics does have to do with promoting human welfare in the long run, human welfare is more complex than the preference-utilitarians and hedonistic utilitarians indicate. Furthermore, the relationship of our duties and responsibilities to human well-being is not as simple or direct as they would suggest. Advocates of such views are likely to draw on Aristotle, but have more to say about duties and obligations than Aristotle said. Such a position, which in the long run may seem the most plausible, may be overlooked in an ethics textbook because it is not associated with any particular major historical figure such as Hobbes, Kant, or Bentham. In this chapter, the works of a variety of philosophers are drawn from to set forth and to defend such a point of view.

VALUE, INTRINSIC GOODNESS, AND THE GOOD LIFE

Happiness and Meaning

In the last chapter, the deficiencies of the hedonist's understanding of happiness were pointed out, and support was given to a definition of happiness as "satisfaction with one's life as a whole." But what contributes to such satisfaction? A psychiatrist, Victor Frankl, reflecting on his experiences in German concentration camps, came to the conclusion that the main concern of human beings "is not to gain pleasure or to avoid pain but rather to see a meaning" in their lives.[1] Even suffering is endurable if there is some meaning to be found in it. Robert Nozick writes that meaning has to do with transcending the limits of an individual life and making a connection with something larger.[2]

One way of making contact with something larger is making an impact on the world beyond oneself. The anthropologist and social theorist Ernest Becker writes:

> What man really fears is not so much extinction, but extinction *with insignificance*. Man wants to know that his life has somehow counted, if not for himself, then at least in a larger scheme of things, that it has left a trace, a trace that has meaning.[3]

The remarks of Nozick and Frankl suggest three ways of finding meaning: (1) through creative activity that has to do with fostering and striving to realize value, (2) through experiencing things of value, which has to do with being inspired by or resonating with values, and (3) through protecting and preserving value, which would include preserving one's character from corruption, even under adverse circumstances.[4] All of these have to do with transcending the individual self and making a connection with something larger.

Other Ingredients of the Good Life

Not Being Deceived about the Source of One's Happiness.   A person may be happy, and may be happy because he or she finds a sense of meaning in his life, but that happiness may be based on illusion. We might look back on someone's life and say of that person that he found satisfaction and meaning in bringing up his children to be honorable and good people (and thus leaving a valuable trace), but without his knowing it, they were totally rejecting his example and his good advice and were becoming more and more despicable. This person found meaning in his life because he thought he was accomplishing something, but he was deluded since, in fact, he was not succeeding. So a good or *eudaimonistic* life consists of at least two ingredients, happiness and not being deceived about that in which one finds happiness. This would also be the case when a source of one's happiness or satisfaction is an experience of value, rather than a meaningful activity. Suppose one source of a person's happiness is awareness of a good reputation, or the experience of a loving relationship with another person, or the experience of visions of God. But perhaps that reputation does not in fact exist, and the relationship is imaginary, and the source of the visions is not God. These facts would count against the belief that the person had as good a life as he or she might have had.

The Value of What One Finds Happiness In.   We can, however, imagine a person who is happy and who was not deceived about that in which she finds happiness, yet whose life we would not want to call good. Perhaps that person has happily and successfully devoted her life to being a "good" Nazi, or to engraving the Lord's Prayer on the head of a pin, or to trying to defend some crackpot pseudoscientific theory. Perhaps a person finds meaning in a certain experience, but it is the experience of a malicious or vindictive pleasure. Perhaps a person finds meaning in a certain experience because she believes it to have some metaphysical significance that it does not really have. One may find meaning and satisfaction in accomplishing something or experiencing something, but it is possible that the something is not really worthwhile, either because it is evil (as with the Nazi enthusiasm, or the malicious pleasure), or because it is trivial and pointless (as in the other examples). One may find meaning in maintaining one's character against great pressures to change, but perhaps the character traits one is maintaining are based on mistaken values.

So a third ingredient we need to add in our idea of a good life is that what one finds happiness in is actually something of value. As Nozick puts it, an objectively meaningful life involves "a transcending of limits in a wider context of [actual] value."[5] Thus, the good life has three ingredients: (1) happiness understood as satisfaction with one's life, which involves having a (subjective) meaning for one's life; (2) not being deceived about one's relationship to that which one regards as being a source of meaning (e.g., being certain that one really is accomplishing one's goals); and (3) being related to that which is neither trivial nor evil, but which has real value.

Intrinsic Value for Human Beings

Talking about preserving value, and about contemplating, appreciating, or resonating with value, raises the question of what has intrinsic value for human beings. One way of seeking to answer the question of what sorts of things are intrinsically valuable for human beings is to look at human nature and then make inferences about what would further the fulfillment or flourishing of the kind of beings human beings are. This approach was taken, at least part of the time, by Aristotle and St. Thomas Aquinas. This is also the approach taken by a contemporary writer, William Galston:

We exist as beings of a certain kind, endowed with organs of sense, practical abilities, and intellectual capacities. These facts carry with them an evaluative force: in general we believe that it is preferable to develop and exercise these powers and that their full development constitutes the norm through which partial realizations are judged. This belief is not merely imposed on our existence. Children have a natural impulse to develop themselves by sharpening their senses, gaining physical dexterity, and satisfying their curiosity. Good child rearing fosters, and, when necessary, regulates this impulse; the bad represses it.[6]

Do all types of human potential have an equal claim to be developed? Or is there one supreme area of fulfillment? There is a middle way that lists various criteria for distinguishing "higher" capacities from "lower." According to Galston, the higher capacities include those that are distinctively human (e.g., morality and theoretical inquiry), are relatively rare, more difficult or demanding, are capable of serving as a unifying factor in life, have positive side-effects on others, and "have been accorded wide and enduring respect."[7]

A second approach, sometimes taken by Aristotle and St. Thomas, is not to look toward human nature and human potential, but to look outward toward the things that human beings actually pursue or might pursue. Then one can ask which of these seem to be worth wanting for their own sake and/or as part of a way of life that is intrinsically worthwhile. Aristotle sometimes speaks about "what everyone [or no one] would say [or choose]."[8] Galston asks about what has been accorded wide and enduring respect. Mill refers to the opinions of competent judges who have wide experience. Perhaps the two approaches will tend to yield similar results. We can also ask what is evil by asking what would be avoided by all rational persons, unless they had some good reason not to avoid it.[9] Those things the absence of which would be evil would themselves be good.[10]

What Possesses Intrinsic Value?

As one takes either of these approaches, a list something like the following emerges. This list is a composite drawn from the largely overlapping lists of a number of philosophers.[11] It is meant to be neither necessarily exhaustive nor unrevisable.

Happiness. Most philosophers agree that this is the primary intrinsic value.

Pleasure and pain. By these criteria, pain is certainly evil, the absence of pain one good, and pleasure, as an ingredient of happiness, another good.

Existence and life. The evidence that life is an intrinsic value is, as Aristotle said, "the fact that everyone desires it."[12] Death is an evil because it deprives one of life.[13] Normal psychological and physical functioning are related values.

Knowledge. Human beings generally see knowledge, especially some understanding of humanity's place in the universe, as a basic good. One philosopher writes:

> Imagine yourself in a situation where you would be offered all of the usual and perhaps unusual necessities and even goods of life . . . but at the price of . . . not having any genuine knowledge or understanding either of yourself or of the nature of things generally—that is to say, at the price of your not asking any questions . . . and so of your not really knowing the what or the why of anything. Would you settle for this? Presumably not.[14]

One political philosopher persuasively argues that a free society depends on there being people with "truth respecting integrity,"[15] which may depend on treating either respect for truth or knowledge, or truth (or knowledge) itself, as an intrinsic good, independent of social utility.

Friendship, social existence, and love. Aristotle regards friendship as an intrinsic good, as well as an instrumental good, when he writes that it is "not only necessary but also noble," and that "no one would choose to live without friends, even if he had all other goods."[16] Friendship is a state of affairs that requires going beyond self-love and caring about another person for his or her own sake.

Aesthetic experience and aesthetic excellence. Art seems to be something that is valued in all societies. Joseph Raz writes: "A life with art is a good in itself; the existence of works of art is a constituent good; and the quality of life with art that explains its value is the ultimate good. All three are intrinsic goods."[17]

The natural order and humanity's harmony with it. Aldo Leopold found intrinsic value in the "integrity, stability, and beauty of the biotic community."[18] Whether features of the natural order have intrinsic value apart from their effect on the quality of human life is a matter of great controversy. Without trying to decide that question, and in focusing on what is good for human beings, we can paraphrase the above quote from Joseph Raz in the following way: Life in harmony with nature and involving "love, admiration and respect" for the natural world is a good in itself; the "order, integrity and life"[19] of the natural world is a constituent good; and the quality of life with such a relationship to nature that explains its value is the ultimate good. All three are intrinsic goods.

Rationality and practical reasonableness. According to John Finnis, "Rationality and rational belief are similarly intrinsic goods. There is value in rationally acquiring knowledge, in rational activities of all kinds, and in rationally held belief."[20] One of the reasons for not being willing to accept the choice of living a pleasurable child's life for the rest of our lives (an example from Aristotle mentioned previously) is that we should be choosing against rationality.

The development and use of abilities in work and other activity. Human beings find enjoyment in and value activity, play, use of physical and intellectual abilities, expenditure of energy, and the development of skill apart from any utilitarian benefit.[21] As Alan Brown writes, "Work, rest and play; these constitute the basic activities that human beings must engage in if their lives are to be well-balanced, if they are to develop as human beings."[22] That one would not wish to be deprived of these things would be one of the reasons one would reject the option (mentioned in the discussion of hedonism) of spending one's life connected to a machine that would stimulate the pleasure centers of the brain. According to Aristotle, the person who is leading the good life is "one who exercises his faculties in accordance with excellence," especially intellectual excellence.[23] The opportunity for women to develop and use their abilities fully is, of course, a major concern of contemporary feminism.

Virtue and moral goodness. The excellence that Aristotle referred to includes moral excellence as well as intellectual excellence. We will discuss moral virtue as an intrinsic good in chapter 10.

Autonomy and liberty. Freedom or autonomy is often regarded as one of the most important values in our Western liberal society, especially in the United States with its frontier tradition. To be autonomous is to rule oneself. One aspect of autonomy is freedom from being ruled by other people. The person who is ruled by his own passions, however, also lacks autonomy. The drug addict who cannot choose other than to devote her life to pursuing a particular drug does not "rule herself" any more than the person living under a tyrant does. A contemporary philosopher, Joseph Raz, sets forth the ideal of the autonomous person:

> [Significantly] autonomous persons are those who can shape their life and determine its course. They are not merely rational agents who can choose between options after evaluating relevant information, but agents who can in addition adopt personal projects, develop relationships, and accept commitments to causes, through which their personal integrity and sense of self-respect are made concrete. In a word, significantly autonomous agents are part creators of their own moral world. Persons who are part creators of their own moral world have a commitment to projects, relationships, and causes which affects the kind of life that is for them worth living.[24]

Freedom or liberty, because of its connection with autonomy, can also be regarded as an intrinsic value. Raz goes on to write that "having a sufficient range of acceptable options is of intrinsic value, for it is constitutive of an autonomous life that it is lived in circumstances where acceptable alternatives are present."[25] Therefore, if having an autonomous life is of value, then women, minorities, and others who wish to be liberated from a narrow range of role descriptions that have been imposed on them certainly have a legitimate claim. If freedom gets its value from its connection with autonomy, then it would seem to have value only insofar as people are autonomous, or insofar as such freedom "serves to nurture development of the capacity for autonomy."[26]

Is There One Supreme Intrinsic Good?

We have rejected the hedonist theory that pleasure (and the absence of pain) is the one supreme good. Some contemporary liberals see autonomy or the freedom of the individual as the one supreme good. A pluralistic view of the good, as we have developed here, supports the view that autonomous choosing between worthwhile goals is a good, but, of course, it is not the only good. In chapters 1 and 2, we referred to the contemporary emphasis on liberty rights. According to the view to be developed in this chapter, rights derive their importance from the interests on which they are based. Liberty rights are not necessarily more important than other considerations and should not be regarded as trumps that override all other considerations.[27] Kant's principle of respect for persons should not be understood only as respect for autonomy or for liberty rights, but as respect for all the interests of a person.[28]

While it is impossible to exercise autonomy unless one has a range of choices, this does not mean that there must be an infinite range of choices. That idea makes no sense.[29] Since autonomy is not the only good, choices can be ruled out on other grounds. As Joseph Raz writes:

> Very rarely will the non-availability of morally repugnant options reduce a person's choice sufficiently to affect his autonomy. Therefore, the availability of such options is not a requirement of respect for autonomy. . . . Autonomy is valuable only if exercised in pursuit of the good. The ideal of autonomy requires only the availability of morally acceptable options.[30]

Of course, even if freedom to choose morally unworthy alternatives is not intrinsically valuable, it is still often instrumentally valuable when the alternative is to put the power to restrict that freedom into someone else's hands.

The Good Life

The Good Life Combines Intrinsic Values.   Since there is no one supreme good, we can regard the good life as "one that successfully combines various desirable activities and goals."[31] Since it is extremely unlikely that one who lives from moment to moment will participate in many of the basic goods, and even more unlikely that he or she will successfully combine them, to some extent one needs an overall coherent and rational plan of life.[32] As John Rawls writes, "We see our life as one whole, the activities of one rational subject spread out in time."[33] Forming such a life plan "will be rational only if it is on the basis of one's assessments of one's capacities, circumstances, and even of one's taste."[34] According to the view set forth in this chapter, it will also be rational only if it gives preference to intrinsic goods (health, friendship, moral character) over instrumental goods (e.g., money), and if it does not arbitrarily eliminate from possible consideration any of the intrinsic goods. One prerequisite for fulfilling the latter requirement may be to refrain from giving any particular goal "overriding and unconditional significance" even while one remains committed to it.[35]

Religion, Meaning, and the Good Life.   Religion may instrumentally enhance the worth of a person's life or detract from it, depending on whether it furthers or obstructs his or her pursuit of worthwhile goals. It also contributes to the happiness of many people by giving them a sense of meaning. But if the religion is completely false, the sense of meaning may be based on illusion. This is a problem for the nonreligious person as well. Robert Nozick asks whether it is possible for such a person to have a sense of meaning that is not based on illusion. His answer is "Yes, but." According to Nozick, "Limited transcendence, the transcending of our limits so as to connect with a wider context of value which itself is limited, does give lives meaning—but a limited one. We may thirst for more."[36]

For example, we can keep on asking about the significance of the trace one's life leaves from the point of view of some larger context, such as several generations or world history. From this larger point of view, the trace may be insignificant, and thus a larger perspective may undercut the individual's satisfaction with his or her life. Suppose, however, that we reach a perspective that cannot be transcended by some larger perspective. Nozick suggests that if there is a self-sufficient unlimited being, that being is its own meaning, and then perhaps it is possible to connect "up with this self-sufficient source of meaning in a way so that meaning flows to us."[37] If religion does connect human lives to such a transcendent reality, then not only does it give people a sense of meaning that might be illusory, but it in fact does give their lives meaning. Religion would also relate to the value of knowledge, especially knowledge of one's ultimate place in the scheme of things, and, if Ultimate Reality is in fact personal, to the good of friendship—friendship with that Reality.

THE BASIS OF OUR DUTIES

How do we get from the ideas of intrinsic values and the good life to a determination of what we ought to do or not do? The principle of impartiality may contribute to the answer. I cannot maintain that participation in what is intrinsically good is desirable for me, but not for someone else. In accordance with the first version of Kant's Categorical Imperative, or the principle of universal applicability, I cannot reasonably maintain that something is wrong for you to do but permissible for me to do if there are no significant differences between our two situations. But where do we go from there?

Two Inadequate Approaches

There are some popular approaches that we have previously dealt with that seem inadequate. These are the utilitarian and the natural rights approaches.

Basing Duties on Utilitarian Calculation.   Should impartiality be exhibited by pursuing the utilitarian goal of providing the most good for the most people in a manner that is impartial, in that each individual's own good counts for no more in his or her deliberations than the good of every other individual? The idea that we should do what produces the most good for the most people depends on ideas we reject in this chapter, namely, that there is only one thing that is intrinsically good, and that it is measurable. A second reason for rejecting the utilitarian approach is that many of the ingredients of the good life, such as meaning, autonomy, and virtue, must be pursued by individuals for themselves and cannot be distributed to other people. What we can do for other people is to meet their needs by removing obstacles to their achieving good lives.

Basing Duties on Respect for Rights.   In the first two chapters, we referred to moral arguments that appeal to rights as the most fundamental moral consideration on which all other moral considerations are based. But that approach seems to be wrong. One reason for rejecting this approach is that there are moral considerations that cannot be based on rights. These include considerations of virtue, moral excellence, and supererogation (going beyond one's duty). They also include duties that do not seem to be related to rights, such as a duty not to destroy a great work of art that I own. A second reason is that it would seem that rights themselves have to be justified in terms of something more fundamental, namely, their contribution to human life and its quality.[38] Joseph Raz defines a right in this way: "If an individual has a right then a certain aspect of his well-being is a reason for holding others to be under a duty."[39]

Perfect and Imperfect Duties

Responsibilities, or Imperfect Duties.   We have said that morality is based on human interests. A fundamental principle of morality is that human beings have some responsibility for furthering what is good for human beings (and perhaps to some extent for animals). "Responsibility" is here equivalent to *imperfect duty*, that is, a duty to bring about certain results, or to contribute to bringing them about, but one that does not specify precisely what one must do or refrain from doing. If we have a responsibility to the hungry, then we "ought" to do something to help the hungry, but we might not have a duty or obligation to do any one specific thing. Perhaps Abigail tells Donald that he ought to write a letter to his congressional representative about the problem of world hunger, or that he ought to help his friend Richard with a project that he is behind schedule on. If these are imperfect duties, Donald might legitimately answer that although he "ought" to do these things, and although he has done these things in the past and will do so again in the future, at this particular juncture of his life he has other things he is concentrating on.

Obligations, or Perfect Duties.   If Donald had promised Abigail that he would write such a letter as part of a united campaign, or had promised Richard that he would help him, then we can say that Donald has no choice in the matter, that he has an obligation, or *perfect duty*, to join in the effort, and that not to do so is morally wrong. That could be called a directly created obligation.

But one can have a perfect duty or obligation without making a promise or directly creating it in some other way. As one author puts it, "Obligations are created indirectly when other sorts of morally relevant considerations . . . mount up and grow to such a pitch that they result in an individual *having* to behave in a given way."[40]

Suppose that the failure of the bill facing Congress would have grave consequences, and that Donald's congresswoman might cast the deciding vote in committee, and that she has not yet declared which way she will vote, and that Donald has been made aware of all of this, and that Donald has in the past been identified with this particular cause, and that the church or group or club to which he belongs is sponsoring the letter-writing campaign. Suppose that Richard's project means a lot to Richard, who has helped Donald in the past, that they have been close friends for a long time, and that nothing Donald is doing is such that it cannot be postponed. At some point, the morally relevant considerations are likely to reach a point where Donald will feel that he has no choice in the matter, that he has an obligation that it would be wrong not to act on. Why should we think he is wrong about this? Wouldn't we wonder about his moral sensitivity if he did not reach that point?

Duties and Rights.   It was claimed above that not all duties can be based on rights. Can any duties be based on rights? We can speak of concrete rights that an individual has in a particular situation. If Donald does not have a duty to help Richard, then we can say that although he "ought" to help, he has a right (a liberty right) not to. If Donald does have a duty to help Richard, then the same "direct or indirect considerations that impose an obligation on [Donald] also justify [Richard] in insisting on the performance of the obligation."[41] On this view, duties are not based on rights, but concrete claim rights are based on duties, and concrete liberty rights are based on the absence of duties.

We can also speak of *general rights*, such as the right to food, or the right to make basic decisions about one's life. Some people have argued that some duties are based on such rights. An argument for this position is that one can be convinced that children have a right to food and a right to an education without being sure who has what duties to do something about these rights. As Raz notes, "Rights are the grounds of duties in the sense that one way of justifying holding a person to be subject to a duty is that this serves the interest on which another's right is based."[42]

However, some people take the opposite point of view and say that rights are not the grounds of duties because we can know that some things are wrong—such as neglecting one's children, or pouring poison in a river, or destroying the ozone layer for future generations—without knowing whose rights are violated, or whether people who are not yet alive have rights, or even if there are such things as rights. Second, we cannot know whether children on a remote island have a right to food or an education until we know whether they would have a legitimate complaint about not getting these things, and that depends what their needs are, what resources are available to meet those needs, and who is available to make use of those resources. On this view, most individual human beings in the world do have specific or concrete rights to political freedom, food, and an education. But the duty to see that they get these things is not based on a general right to these things. Rather, the duty to see that they get these things is based on their need for these things, the availability of resources, and the fact that other people are in a position to do something about those needs, as well as other relevant moral considerations. Their rights are in a sense based on duties, since they have a right to these things because they have a legitimate complaint if those who have a duty to meet these needs do not do so.[43] Whether it is closer to the truth to say that some duties are based on general rights, or that rights are really based on duties, in either case both rights and duties are ultimately based on what is good for human beings.

The Basis for Responsibilities and Obligations

Responsibilities and Obligations to Further the Good.   As the last section concludes, ultimately our duties are based on the possibility of furthering human interests, or human participation in what is intrinsically good. Since there are various goods and various acceptable ways of life, it is not very often that one would have an obligation to further some specific good for people in general, unless one happens to be faced with some unique opportunity.

Responsibilities and Obligations to Protect the Vulnerable.   Some people face more obstacles to participating in a good life than others and are in more danger of failing to do so, and all people face more obstacles and dangers at some times than at others. Obstacles and dangers can come from various directions. As Robert Goodin claims, many of our obligations (or perfect duties) and responsibilities (or imperfect duties) derive, at least in part, from the fact of vulnerability.[44] This view is also compatible with the Western religious tradition, for which the paradigm cases of moral evil are often those of taking advantage of people who are vulnerable because of their economic, political, or legal position. It is our instinct to feel particularly outraged against those who physically, sexually, or psychologically abuse children or the elderly, or who exploit people under their influence or control (such as a therapist who exploits a patient). From this point of view, the strongest considerations in matters of sexual activity, divorce, abandonment, child support, and so on should not be the supposed rights of the most articulate, but the well-being of those who are most vulnerable, namely, children.

People can be as vulnerable to the inaction of others as to their actions. If we meet a person in the desert who is without water, and we have an excess supply, then that person is vulnerable to our decision as to whether or not to give him or her water. A moral code that would not demand such an action would not adequately respond to the vulnerability of human beings, or further the good of human beings. When there are many people facing severe deprivations, they are often vulnerable not so much to the action or inaction of specific individuals as to the action, or more often inaction, of groups of individuals. Similarly, people who are vulnerable to direct harm (e.g., abused children) are also vulnerable to the inaction of those who fail to protect them. In both of these kinds of cases, individuals have a responsibility to protect the vulnerable by promoting social attitudes and setting up social institutions to protect them. (See chapters 9 and 11.)

People are most vulnerable to being objects of cruelty or indifference when there is an imbalance of power. Philip Hallie writes that

> cruelty . . . is a kind of power relationship, an imbalance of power wherein the stronger party becomes the victimizer and the weaker becomes the victim. . . . The absence of cruelty lay in a situation where there is no imbalance of power. The opposite of cruelty, I learned [from studying the Nazi era], was freedom from that unbalanced power relationship. Either the victim should get stronger and stand up to the victimizer, and thereby bring about a balance of their powers, or the victim should free himself from the whole relationship by flight.[45]

Fulfilling duties to protect the vulnerable can take the form of (1) refusing to victimize others, (2) rescuing victims or potential victims from unbalanced power relationships, (3) restructuring family, social, economic, legal, or political institutions so that "the victim gets stronger" and large power imbalances do not occur, (4) encouraging the development of moral characteristics that incline people not to take advantage of situations in which they have power over others, and (5) punishing those who do exploit others.

One of the most obvious imbalances of power is that between the present and the future. Future generations are potential victims of those living today and are incapable of freeing themselves from the relationship by flight. Just what our duties are to future generations is a matter of ongoing discussion, but at the very least, we can say with Joel Feinberg, "Surely we owe it to future generations to pass on a world that is not a used up garbage heap."[46]

NEGATIVE DUTIES AND PROHIBITIONS

Absolute and Near-Absolute Prohibitions

Duties often conflict. Aristotle considered the possibility that adultery could be permissible for the sake of overthrowing a tyrant. One of the questions that people have disagreed about has to do with whether there are any moral prohibitions that are absolute or nearly absolute. We have seen that Kant thought so. People have argued for absolute duties in other ways as well. Some (primarily Catholic) philosophers have argued that it is absolutely morally impermissible to choose "directly against a basic value,"[47] so that killing the innocent through abortion (and even contraception) is always wrong. This author has not heard any convincing explanation of why the consideration of acting against a good should invalidate all other considerations, nor a convincing account of the distinction between acting directly and acting indirectly.[48] Some people try to base absolute prohibitions on rights, even to the point of saying that it would be absolutely wrong to interfere with someone's liberty rights by stopping him or her from committing suicide, or to interfere with the property rights of the rich by taxing them to feed the starving. (See chapters 9 and 11.) But since rights are based on human needs and interests, as are other moral considerations, then "it cannot be claimed that they are trumps in the sense of overriding other considerations based on individual interests."[49]

Absolute and near-absolute prohibitions can be based on protecting the vulnerable. The more vulnerable we are to a harm, the more helpless we are to do anything about it, and the greater that potential harm (or the greater the good we are in danger of losing), the greater the need to be protected by the law and by the moral rules. The possession of truth is of such importance to us, both as an intrinsic good and as a necessary means of rationally planning our lives, that the prohibition of lying is a stringent moral rule, and the more important the truth is to the person who might be deprived of it, the more stringent the rule must be. So also, a prohibition against deliberately or recklessly killing others or endangering their lives decreases our vulnerability. A rule against lying that does not allow for exceptions, and a rule against killing that includes no exception for self-defense, would increase rather than decrease the vulnerability of the innocent.

There are cases, however, in which it is difficult to imagine how any exception to the rule would make people less vulnerable. Prohibitions against deliberately or recklessly killing nonaggressive people or endangering their lives in peacetime, or against physical, psychological, or sexual abuse of children and the elderly, can be regarded as moral absolutes. Prohibitions protecting people from harm should be regarded as absolute unless and until we can find some persuasive argument that allowing some exceptions would decrease rather than increase our vulnerability. For some cases, it seems unlikely that such arguments could ever be found. Specific relationships that involve an imbalance of power and increased vulnerability bring with them special moral prohibitions, some of which would seem to be absolutes (e.g., the prohibition of sexual relationships between psychiatrists and patients and between authority figures and children).

If someone lies under oath in court, we as individuals are helpless to prevent it or to protect ourselves from the harm that is caused thereby. And not only are we helpless as individuals, but the system on which we all depend is threatened. Individual vulnerability to harm, then, is not the only reason for absolute or near-absolute prohibitions. The pursuit of the good life or the good society requires the existence of human cooperation on various levels. As pointed out in chapter 4, certain practices, such as killing the innocent and lying in court or under oath, are "so fundamentally destructive of human relationships that no difference of century or society can change their character."[50] Arthur Dyck puts it this way:

> We might say that lying, breaking promises, and unfair procedures would be destructive of the human relationships that are endemic to the formulation and acceptance of any standards, laws and procedures needed for cooperative behavior in community, and that all communities recognize, implicitly or explicitly, their general wrong-making character.[51]

Prohibitions of such practices ought to be regarded as nearly absolute.

The Principle of Double Effect

In the last chapter, we used the examples of a doctor's letting one person die in order to save four people and his killing of one person in order to save four people. Our moral intuition tells us that the person who does the first has done what is morally permissible, while the person who does the second has done a serious wrong to the person who is killed. Sometimes the distinction is made between duties not to harm and duties to benefit. Since we are usually more vulnerable to harm than to failures to help, the duty not to harm is rightly regarded as generally more stringent than the duty to help.

This may not always be true. If, in order to get an inheritance, an adult refrains from saving a drowning child, his action is just as bad as if he had drowned the child.[52] The difference between this case and the doctor examples has to do with intention. In this example, the adult intends the death of the child, whether by action or inaction. When the doctor let one person die to save four others, there was no intention that the fifth person die. (Our lives would be more precarious if we had a moral rule that people could never do any good if, as a side effect of their doing good, some other good were neglected.) In the case in which the doctor killed one person in order to save four, he deliberately and intentionally brought about that person's death. The death was intended as a means to his goal.

The principle of double effect states that it is always (or perhaps almost always) morally prohibited to intend something that is evil, either as one's ultimate goal or as a means to some further goal. However, it is *frequently* morally permissible to allow some evil to occur as a side effect of acting to achieve some morally permissible goal. For example, in warfare it is morally prohibited to deliberately seek the death of civilians as an end in itself. It is also always, or almost always, morally prohibited to attack civilians as a means to some worthy end, such as bringing a quicker end to the war so that fewer civilians will be killed in the long run. It is *frequently* morally permissible to attack a military target in a cause one believes to be just, even though civilians will be killed as a side effect. Whether it is permissible to do so in any particular case depends on a comparison of the amount of harm done to civilians with the importance for the war effort of destroying the military target.

If we could never do anything that brings about evil, then we could not build highways, which enable our economy to function but on which people are killed in predictable numbers. The principle of double effect makes a distinction between this sort of permissible action and deliberate killing, which is morally prohibited because it threatens the vulnerable. But we are equally vulnerable to those who recklessly kill or harm, such as those who knowingly sell defective bolts that may be used in cars, buildings, bridges, or space shuttles, and those who drink and drive. The moral prohibition against such actions should be equally as stringent as the prohibition against intentionally harming, and those who knowingly put others at risk in such cases are as morally defective as deliberate killers, because they put just as small a value on the lives of the innocent in comparison with the value they place on their own whims and wishes.[53]

We are also vulnerable to those for whom the truth counts for nothing. Those who deliberately say what they know to be false, and those who are simply reckless about the truth in important matters, equally deprive us of what we need to act as rational beings. The most fundamental moral rules prohibit intending the deaths of other human beings or recklessly endangering their lives, and intentionally or recklessly endangering the truth, especially in matters that are important for the lives of individuals and social institutions. Other moral rules prohibit the intentional destruction or reckless endangerment of other intrinsic goods. Of course, deciding what counts as reckless endangerment requires an evaluation of the various goods that are involved in alternative courses of action. Inescapably, these various goods must be weighed against one another.

FURTHER REFLECTIONS ON THE CONTENT OF OUR DUTIES

The Claim of Conventional Morality

We expect more of people than that they simply refrain from violating the most fundamental moral rules. How do we derive other moral duties? The good of friendship, for example, and similarly the good of citizenship, may be seen as the basis for our various duties to people with whom we are in relationship in different degrees of intimacy. There are some moral requirements that are always conducive to the good of friendship and to the existence of a worthwhile society. To a large extent, however, what is appropriate in our behavior toward our friends and our fellow citizens, and thus the determination of our duties, depends to a significant extent on their expectations, which in turn depend to a large extent on the nature of the traditions and institutions of the particular society in which we live. John Kekes writes:

> Good societies are cohesive and enduring partly because their members largely agree about how they should treat each other, what sort of lives are good, and what constitutes benefit and harm. Their agreement rests on shared values and conventional morality embodies them. . . . This makes it possible for people to have reasonable expectations about each other's conduct. These expectations rest on the justified assumption that members of a society are guided by many of the same values and rules. . . . Thus members of a society can count on each other. And because they can do that, there is a social bond between them.[54]

These considerations support what has been called *moral conventionalism*. Since all societies need a conventional morality, individual members of a society have a *prima facie* duty to abide by the directives of that conventional morality, and the society is justified in teaching, encouraging, and in some cases enforcing that morality.[55] This may sound obvious, but some people who see themselves as liberal advocates of freedom and individuality "regard conventional morality as a restriction on freedom and a hindrance to the development of individuality."[56] But freedom and individuality need a background of stability. Kekes writes that "just as language supplies the forms in which whatever one wants to say can be said, so conventional morality supplies the forms of life among which members of a society can freely choose and thus develop their individuality."[57]

Conventional morality is not the final determinant of our duties. Our responsibilities to further what is good and especially to protect the vulnerable are sources of criteria by which to judge the adequacy or inadequacy of any existing conventional morality, as well as sources of duties to go beyond conventional morality. We have said that from the point of view of protecting the vulnerable, the most urgent considerations in such matters as sexual activity, divorce, abandonment, and child support should be the well-being of children. It is not clear that what has come to be conventional morality in parts of our society reflects this priority; rather, conventional morality sometimes seems to be concerned with protecting the autonomy of the least vulnerable.

Special Duties to Particular People

Our special duties to particular people derive in part from the conventional morality of our society. A duty of reciprocity, which is part of the conventional morality of all (or almost all) societies, creates specific duties to specific people such as parents, friends, and benefactors. Particular duties also derive in part from the fact of vulnerability.[58] One person (e.g., a child) is vulnerable to a second person (e.g., a parent) because the second person is in the best position to provide what is needed by the first, and/or because the first has a need to receive certain things that only the second can give (e.g., parental love). This view is opposed to the view that all our specific moral duties derive from contracts, promises, or mutual consent. It says that we have significant duties that we have not consented to (for example, duties to aged parents), as well as duties to those who have not consented and perhaps cannot consent (for example, our children).

To a significant degree, conventional morality determines which person is in the best position to provide a specific individual with what he or she needs, and thus determines what particular moral duties or responsibilities that person has. While conceivably the material needs of children, for example, could be provided for in various ways, children are particularly vulnerable to the failure by their parents to meet their emotional and psychological needs, and parents generally have emotional bonds to children that put them in the best position to provide for such needs. Thus parents have special responsibilities to their own children. In modern society, children who grow up without taking an interest in their own education are handicapped in their efforts to build a worthwhile adult life, for economic as well as other reasons. Since the home environment is probably the major factor in a child's involvement in the educational process, the child is particularly vulnerable to the attitudes of parents, and parents, therefore, have particular responsibilities in this regard.

Similarly, moral responsibilities between husbands and wives are based only secondarily on the fact "that they have made each other certain promises in the wedding ceremony," but primarily on the fact "that they have placed themselves, emotionally and sometimes physically and economically as well" in a position of vulnerability to each other.[59] Obviously, then, unmarried couples can also have strong moral responsibilities to each other, and the fact that they have not voluntarily consented to accept such responsibilities does not alter the fact.

Duties of children to support their parents have always been thought to exist when, and only when, the parents are in need. Only some parents are in need of financial help from grown children, but most parents would feel that something was missing from their lives if the children whom they loved and nurtured provided no love in return. Again, both sorts of duties relate to the fact of dependency and vulnerability. Responsibilities toward friends spring from the emotional vulnerability inherent in friendship, a vulnerability one does not incur with mere acquaintances. These responsibilities have to do primarily with "mutual consideration for the feelings of the other."[60]

The purposes of any organized group, be it a company, a government, or society in general, are vulnerable to being undermined by the failure of the people within it to fulfill their voluntarily accepted responsibilities. Fellow members of that organization are vulnerable to having their time, money, hopes, and efforts wasted if others fail to fulfill their understood or specifically assigned tasks. So people have a *prima facie* duty to fulfill their institutional roles. Fulfilling one's institutional role tends to be one's duty, and it is one's duty if it is not displaced by some other overriding moral consideration.

Special Duties versus General Duties to Others

One person can be vulnerable to another either because some special relationship exists between them, or simply because one person is in need and the other is in a position to help. Sometimes, though perhaps infrequently, people neglect their responsibilities to family members and associates to spend time doing good for strangers. More frequently, people ignore the needs of strangers, claiming that all their time, money, and energy is used in fulfilling their responsibilities to family and immediate associates.

A common view is that duties to specific people, such as children, spouses, employees, and employers, are based on various implicit or explicit promises. The position taken in this book is that many of our specific responsibilities and our general responsibilities are based on the same factor, the vulnerability of persons toward others. Therefore, there is no reason why, in general, responsibilities to friends, neighbors, fellow students, fellow church members, residents of the same city, or inhabitants of the same country should always override responsibilities to strangers.

Other Special Duties

Kant's Categorical Imperative states that it cannot be permissible for me to do what it would be impermissible for others to do in the same circumstances, but that may not mean that anything that it is permissible for others to do it is also permissible for me to do. For not only do I have to meet the minimum requirements of morality; I also have to live a life defined by my own ideals, the ideals that are part of my rational life plan, and these may require more of me. I may not only ask what is required of me as a conscientious person, but also what is required of me as a certain kind of person (e.g., a kind person, a loyal person, a friend, a Buddhist, a Christian, a person who has identified his or her life with a certain cause). What my duties are depends on the vulnerability of other people to my actions, but also depends on my image of myself.

There is another question that may be as important as any we can ask about our duties. It is this: How much sacrifice do our positive moral duties require of us? How demanding is our responsibility for or duty to help those who are fellow citizens or members of the same society? This question is of such importance that a separate chapter, chapter 9, will be devoted to it.

A METAETHICAL POSTSCRIPT

Most of this book, including the section that asks about what has intrinsic or objective value, deals with what is called *normative ethics*. To ask whether there is any such thing as objective value is to ask a *metaethical question*. (Metaethics is the study of the nature, meaning, and varieties of ethical arguments.) We have been proceeding on the assumption that there are such things as intrinsic values. In chapter 2, however, we dealt with skeptical approaches that deny that values have any objective reality, but insist that values exist wholly in the subjective reactions of individuals.

Why does the moral skeptic reject the objectivity of judgments about intrinsic goodness? A major reason is that "goodness" is not a property belonging to certain states of affairs in the way that largeness or heaviness belongs to physical objects. If "goodness" were a property, it would be a queer sort of property; hence it must, according to the skeptic, be something our feelings and desires project on states of affairs (as Hobbes thought), something that is not really there.

One can, however, make a distinction between different types of properties, such as between basic properties (e.g., the molecular structure of something) and properties that are supervenient on the basic properties (e.g., fragility, which depends on the molecular structure). Sometimes these distinctions are also distinctions between primary qualities of objects (those that are thought of as being in the objects, independent of anyone's observing them) and secondary qualities, such as colors, which in some sense depend on the observer. So it has been argued by some philosophers that the way in which goodness belongs to a state of affairs is no queerer than the way in which supervenient properties such as fragility belong to

138 INTRODUCTION TO ETHICS

objects,[61] and by others that it is no queerer than the way in which secondary qualities (like redness) belong to objects, or the way in which truth belongs to propositions.[62]

QUESTIONS

1. This chapter defends a pluralistic conception of the good. On such a view there is no possibility of determining what is the most good for the most people. Does that make ethics unscientific? Should ethics be scientific?

2. Can you think of anything that should be added to or deleted from the list of intrinsic goods? What are your arguments?

3. Certain religious groups, when accused of such things as having terrible taste in music, or following questionable money-raising gimmicks, or staging fake miracles, say that whatever brings people in and so "saves souls" (their view of the one dominant good) is justified. Some representatives of the American political right regard any action, no matter what law it breaks or what other values it violates (e.g., respect for truth), as justified if it combats communism. Are these examples of the dangers and totalitarian potential of any theory that believes in one dominant goal? Is a pluralistic view of the good a protection against such consequences?

4. What are the reasons why, other things being more or less equal, we have a duty to abide by the conventional morality of our society? Kekes gives the following account of conventional morality in the United States today:

> Parents are responsible for their children, breaking one's promise requires an excuse, politicians speaking in their public capacity should not lie, winners must not gloat over losers, one ought not to brag about his talents, a life of idleness is wrong, following one's conscience is right, eating people is wrong, one must not torture animals, parents should not have sexual intercourse with their children, disagreements should not be settled by physical violence, people should be allowed to express unpopular views, it is wrong to spread malicious lies about one's rival, one must ask for permission before borrowing anything, handicapped people should not be laughed at, white lies are permissible, one cannot publicly rejoice at his enemy's misfortune, deliberate cruelty is wrong, one should be loyal to friends, confidential information ought not to be made public, courage, honesty, and fairness are good and their opposites are bad.[63]

Is there anything on this list that you would challenge as being part of conventional morality in the United States today? Is there anything on this list that is part of conventional morality in the United States today that you think should not be part of it? The list is not meant to be exhaustive, but in your opinion, are there any glaring omissions?

5. This book takes the position that special responsibilities for (or duties to) parents, children, spouses, relatives, employees, friends, and so on, are based to a significant degree on the vulnerability that people have to each other in these

relationships. A principal alternative view is that they are duties that are voluntarily incurred through an action (such as conceiving children), an explicit promise (as in marriage), or an implicit promise. Is this alternative view related to the minimalist view discussed in the first chapter, which maintains that I don't have any duties I don't voluntarily accept? What arguments can you think of for each side of this debate? Which view is correct, or are they both partly correct? Can you think of, and argue for, some third position?

FURTHER READINGS

The pluralistic view of intrinsic goodness found in this chapter is similar to that in:

Finnis, John. *Natural Law and Natural Rights.* New York: Oxford University Press, 1980.

Parts of the view of moral duty in this chapter are influenced by or are similar to the views of the following:

Benditt, Theodore M. *Rights.* Totowa, N.J.: Rowman and Littlefield, 1982.
Goodin, Robert. *Protecting the Vulnerable.* Chicago: University of Chicago Press, 1985.
Raz, Joseph. *The Morality of Freedom.* New York: Oxford University Press, 1987.

For a discussion of and application of the theory of double effect, see:

Nagel, Thomas. "War and Massacre." *Philosophy and Public Affairs* 1 (Winter 1972): 129–33.

Much of contemporary writing that is relevant to the section of this chapter entitled "A Metaethical Postscript" can be found in:

Sayre-McCord, Geoffrey, ed. *Essays on Moral Realism.* Ithaca, N.Y.: Cornell University Press, 1988.

Other highly recommended readings are:

Held, Virginia. "Non-Contractual Society." In *Science, Morality and Feminist Theory, Canadian Journal of Philosophy* Supplementary Volume 13, edited by Marsha Hanen and Kai Nielsen, 111–38. Calgary: University of Calgary Press, 1987.
Sommers, Christina Hoff. "Philosophers against the Family." In *Person to Person*, edited by Hugh LaFollette and George Graham, 82–105. Philadelphia: Temple University Press, 1989.

Steinbock, Bonnie. "Drunk Driving." *Philosophy and Public Affairs* 14 (Summer 1985): 278–95.

NOTES

1. Viktor Frankl, *Man's Search for Meaning: An Introduction to Logotherapy* (Boston: Beacon Press, 1962), 115.
2. Robert Nozick, *Philosophical Explanations* (Cambridge, Mass.: Harvard University Press, 1981), 594, 610.
3. Ernest Becker, *Escape from Evil* (New York: Macmillan, 1976), 4.
4. See Frankl, *Man's Search*, 66–67, and Nozick, *Philosophical Explanations*, 429.
5. Nozick, *Philosophical Explanations*, 618. See also 610–11.
6. William Galston, *Justice and the Human Good* (Chicago: University of Chicago Press, 1980), 61.
7. Ibid., 63.
8. Aristotle, *Nicomachean Ethics* 1, 7: 1097b6; 9, 4:1166a19–22; 9, 9:1169b17; 10, 3:1117a1–3; etc.
9. This criterion is set forth by Bernard Gert in *The Moral Rules* (New York: Harper and Row, 1966), 46f.
10. This paragraph reflects the views of John Finnis in his *Natural Law and Natural Rights* (New York: Oxford University Press, 1980), 59–92, and his *Fundamentals of Ethics* (Washington, D.C.: Georgetown University Press, 1983), 42–53.
11. Philosophers producing such lists include John Finnis, Nicolai Hartmann, William Frankena, Elizabeth Telfer, and H. J. McClosky.
12. Aristotle, *Nicomachean Ethics* 9, 9:1170a25–26. See also 9, 4:1166a19–22, as well as Galston, *Justice*, 58–61.
13. As Thomas Nagel writes, life is not just a neutral opportunity to have positive and negative experiences, but is itself "emphatically positive" and "is worth living even when the bad elements of experience are plentiful, and the good ones too meager to outweigh the bad ones on their own." This quotation is from his "Death," in *Moral Problems*, ed. James Rachels (New York: Harper and Row, 1971), 362.
14. Henry Veatch, *Aristotle: A Contemporary Appreciation* (Bloomington, Ind.: Indiana University Press, 1974), 106–7. Similar arguments are found in F. C. Sharp, *Ethics* (New York: Century, 1928), 372–73; in H. J. McClosky, *Meta-Ethics and Normative Ethics*, 183; and in W. D. Ross, *The Right and the Good* (Oxford: Oxford University Press, 1930), 139. See also John Finnis's argument that the assertion "Knowledge is a good" cannot coherently be denied, in his *Natural Law*, 61–75.
15. Kenneth R. Minogue, *The Liberal Mind* (New York: Random House, 1963), 167–68. See also Kenneth Spragens, *The Irony of Liberal Reason* (Chicago: University of Chicago Press, 1981), 383.
16. Aristotle, *Nicomachean Ethics* 8, 1:1155a29, 1:1155a5. John Finnis writes that a person can "scarcely think of himself as really well-off if he has no friends" (*Natural Law*, 74–75). See also John Kekes, who writes—in "Moral Intuition," *American Philosophical Quarterly* 23 (January 1986): 89—"A conception of good life must leave room for intimate personal relationships based on love and friendship; without them, a life cannot be satisfactory."
17. Joseph Raz, "Right-Based Moralities," in *Utility and Rights*, ed. R. G. Fey (Minneapolis: University of Minnesota Press, 1984), 48. See also Finnis, *Natural Law*, 89–90, and McClosky, *Meta-Ethics*, 166.
18. Aldo Leopold, *Sand County Almanac* (New York: Oxford University Press, 1949), viii, x.
19. The quotes are from Mark Sagoff, *The Economy of the Earth* (New York: Cambridge University Press, 1988), 147, 148.
20. Finnis, *Natural Law*, 87.

21. Ibid.

22. Alan Brown, *Modern Political Philosophy* (New York: Penguin, 1986), 159.

23. Aristotle, *Nicomachean Ethics* 1, 10, 13. See also McClosky, *Meta-Ethics*, 171.

24. Joseph Raz, *The Morality of Freedom* (Oxford: Oxford University Press, 1987), 154.

25. Ibid., 205.

26. Lawrence Haworth, *Autonomy* (New Haven: Yale University Press, 1986), 130.

27. In agreement with Raz, *Morality of Freedom*, 191.

28. Ibid., 189.

29. Joseph Raz writes: "Autonomy is possible only within a framework of constraints. The completely autonomous person is an impossibility. . . . An autonomous personality can only develop and flourish against a background of biological and social constraints which fix some of its human needs. Some choices are inevitably determined by those needs." Ibid., 155–56.

30. Ibid., 381.

31. Alan Brown, *Modern Political Philosophy*, 161.

32. See Finnis, *Natural Law*, 103–4.

33. John Rawls, *A Theory of Justice* (Cambridge: Harvard University Press, 1974), 420.

34. Finnis, *Natural Law*, 105.

35. Finnis, *Natural Law*, 110. This position is largely a restatement of views set forth in chapter 5 of Finnis's book.

36. Nozick, *Philosophical Explanations*, 618.

37. Ibid., 606.

38. These considerations come from Raz, *Morality of Freedom*, 194–96, 212, and from Theodore M. Benditt, *Rights* (Totowa, N.J.: Rowman and Littlefield, 1982), 46.

39. Raz, *Morality of Freedom*, 172–73.

40. Benditt, *Rights*, 46.

41. Ibid., 49.

42. Raz, *Morality of Freedom*, 212.

43. These points are made by Benditt, *Rights*, 46; Elizabeth Wolgast, *The Grammar of Justice* (Ithaca, N.Y.: Cornell University Press, 1987), 48; and Michael Perry, *Morality, Politics and Law* (New York: Oxford University Press, 1988), 308.

44. Robert Goodin, *Protecting the Vulnerable* (Chicago: University of Chicago Press, 1985).

45. Philip Hallie, "From Cruelty to Goodness," *Hastings Center Report* 11(June 1981): 25.

46. Joel Feinberg, "The Rights of Animals and Unborn Generations," in *Philosophy and Environmental Crisis*, ed. William T. Blackstone, 64–65. (Athens, Georgia: University of Georgia Press, 1974).

47. Finnis, *Natural Law*, 123.

48. On this view, killing and contraception are both regarded as acting directly against the good of life. To me, this view seems silly. Killing harms some individual by depriving him or her of participating in the good of life. The use of contraception does not harm any individual. The basic values should be considered intrinsically good as goods for human individuals and communities, not as abstract goods.

49. Raz, *Morality of Freedom*, 187.

50. J. A. T. Robinson, *Christian Morals Today* (London: SCM Press, 1964), 18.

51. Arthur Dyck, *On Human Care: An Introduction to Ethics* (Nashville: Abingdon, 1977), 53.

52. James Rachels discusses such an example in "Active and Passive Euthanasia," *New England Journal of Medicine* 292 (January 9, 1975): 78–80.

53. See Bonnie Steinbock, "Drunk Driving," *Philosophy and Public Affairs* 14 (Summer 1985): 278–95.

54. John Kekes, "Moral Conventionalism," *American Philosophical Quarterly* 22 (January 1985): 44.

55. Ibid., 37. For an account of Kekes's view of the content of conventional morality in the United States today, see question 4 at the end of this chapter.

56. Ibid., 44.

57. Ibid.

58. Goodin, *Protecting the Vulnerable*, chaps. 3 and 4.

59. Ibid., 79.

60. Ibid., 98.

61. David O. Brink, "Moral Realism and the Skeptical Arguments from Disagreement and Queerness," *Australasian Journal of Philosophy* 62 (1984): 111–25; John Campbell and Robert Pargetter, "Goodness and Fragility," *American Philosophical Quarterly* 23 (April 1986), 155–64.

62. John McDowell, "Values and Secondary Qualities," in *Morality and Objectivity*, ed. Ted Hondrich (Boston: Routledge and Kegan Paul, 1985), 110–29; David Wiggins, "Truth, Invention, and the Meaning of Life," in *Essays on Moral Realism*, ed. Geoffrey Sayre-McCord, 127–65 (Ithaca: Cornell University Press, 1988).

63. Kekes, "Moral Conventionalism," 38.

9

Toward an Adequate Moral Theory (Continued): The Extent of Our Positive Duties

PERSONAL AND COLLECTIVE RESPONSIBILITY

The Question of Sacrifice

If we have duties to those in need, how much do those duties demand of us in terms of personal sacrifice? Henry Shue correctly observes that "how much sacrifice can reasonably be expected from one person for the sake of another, even for the sake of honoring the other's rights, is one of the most fundamental questions in morality."[1]

This is a question that was left unanswered in the last chapter. It is a question that stares us in the face through the eyes of starving and malnourished people, particularly children. Estimates of the number of severely malnourished people in the world range from 70 million[2] to 460 million[3] to 1 billion.[4] What duties do individuals have to help?

Duties Not to Harm and to Compensate for Harm

Before pursuing the question of what duties we have to people in need simply because they are in need, it is worth pointing out that there may also be a duty to compensate those in need for past injustices that helped render them needy. The decisions of some countries often inadvertently cause harm to other countries. For example, the massive secret sale of American grain to the Soviet Union in 1972 eliminated surpluses and caused food prices to soar, resulting in hunger for many in poor nations. Pricing decisions of oil-exporting countries similarly drove up fertilizer prices, increasing hunger for many people. Nations have also acted directly to perpetuate poverty, as the United States did in 1954 when the Central Intelligence Agency helped overthrow the democratically elected government of Guatemala to protect the interests of the United Fruit Company.[5] Corporations acting in their own interests also contribute to poverty, as did the banana companies whose officers bribed government officials in Honduras to keep their taxes low.

When harm is caused to people, either deliberately or because of reckless disregard for their interests, those who cause the harm first have a duty to stop harming, and then they have duties of compensation. Consider the following case:

> Bengal (today's Bangladesh and the West Bengal state of India), the first territory the British conquered in Asia, was a prosperous province with highly developed centers of manufacturing and trade, and an economy as advanced as any prior to the industrial revolution. The British reduced Bengal to poverty through plunder, heavy land taxes and trade restrictions that barred competitive Indian goods from England, but gave British goods free entry into India. India's late Prime Minister Nehru commented bitterly, "Bengal can take pride in the fact that she helped greatly in giving birth to the Industrial Revolution in England."[6]

Those who benefited from the Industrial Revolution in England, including those alive today, would still have duties to aid Bengal, just as those who inherit stolen money have a duty to return it, with interest, to the victims or their heirs. It can be argued that every reasonably well-off person in the industrialized countries has such a duty.[7] Of course, in light of the complexity of both the causal chains of harm and the causal chains of benefit, it is often difficult to say where the responsibility for correcting for past injustices lies.[8]

DUTIES TO AID OTHERS

Minimalist Approaches

Apart from any duties to compensate for past injustices, and apart from any duties based on a social contract, what duties do we have to those in need? On one extreme are those who say we have no such duties. Some of those who take a social contract approach might say that we have no duties to those who are not part of the same social contract. Robert Nozick takes a natural rights approach.[9] He says that while we do have duties not to harm and duties to compensate for past harms, we have no positive duties to aid strangers. For Nozick, duties are based on rights. The positive rights of some people to food cannot override the negative rights of other people not to be interfered with in the use of their own resources. That is because, according to Nozick, there are no such things as positive natural rights. We argued against the idea of basing morality on rights in the last chapter and will deal with Nozick's views in more detail in chapter 11.

Demanding Utilitarian Approaches

On the other extreme are utilitarian approaches that claim that the very fact of widespread hunger imposes a duty on each person to do whatever he or she is capable of doing to accomplish whatever is necessary to prevent hunger and starvation. So Peter Singer writes:

> I begin with the assumption that suffering and death from lack of food, shelter, and medical care are bad. . . . My next point is this: if it is in our power to prevent something bad from happening without thereby sacrificing anything of comparable moral importance, we ought, morally, to do it.[10]

Governments of prosperous countries could conceivably require citizens to fulfill this duty by taxing them and using the money appropriately.[11] Suppose governments do not do this. Suppose I give a considerable amount to hunger relief and discover that there is still a great need because many other people have not given. Do I have the duty to keep on giving more? If I save one drowning person and have the opportunity to save a second one, then a third, and so on, do I not have a duty to do it, even if other people could have saved the second drowning person but failed to do so? If the answer is yes, would I not then also have a duty to keep on giving more to save the hungry, even though I have to sacrifice a great deal of what I could have had for myself? If we reach the conclusion that we have a duty to do all we can, just as in the case of the drowning people, we are faced with the problem of being overwhelmed with obligations. The area of moral duty is expanded to the point of obliterating both the area of the morally indifferent and the area of the morally supererogatory (i.e., doing good beyond what duty demands).[12]

Alternative Utilitarian Approaches

Others who take a utilitarian approach reach different conclusions. People who have been labeled "crisis environmentalists" and "neo-Malthusians" (after Henry Malthus, the early-nineteenth-century English economist who warned of the dangers of excessive population growth) argue that population growth is outstripping food production while at the same time leading to the depletion of the world's natural resources and the pollution of the environment. Thus, the more people who are saved now, the more misery there will be in the long run. One writer, Garrett Hardin, compares rich nations to lifeboats and the poor of the world to drowning people trying to get into the lifeboats. To allow too many to get in would be to risk sinking the lifeboats and bringing disaster on everyone. Furthermore, the high rate of population growth among the poor nations insures that eventually the lifeboats will be swamped.[13] On this view, treating the world food supply as common property to which everyone is entitled undermines any incentive among the poor of the world to increase production and limit population growth. The increasing population will continually reduce the amount available for each individual while at the same time increasing pollution and putting other strains on the environment.[14] So Hardin writes that "for posterity's sake we should never send food to any population that is beyond the realistic carrying capacity of its land."[15] The idea that certain countries should be left to have "massive diebacks of population"[16] while others should perhaps be helped has been called *triage*.[17] This point of view does not only say that we have no duty to help; it says we often have a duty not to help.

One way of responding to Hardin's argument is to raise questions about the choice of metaphors and their applicability. For example, some Western industrialized countries are overpopulated while some African countries are underpopulated with respect to their potential carrying capacity.[18] One can ask various questions about this point of view: Why should we use the metaphor of lifeboats rather than of luxury liners? Why should we view the Third World poor as the primary threat to the resources of the world rather than the people of developed countries such as the United States,[19] since the average American uses up thirty times the amount of the earth's resources as the average Asian or African?[20] How are the lifeboat metaphors applicable when, apart from particularly bad years, most countries in the world have the resources necessary to feed their people as long as they are used primarily for that purpose?[21] How is the lifeboat metaphor applicable when developed nations, including the United States, import more protein from the developing nations than they export to them?[22]

Apart from these problems, how would someone like Singer respond to Hardin?[23] One could reply that the considerations Hardin points out only affect the question of what one should do to help, not how much one should do. Perhaps these considerations merely impose on all people a duty to redouble their efforts to find and support solutions that avoid both short-range hunger and long-range disaster. But that only increases the problem already mentioned, of an overload of duties.

Many other questions can be raised about the best way to help. Government aid has often not benefited the most vulnerable in the past, and may not do so in the future, so aid through private and religious organizations may be better.[24] Changes in trade and other policies of the industrialized countries may be more important than giving food aid. Perhaps a major duty individuals have is that of exerting pressure on government to make sure that policies do protect the vulnerable.[25] (See the project at the end of the chapter.) But while these considerations are relevant to the question of how help can best be given, they do not affect the question of how much a person has a duty to sacrifice in order to help.

HUNGER, POSITIVE DUTIES, AND THE IDEA OF A FAIR SHARE

Peter Singer says we have a duty to do all we can; Robert Nozick says we have no duty to benefit others at all. Many others say we have "some" duty to help but give no clear guidance. Can we find a middle way between Singer and Nozick that is more precise than this? Perhaps the following provides some guidelines. An estimate can be made of what resources would be needed to feed the hungry, bring about political and economic change, promote development, limit population growth, and do whatever is necessary to see that all people have a minimally decent standard of living. Some formula based on ability to help could determine what a fair share would be for each citizen of a developed country (and each wealthy citizen of a developing country) to contribute to the needs of those in distress in that country and to that country's share of helping people of other nations. To the extent that nations adopt this procedure and make it part of their tax structure, a person could fulfill the duty of doing her or his share by paying her or his taxes.[26] The ideal would be for nations to do this so that the responsibilities would be carried out and the burden would be distributed fairly.[27] To the extent that nations have not done this, and it is unlikely that any have, each individual could and should still make some sort of estimate of what a fair share would be and give at least that amount, or what remains of that amount after taking into consideration that part of her or his taxes that are used for the appropriate purposes, through private or religious agencies.[28]

I would claim that it would be a strict duty or duty of perfect obligation for an individual to give at least her or his fair share, according to some plausible formula, toward seeing that all human beings have the basic necessities of life insofar as that can depend on the actions of others. This conclusion can also be supported by a generalization argument. If everyone contributed at least his or her fair share of time, effort, and money, the basic needs of human beings would be met, since that would be one of the criteria for deciding on a fair share.

We have noted that when some people fail to try to save people who are drowning, the individual who has already done her or his fair share of rescuing now has a duty to do more. But aiding the hungry is not exactly like this. Saving people from drowning is dealing with an emergency situation. When the emergency has passed, the rescuer can return to a life of pursuing goals she or he sets for herself or himself. Hunger and poverty, however, are chronic problems. A duty to keep on giving of one's resources, even after one has done a fair share, would threaten to eclipse everything else in one's life, including developing one's talents, raising a family, sending children to college, and so on, so that a person would become nothing but a means to meeting the needs of others. Doing more than a fair share is certainly admirable, but a strict duty to do as much as one possibly can would seem to be a duty, not of loving one's neighbor as oneself, but of loving one's neighbor instead of oneself.

The idea of a strict duty to do at least one's fair share draws a line at a plausible point somewhere between doing nothing and sacrificing one's whole life to the cause of relieving the distress of others. Failure to recognize a duty to give a fair share is to indicate that one believes either that it is not important that the needs of those in distress should be met, or that other people should do more than their fair share. It might be said that the first is at least a sin against compassion and the second is a sin against fairness or justice. In either case, one is treating the interests of others as having less validity than one's own, or, from another point of view, one is not loving others as oneself. So our view of positive duties is that each individual has a duty to do a fair share of what needs to be done to meet the basic needs of other people, even if this requires considerable sacrifice. Most people in industrialized countries are probably not fulfilling this duty. The wealthy, in particular, are not fulfilling it, since studies of United States federal income tax returns indicate that on the average the wealthy give a lower percentage of their incomes to charity than the less well-off.

CALCULATING A FAIR SHARE

Although the idea of a fair share does provide a basis for objectively deciding what one's duties are (at least up to a point), in the absence of any official calculation of such a share individuals generally do not have enough information to assess their own fair share, and if they did, they would probably tend to underestimate their share. What people tend to think of as their fair share depends much less on any knowledgeable calculations than on what they think their neighbors, fellow citizens, or fellow church members are contributing.[29] People console themselves with the thought that it cannot really be their duty to do more than others are doing. But since each person tends to think that he or she is doing more with respect to his or her resources than others (owing to self-interest and the vice of pride), the idea of a duty to do a fair share is in danger of succumbing to a downward pressure to require less and less. If the ultimate goal of our duties and responsibilities is to protect the vulnerable, then the duty to do one's fair share to meet their needs should be supplemented with a duty to put upward pressure on the prevailing idea of a fair share. This can only be done by people who do considerably more than what is generally perceived as a fair share. Christian ethics speaks of the ideals of living as a light set on a hill to witness to a higher and more demanding way of life, and of being the salt of the earth that preserves it from the decay brought about by the decline of prevailing standards. Others may accept secular counterparts to these ideals, or equivalents drawn from other religious traditions.

THE LIMITS OF DUTIES TO AID OTHERS

The principal concern of this chapter has been the individual's responsibility. Government action can be a channel through which an individual carries out *some* of his or her responsibility.[30] Here we will note some implications for government action of certain considerations about duties to help that were mentioned in chapter 6. First, wealthy nations have frequently violated the prohibition against giving help in a manner that makes the recipients more dependent in the long run, rather than more self-sufficient. Second, Kant would seem to be right when he says that giving for the sake of obligating the recipient does not fulfill a duty of benefiting others. So Americans ought not to congratulate themselves on their generosity when aid is given, as it often is, for ulterior purposes, such as to get rid of surplus farm products, to help boost farm prices, to gain political influence, or to stimulate markets and/or a favorable climate of investment for American companies. Such acts are based neither on compassion nor on a sense of duty.

Third, wealthy countries would seem to have a right to make aid contingent on a good-faith effort on the part of the receiving country to bring about necessary changes to prevent its situation from getting worse, if this can be done without causing undue suffering to people who are not in a position to influence their government. Otherwise, the people who give can claim that they are being used solely as means to the ends of the underdeveloped country or its people.[31] Perhaps developed nations have seldom given enough nonmilitary aid to a particular developing nation to be in a position to dictate what steps it should take to improve the ability of its people to be self-sufficient, or perhaps the developed nations, for reasons having to do with political strategy, military effort, or business investment, have seen fit not to demand such remedial steps. But it would seem to be legitimate for them to make such demands.

QUESTIONS

1. The author indicates that if the careless or self-serving actions of the wealthy have caused harm to the poor, then the wealthy have a duty to compensate those who have been harmed. Suppose, however, that problems in Third World countries have inadvertently been caused by the benevolent efforts of Western nations (e.g., such as Western health-care efforts that have reduced the infant mortality rate and thereby have contributed to the population explosion). Does that also impose special duties of compensation on the Western nations?

2. Suppose people are hungry in poor countries because of facts such as this one: in 1954 it cost Brazil 14 bags of coffee to buy one American Jeep, but by 1968 it cost Brazil 45 bags of coffee to buy one Jeep.[32] Is anyone accountable for such a change? In the ten-year period from 1959 to 1969 the United States invested $27 billion in Europe and Canada, from which it made a profit of about 44 percent; but in the same period it invested $5.8 billion in Third World countries, from which it made a profit of 250 percent.[33] Should some of the difference in profits have stayed in those countries (e.g., by paying higher wages to workers, or through higher taxes)? If advantages to the developed countries are a by-product of chance conditions and the operation of the free-market system, do those who benefited from these conditions have duties to those who were harmed? Would the fact that certain trade policies benefit some people (usually the already well-off) to the disadvantage of others (usually the already badly off) be enough to show that the policies are unjust? If not, what would show them to be unjust?

3. The author claims that we have a strict duty to do a fair share toward meeting the needs of others, whether they are part of our society or not. What does he mean by a fair share? What he regards as a fair share is probably much more than most people recognize a duty to do, but less than Singer would demand. Do you think our duties are less demanding or more demanding than the author does? How would you argue for that position?

4. One of the advantages of the idea of a fair share is that it would not normally put the individual under a duty that would overwhelm him or her and take up his or her whole life. We could imagine, however, a situation in which the need of those in distress is so great, and those able to help so few, that if everyone did everything he or she could do to help, that would still not be enough, or would be barely enough. In such a case, trying to do a fair share would require just as much as trying to follow Singer's requirements, and would take up the individual's every effort. Would the individual still have a duty to do his or her fair share, or would he or she not have such a duty because doing one's fair share would then require loving one's neighbors instead of oneself rather than as oneself? Would it matter whether this situation of overwhelming need were temporary or long-term? The author has not answered all these questions. Can you?

5. When people are asked to give to a charity, they often ask how much other people who have also been asked are giving. Are there situations in which the answer to that question is relevant to how much you should give? Are there situations in which it is not relevant? What would make it relevant or not relevant?

PROJECT

The author suggests that a major duty individuals have is that of exerting pressure on government to make sure that policies do protect the vulnerable. In American society people are not quick to recognize this as a moral duty. Churches have much more success in getting their members to contribute to "One Great Hour of Sharing" and "Hunger Fund" offerings than they do in getting them to write letters to their senators and congressmen about hunger issues. Whatever a fair share of political influence is, an individual who fails to write one such letter a year would seem to be failing to do a fair share and so is violating a strict duty. An individual could write many such letters a year, and encourage others to do likewise, without sacrificing anything significant. Find out from an organization such as Bread for the World (802 Rhode Island Avenue N.E., Washington, D.C. 20018) what hunger-related issues are facing Congress this year, and write a letter to your senators and representative. Perhaps you could organize a class project to do this.

FURTHER READING

Two anthologies dealing with this subject and containing some of the essays referred to in the notes are:

Aiken, William, and Hugh LaFollette, eds. *World Hunger and Moral Obligation.* Englewood Cliffs, N.J.: Prentice-Hall, 1977. This includes the essays by Singer and Hardin discussed in this chapter.
Lucas, George R., and Thomas W. Ogletree, eds. *Lifeboat Ethics: The Moral Dilemmas of World Hunger.* New York: Harper and Row, 1976.

Other works dealing with this issue from a philosophical point of view are:

Care, Norman S. *On Sharing Fate.* Philadelphia: Temple University Press, 1987.
O'Neill, Onora. "The Moral Perplexities of Famine Relief." In *Matters of Life and Death: New Introductory Essays in Moral Philosophy,* edited by Tom Regan, 260–97. New York: Random House, 1980.
Shue, Henry. *Basic Rights.* Princeton, N.J.: Princeton University Press, 1980.
Van Wyk, Robert N. "Perspectives on World Hunger and the Extent of Our Positive Duties." *Public Affairs Quarterly* 2 (April 1988): 75–90. The present chapter is an abbreviated version of this essay.

Other works on the issue of hunger that are not necessarily philosophical include the following:

Lappé, Frances Moore, and Joseph Collins. *World Hunger: 10 Myths*. 4th ed., San Francisco: Institute for Food and Development Policy, 1982.
Sidor, Ronald J. *Rich Christians in an Age of Hunger*. Downers Grove, Ill.: Intervarsity Press, 1977.
Simon, Arthur. *Bread for the World*. Rev. ed. Grand Rapids, Mich.: Eerdmans, 1984.

NOTES

1. Henry Shue, *Basic Rights* (Princeton, N.J.: Princeton University Press, 1980), 114.
2. This is an estimate reported by Nick Eberstadt in "Myths of the Food Crisis," *New York Review of Books*, February 19, 1976.
3. This figure was prepared by the United Nations for the 1974 World Food Conference in Rome.
4. Lester Brown, *In the Human Interest* (New York: Norton, 1974), 98.
5. At that time, the U.S. secretary of state was John Foster Dulles, past president of United Fruit and a large shareholder. His brother, Allen Dulles, was head of the Central Intelligence Agency. Allen Dulles's law firm had written agreements between United Fruit and Guatemala in 1930 and 1936. See Carl Oglesby and Richard Shaull, *Containment and Change* (New York: Macmillan, 1967), 104.
6. Arthur Simon, *Bread for the World*, rev. ed. (Grand Rapids, Mich.: Eerdmans, 1984), 47.
7. Onora O'Neill, "Lifeboat Earth," *Philosophy and Public Affairs* 4 (Spring 1975): 286.
8. For some of these problems, see Robert Goodin, *Protecting the Vulnerable* (Chicago: University of Chicago Press, 1985), 159–60, and Charles Beitz, "Global Egalitarianism: Can We Make Out a Case?," *Dissent* (Winter 1979): 60–62.
9. Robert Nozick, *Anarchy, State, and Utopia* (New York: Basic Books, 1974), 30–35.
10. Peter Singer, "Famine, Affluence, and Morality," *Philosophy and Public Affairs* 1 (Spring 1972): 231.
11. The legitimacy of governments' doing so is argued for by Goodin, *Protecting the Vulnerable*, 164, and Shue, *Basic Rights*, 118.
12. This is a problem raised by James Fishkin in *The Limits of Obligation* (New Haven: Yale University Press, 1982), especially chaps. 1–7, 9, and 18.
13. Garrett Hardin, "Lifeboat Ethics: The Case against Helping the Poor," *Psychology Today* 8 (September 1974): 38–43, 123–26.
14. Hardin, "The Tragedy of the Commons," *Science* 102 (December 13, 1968): 1243–48.
15. Hardin, "Carrying Capacity as an Ethical Concept," in *Lifeboat Ethics: The Moral Dilemma of World Hunger*, ed. George R. Lucas and Thomas W. Ogletree (New York: Harper and Row, 1976), 131.
16. Part of the title of an article by Hardin, "Another Face of Bioethics: The Case for Massive 'Diebacks' of Population," *Modern Medicine* 65 (March 1, 1975).
17. The word *triage* is derived from a procedure for rationing medical help in battle situations. Wounded soldiers are divided into three classes (hence the derivation of the term). Immediate treatment is given to those who can be expected to recover if and only if they are aided. Soldiers with little hope of survival, and those who would likely recover adequately without help, are left untreated, at least until the first group has been taken care of. The application of the term to the issue of world hunger, and to nations rather than to individuals,

is controversial. See Stuart W. Hinds, "Relations of Medical Triage to World Famine: A History," in Lucas and Ogletree, *Lifeboat Ethics*, 29–51, and Donald W. Schriver, Jr., "Lifeboaters and Mainliners," in *Lifeboat Ethics*, 141–50.

18. Paul Verghese, "Muddled Metaphors," in Lucas and Ogletree, *Lifeboat Ethics*, 151–56.

19. It has been claimed that the United States uses as much energy for its air conditioners as the billion people of China use for all purposes, and that each American citizen consumes on the average about 1,725 pounds of grain a year (directly and through meat production) compared to 400 pounds per person in poor countries. See Simon, *Bread for the World*, 63.

20. Verghese, "Muddled Metaphors," in Lucas and Ogletree, *Lifeboat Ethics*, 152.

21. Frances Moore Lappé and Joseph Collins, *Exploding the Hunger Myths* (San Francisco: Institute for Food and Development Policy, 1979), 5–7.

22. See citations in Ronald J. Sidor, *Rich Christians in an Age of Hunger* (Downers Grove, Ill.: Intervarsity Press, 1977), 156, and Georg Borgstrom, *The Food and People Dilemma* (Belmont, Calif.: Cuxbury Press, 1973), 64.

23. Radical disagreements concerning policy are not a new problem for utilitarians. John Plamenatz points out that William Paley and Jeremy Bentham arrived at incompatible conclusions on almost all practical issues from very similar theoretical principles. See Plamenatz, *The English Utilitarians*, 2nd ed. (Oxford: Blackwell, 1958), 56.

24. See Frances Moore Lappé and Joseph Collins, *World Hunger: 10 Myths*, 4th ed. (San Francisco: Institute for Food and Development Policy, 1982), 39–45.

25. I would agree with Henry Shue's claim that the positive duties that a government has toward persons outside its jurisdiction are duties it has not directly, but as an agent of its citizens as they employ government to carry out their duties. See Shue, *Basic Rights*, 151.

26. For some suggestions concerning such ways, see Lappé and Collins, *World Hunger*, 49–50.

27. As is also argued for by Shue, *Basic Rights*, 118, and by Goodin, *Protecting the Vulnerable*, 164.

28. Of course, the idea of a fair share is rather inexact. Presumably one should think in terms of placing a graduated income tax on oneself. But with what sort of gradation?

29. See Singer, "Famine, Affluence, and Morality," 237.

30. See note 25.

31. See Shue, *Basic Rights*, pt. 3, "Policy Implications," 155–74.

32. Pierre Ghedo, *Why Is the Third World Poor?* (Maryknoll, N.Y.: Orbis, 1973), 64.

33. Senator Mark Hatfield, quoted in W. Stanley Mooneyhan, *What Do You Say to a Hungry World?* (Waco, Tex.: Word Books, 1975), 129–30.

10

Virtue and Vice

A GENERAL ACCOUNT OF VIRTUE

If we are evaluating a person, or a type of person, even perhaps a type of person we are considering trying to become, we do so in terms of characteristics, capabilities, dispositions, and so on. We might ask what sort of characteristics Jones would have to have, or I would have to have, to be a good athlete, musician, soldier, teacher, or businessman. We can call these the virtues or excellences of athletics, musicianship, soldiering, or business. We might also want to ask what makes Jones, or myself as I now am, or some future self I might strive to become, an example of a good human being simply as a human being. Those characteristics we would call the virtues or excellences of human beings.

THE CLASSICAL ACCOUNT OF VIRTUE IN ARISTOTLE AND ST. THOMAS

The philosopher who is most noted for his consideration of the topic of virtue or excellence was Aristotle. We have seen in chapter 4 that Aristotle came to the conclusion that the person who is leading a good life, or has *eudaimonia*, is the person "who exercises his faculties in accordance with perfect excellence, being duly furnished with external goods, not for any chance time, but for a full term of years."[1]

Intellectual and Moral Excellence

Intellectual Excellence, or Intellectual Virtue.   For Aristotle there are two sorts of excellence, moral excellence and intellectual excellence. Intellectual excellence consists of excellence in practical reasoning and excellence in theoretical reasoning or intellectual contemplation. In some places, he regards a life engaged in intellectual contemplation to be the highest form of life, similar to the life of God (or the gods), who (in Aristotle's view) is not involved in practical concerns. If we emphasize this aspect of Aristotle's thought, we end up with a view of the good life for a privileged few. But there is also in Aristotle an account of practical reasonableness that has been defined as

> being able to bring one's own intelligence to bear effectively on the problems of choosing one's actions and life style and shaping one's own character; positively, it involves that one seeks to bring an intelligent and reasonable order into one's own actions and habits and practical attitudes.[2]

Both aspects of intellectual excellence are aspects of human flourishing as well as means to it. Aristotle writes that both

> prudence [excellence in practical reasoning, or practical reasonableness] and wisdom [excellence in theoretical reasoning] must be desired for themselves, since each is the virtue [or excellence] of one of the parts of the soul, even if neither of them produces anything.[3]

Eudaimonia, Virtue, and Moral Goodness.   The person who is leading a good life is "one who exercises his faculties in accordance with" both intellectual and moral excellence.[4] The traditional view, found in Aristotle and in St. Thomas Aquinas, is that the virtues are qualities that aid human beings in achieving their highest good, and the absence of which interferes with moving toward that good.[5] There are similar views in Hinduism, where "every ethical activity must be judged as a means to the attainment of"[6] the highest state of mind, and in Buddhism, where undesirable character traits are those that stand in the way of enlightenment and mental development. (In Buddhism these vices are the five hindrances: sensual desire, ill will and anger, sloth and torpor, restlessness and worry, and doubt.[7])

For much of the Western tradition, there is less emphasis on any one dominant goal of human life. Those who emphasize the plurality of valuable activities and experiences that go to make up human flourishing can define moral virtue in this way: "Moral virtues are the attitudes, habits, dispositions, willingnesses . . . which can be justified as reasonable modes of response to the opportunities [for participating in the basic goods] which intelligence makes evident to us."[8] The intellectual virtue or excellence that is relevant to morality is practical reasonableness, that is, excellence in the use of the faculty of practical reason. Moral virtue directs one toward the right goals or ends and practical wisdom aids one in choosing wisely the means to these goals.[9]

Strength-of-Character Virtues and Virtues as Correctives

Virtues are to be sought as characteristics that contribute to human good, and part of the human good is living according to reason.[10] So living according to reason is an intrinsic good as well as an instrumental good. One obstacle to living according to reason is being swayed by passions and emotions. The person who never uses reason to set goals to be pursued, but who just drifts along, being swayed by this emotion and then by that emotion, is not leading a fully human life. So for Aristotle and St. Thomas, among others, at least one purpose of moral virtue is to prevent passions and emotions from interfering with living according to reason. G. H. von Wright writes: "The role of virtue, to put it briefly, is to counteract, eliminate, rule out the obscuring effects which emotion may have on our own practical judgment, e.g., judgment relating to the beneficial or harmful nature of a chosen course of action."[11]

One emotion that has such obscuring effects is fear. Courage is the virtue that counteracts the effects of that emotion, and cowardice is the lack of that virtue. Another factor that has such obscuring effects is the inclination to pursue "simple, easily accessible pleasures and amusements" so that a person is "unwilling or unable to forego an immediate pleasure when considerations indicate that he should."[12] Why do people in business and government get involved in crooked deals? Why is there an epidemic of drug use and teenage pregnancies? One answer has to do with the inability of people to say no to temptations for immediate gratification. The virtue needed to counteract this human inclination is self-restraint, or what Aristotle called temperance (or moderation); the lack of self-restraint is self-indulgence. Courage and moderation are strength-of-character virtues. One contemporary philosopher, Anthony Quinton, defines strength of character as

> the disposition or habit of controlling one's immediate, impulsive desires, so that we do not let them issue in action until we have considered the bearing of that action on the achievement of other, remoter objects of desire. Understood in this way, character is much the same thing as self-control or strength of will.[13]

One philosopher, James Wallace, points out that there are two places at which virtue can combat the influence of passion. People may rationally decide on a plan of action but then be swayed off course because of desires that conflict with that plan, or because of fear (or possibly of rashness). Or people may be so controlled by impulse and desire, or so affected by fear, that they may never think about any long-range plans of action. Thus we have two types of self-indulgent persons. "One is weak and abandons his plans when he can pursue easy pleasures and amusements. The other pursues easy pleasures without any reservations, because he has no plans to abandon."[14]

Likewise, we have two types of cowards. One allows excessive fears to prevent him from carrying out plans; the other is so influenced by fear that he never makes any plans. In order to live well, one must avoid being either sort of self-indulgent person and either sort of coward, so one must have the virtues of temperance, or self-restraint, and courage.[15]

These virtues, "which are all dispositions to resist the immediate solicitations of impulse,"[16] are ingredients in the *eudaimonia* conceived of by Aristotle and St. Thomas. But even if one does not accept either of their particular views of the good life, any reasonable conception of the good life requires commitment to long-range projects. Carrying out such commitments requires the strength-of-character virtues. The moral virtues have, thus, also been characterized as those dispositions that are needed in order to achieve "any large scale worthy enterprise,"[17] and in particular cooperative enterprises.

Virtue, Reason, and Emotion

None of this should be taken to mean that Aristotle sees emotion and reason as necessarily in opposition to each other, so that emotion must be eliminated from influencing action. Rather, it is a matter of having appropriate emotions.

> Aristotle's moral theory must be seen as a theory not only of how to *act* well but also of how to *feel*, for the moral virtues are states of character that enable a person to exhibit the right kinds of emotions as well as the right kinds of actions.[18]

The courageous person, then, is not only the person who acts in spite of his or her fear, but also the person who does not feel inappropriate fear, or for that matter inappropriate confidence. The experience of feelings, for Aristotle, can themselves be more rational or less rational. Reason may or may not be present in them. Reason is in the emotions when they are appropriate to the circumstances.

> In feeling fear, confidence, desire, anger, pity, and in general pleasure and pain, one can feel too much or too little; and both extremes are wrong. The mean and the good is feeling at the right time, about the right things, in

relation to the right people, and for the right reason; and the mean and the good are the task of virtue. [19]

Although Aristotle's famous doctrine of the mean, stated here, is rather imprecise, there are certainly some circumstances in which we can say that an emotion does not occur at the right time to the right extent with respect to the right objects. If I am furious over some minor slight from someone, it would seem that my feelings are irrationally inappropriate to the situation. On the other hand, if I fail to be moved at all when I see some bullies beating up a smaller child, my lack of emotion would seem to be inappropriate to the situation. What factors determine what is appropriate? One factor may be that which is approved of in one's own society. But another factor is that which harmonizes with reality. My feelings may be rational in the sense that they are sensitive to the real nature of the situation. They are not, for instance, distorted by extraneous considerations. If I become furious at my wife over some minor thing because I am really upset with my employer, then my feelings are not sensitive to the real nature of the situation, but rather are distorted by extraneous considerations.

Being and Becoming a Virtuous Person

The Virtuous Person.   Who is the virtuous person? It is not the person who only happens to do something that is or appears to be just or temperate or courageous. The person must perform the act in the manner in which a just, or temperate, or courageous person would perform it. [20] First, she must know what she is doing. If a person is unaware of danger, then her action cannot display courage. Second, the person must choose the act, and choose it for itself. If a person defies a danger only out of fear of a greater danger, then the act was not chosen for itself and does not display courage. Third, the act must be the "expression of a formed and stable character." [21] Whether a person has a formed and stable character of a certain sort is revealed by how she feels about acting in certain ways, and by what she enjoys doing. If you asked Aristotle what you should do, he would not tell you to do what you enjoy doing. He would tell you to first train yourself so that you get a firm and stable character, one that enjoys being virtuous, and then to do what you enjoy doing. "The good man and the bad man will find different activities pleasant, and so when they both aim at pleasure, they are not aiming at the same thing in any [significant] sense." [22]

The just person is not the one who begrudgingly does what is just, but the one who enjoys acting justly, or at least is pained by the thought of acting in any other way. The generous person is not the person who gives but resents doing so, but rather the person who enjoys giving. So Aristotle says that the pleasure or pain that accompanies an act "must be taken as a test of the formed habit or character."[23] A courageous and truthful person finds more pain in the thought of fleeing from danger or getting out of trouble by lying than she does in the thought of risking the danger or accepting the trouble.

Becoming Virtuous.   How do I come to be virtuous, or, in other words, to enjoy acting virtuously in the way in which a virtuous person does? This begins with moral education. Through moral education, a person comes to recognize the appropriate and correct ways to feel or act in certain circumstances; that is, she comes to value certain ways of feeling and acting. She comes to see that some virtue, such as courage, is intrinsically good, so she chooses it for its own sake, or for the sake of becoming or remaining a courageous person. The person who does not have any moral training to start with has a great deal of difficulty seeing the point of a virtuous life. To a certain extent, one has to be virtuous to understand and value virtue, and one has to understand and value virtue to become virtuous. Aristotle writes:

> If a person lives under the sway of his passions, he will not listen to the arguments by which you would dissuade him, or even understand them. . . . The character, then, must be already formed, so as to be in some way akin to virtue, loving what is noble and hating what is base.[24]

Practical reasonableness enables one to see what courage or some other virtue requires under the particular circumstances in which a person finds himself. Insofar as one thinks that his own wisdom is limited, he can act in accordance with the way some person who is a model of virtue and wisdom would act. Some Christians, for example, approach matters by asking, "What would Jesus do?" A person can force himself to act as he would act if he did feel courageous or generous, or as another person whose courage and generosity he admires would act. If he does this, eventually he comes to have the right feelings. So Aristotle says that a person trains himself to feel fear or confidence.[25]

When a person no longer feels inordinate fear in a situation in which a courageous person would not feel such fear, he or she has in fact become such a courageous person.[26] The same would be true for proper anger, for moderation (temperance), and so on. First one has to care about performing virtuous acts. Then one just performs virtuous acts. Each person has the capacity to choose to do that. Eventually one comes to perform them the way a virtuous person would perform them, backed up by the right feelings. Now one enjoys being virtuous and finds repellent what is not virtuous. So Aristotle says that "by doing what is just a man becomes just, and temperate by doing what is temperate, while without doing thus he has no chance of ever becoming good."[27] Moral goodness does not consist of avoiding pleasure in the interests of something else, but of learning to take pleasure in virtuous activity, in the expression of moral and intellectual excellence. Aristotle has some additional practical advice on this. Since virtues are correctives, we have to see where we most need to be corrected. One should try to overcompensate in combating the extremes that are most common for human beings, those that are most common for oneself personally, and those that most entice one with the offer of pleasure.[28]

Interlude: Alternative Points of View

If virtue is something that is, at least in part, acquired by willpower, as Aristotle and much of the Western tradition maintain, then not all points of view have much concern for virtue. According to some points of view, moral excellence is not achieved by study and effort, but rather by getting the intellect and the will out of the way and then by tapping into the individual's "natural spontaneity toward goodness."[29] Ralph Waldo Emerson is regarded as a representative of such a point of view. According to the ancient Chinese religion Taoism, another representative of that point of view, instead of striving after knowledge or goodness one should lose oneself in the Tao (the creative principle) as fish lose themselves in water.[30] Ambition, self-assertion, self-justification, boasting, pride, lack of contentment, and extravagance are the activities of the self that prevent one from losing oneself in the Tao.[31] Out of this would seem to come a kind of nonassertive love. Some Christians believe that moral goodness does not come from any effort of one's own, but rather from some infusion of love and goodness from God or the Holy Spirit, with respect to which the individual plays a purely passive role. There is little doubt that experiences of various sorts, whatever their origin, can have transforming effects on human beings. But this does not rule out the role of human effort in the acquiring of virtue.

Other Virtues in Aristotle

Contemporary writers who wish to reemphasize Aristotle's way of looking at ethics do not necessarily wish to return to Aristotle's list of specific virtues. That list includes courage (a mean between cowardice and foolhardiness), temperance or moderation (between intemperance and an unnamed vice similar to excessive self-control), liberality (between prodigality and stinginess), magnificence (between vulgar display and shabbiness), proper pride (between vanity and undue humility), proper ambition (between overambition and lack of ambition), gentleness or good temper (between irascibility and apathy), truthfulness (presumably about oneself, primarily expressed in modesty), wittiness (a mean between buffoonery and boorishness), and agreeableness in company or friendliness.

There are a number of things to notice about this list. First, as Aristotle himself recognized, not every virtue fits well into the scheme of being a mean between two extremes. Second, some actions are simply wrong; for example, there is no virtue corresponding to a moderate inclination to commit adultery with the right person at the right time under the right circumstances. Third, when Aristotle says that virtue is desire guided by reason, he does not actually give reasons why certain characteristics are on the list of virtues and others are not. Some would be recognized as intrinsically or instrumentally worthwhile by almost everyone, while others seem to be primarily reflections of the prejudices of the Greek upper class to which Aristotle belonged. Some Christians, for example, would consider it an exhibition of virtue for a wealthy member of their group to dress simply so as not to intimidate or humiliate other members of their group. Aristotle would consider it an absence of the virtue of magnificence. Aristotle's virtue of proper pride might involve a kind of arrogant self-sufficiency that looks down on the opinions and life-styles of social inferiors.[32]

Further Considerations on Aristotle and Virtue

Even as Aristotle recognized, virtues are not valued only as correctives. Elizabeth Telfer writes:

"In general, it seems that whereas the virtues are made necessary by deficiencies in man and his surroundings, they have a value which does not derive wholly from their usefulness in dealing with such deficiencies."[33]

Even when virtues are correctives, some would seem to be valuable not as correctives for the passions, but as compensations for the lack of passion or for other deficiencies in human beings or their environment. Furthermore, virtues may not necessarily be correctives at all. Self-confidence and resourcefulness do not seem to be correctives. Neither do some of the characteristics that Edmund Pincoffs calls meliorating virtues,[34] which will be discussed below.

The Social Virtues, Friendship, and Moral Education

Why Be Virtuous?   Someone might ask, "Why should I wish to be virtuous?" We have seen that one answer is that such virtues as courage are beneficial to individuals who have them because they enable these individuals to make and to carry out plans in spite of obstacles. A courageous person is more likely to lead a fulfilling life. Of course, courage might also get one killed. But once one becomes courageous, he or she comes to value courage for its own sake, and cannot choose instantaneously to be some other sort of person when it is inconvenient to be courageous.[35]

The Social Virtues and the Individual Virtues.   When we think of moral virtues, we often think of those characteristics that are beneficial to other people rather than to the agent, such as kindness, generosity, loyalty, and truthfulness. Some people would limit the application of the term *moral virtues* to these, calling courage and other such characteristics *instrumental virtues*, or some other kind of virtues.[36] However, the moral virtues can be characterized as those traits that "would cause an individual moral agent who had them to excel at all the morally justifiable things characteristic of moral agents."[37] Courage and strength-of-character virtues in general would do this, since they would enable a moral agent to better exercise other virtues. P. T. Geach writes that "the exercise of another virtue may always call for courage, the world being what it is, so no virtue can exist in due development without courage."[38]

Virtue and the Good of Others.   So without denying that courage is a moral virtue, we will consider these other virtues that are primarily related to the good of other people. One virtue that is so related is conscientiousness, or what Kant called the good will, that is, the commitment to fulfill one's explicit moral duties. Some authors reserve the name "moral virtues" for those that are explicit forms of regard for the interests of others, such as honesty, caring about justice, sincerity, truthfulness, benevolence, trustworthiness, and nonrecklessness.[39] There are other virtues, sometimes called the meliorating virtues, that make social life better without necessarily intending to do so. These include such things as gentleness, decency, modesty, and even-temperedness.

Lawrence Becker devotes a book to the virtue of reciprocity, or the disposition to return good for good in various appropriate ways. Such a virtue is generally a part of conventional moralities for good reason. The common practice of returning good for good reinforces helping behavior in a society, while its absence would tend to extinguish such behavior.[40]

The Social Virtues and Friendship.   Why should we seek to develop these socially oriented virtues? The biblical tradition says that having such virtues as love for other people is intrinsically related to achieving the highest goal for oneself, namely, being a child of God. (See Matt. 5:43–48.) There is also a secular Aristotelian answer. In chapter 8 we said that morality was concerned with promoting what is intrinsically good. Deficiencies in such virtues as friendliness, sympathy, benevolence, and honesty are obstacles to having friends and participating in an important aspect of a satisfying life, and thus are obstacles to a good life. As we noted in chapter 2 the existence of a deep chasm between serving one's own interest and benefiting other people depends on what is ultimately worthwhile for human beings. To the degree that friendship is an intrinsically worthwhile thing, there is no deep chasm.

The Social Virtues and Moral Education.   Human beings are social beings who ordinarily can find fulfillment only in society. Furthermore, living in a certain kind of society is a necessary prerequisite for participating in many aspects of the good life. Protecting the existence and furthering the quality of society require going beyond self-love and caring both about the common good and about other people. Suppose, however, that someone said to Aristotle, "I acknowledge that my being courageous benefits me personally. I also acknowledge that a major factor in my leading a good life is living in a good community and that each person's possessing the social virtues is very beneficial to the community. However, I feel no displeasure at being unjust, and I will not try to acquire a disposition toward justice unless you show me how my being just directly benefits me personally." Aristotle would probably say that such a person's moral upbringing and background are so deficient that he or she has been rendered incapable of seeing the value of virtue. Thus it would be pointless to pursue the matter.

Virtue and Meaning in Life.   A further answer to the person seeking a reason to develop virtue is given by Peter Singer. A person who pursues only immediate pleasure for him- or herself and is totally indifferent to the welfare of others is a psychopath. Such a person cannot remain satisfied with his or her life in the long run because there is nothing long-term or far-reaching in his life that could give it meaning. Even the more prudent egoist who does have egoistic long-term plans will ultimately find life meaningless, and thus unhappy, if he or she does not acquire interests broader than self-interest. One of the ways of doing this is to acquire a concern for how things look from the moral point of view.[41] In other words, personal happiness and fulfillment require meaning. Meaning requires being related to something beyond oneself, and being concerned with morality is one way to be linked up with a larger framework beyond oneself. Here again there seems to be a convergence between concern for others and one's own good.

KANT AND ARISTOTLE ON THE STRENGTH-OF-CHARACTER VIRTUES

The strength-of-character virtues are as important for Kant as they are for Aristotle. We have seen that for Kant the moral worth of a person is found in the will to do one's duty for its own sake, or, as Kant puts it elsewhere, virtue is "the agreement of the will with every duty,"[42] or "the strength of man's maxim in obeying his duty."[43] Since strength is needed to overcome obstacles, and the obstacles to doing one's duty are one's natural inclinations, virtue may also be called "the moral power of self-restraint."[44] Since for Kant acting according to duty is acting according to reason, the virtuous person is one who as much as possible brings "all his capacities and inclinations under [the] authority [of reason, and does not] let himself be governed by feelings and inclinations."[45] So while Aristotle and Kant are very different (Aristotle would say "does not let himself be governed by inappropriate emotion"), they are similar in emphasizing strength-of-character virtues. Aristotle, however, would seem to say that for the person who has fully acquired the virtues of moderation, courage, and so on, they are no longer a matter of strength of character. This is because the virtuous person naturally acts virtuously, for it is in virtue that he or she finds pleasure and enjoyment. So it would seem that for Kant the person who is most honest is the one who is tempted to steal but through strength of will resists the temptation to do so, while for Aristotle the person who has truly become honest no longer feels any temptation.

Philippa Foot resolves this conflict by raising the question of why a person finds it difficult to be virtuous. Insofar as one person is more strongly tempted than another to be dishonest because of a failure to value and find pleasure in honesty, then the person who feels the least temptation is the more virtuous, and Aristotle is correct. On the other hand, insofar as one person is more strongly tempted than another because of external circumstances (e.g., poverty), then his or her use of more strength of will to resist temptation displays greater virtue, and to that extent, Kant is right.[46]

VIRTUE AND VICE
IN WESTERN RELIGIOUS TRADITIONS

Virtue and Vice in the Hebrew Scriptures and Judaism

When we read Aristotle, we are likely to find it somewhat strange. That is because between us and Aristotle stands the influence on Western thought of the whole biblical tradition. There is nothing in Aristotle about cruelty as the greatest of all vices. There is nothing in Aristotle that compares with the Jewish and Christian views of love, compassion, and humility. We need to pause and take a look at this tradition of religiously oriented ethics. In light of the discussion of the Hebrew Scriptures in chapter 3, it would seem that an important moral virtue in those writings is love or compassion, involving a disposition to care about the poor, the powerless, and the oppressed. Another is a sense of injustice, that is, a disposition to notice and to respond when other human beings, or at least other members of one's community, are being taken advantage of. Both of these could perhaps be derived from a third important virtue, which is loyalty to the covenant. God is praised for being just and keeping his covenant. Psalm 105:8–9 says:

> He is mindful of his covenant for ever,
> of the word that he commanded for a thousand generations.
> The covenant which he made with Abraham.

According to the Hebrew Scriptures, and thus according to Judaism and New Testament Christianity, one of the chief characteristics of God is *Hesed*, perhaps best translated as "mercy" or "steadfast-love." *Hesed* incorporates the sense of loyalty and is associated with the relationship of covenant. God's love is understood to be steadfast, merciful faithfulness to the covenant relationship. We read in Micah 6:8: "He has showed you, Oh man, what is good; and what does the Lord require of you but to do justice, and to love *Hesed*, and to walk humbly with your God?"

There are contrasts between the biblical view and the assumptions that underlie modern culture. Commentators on our culture say that it "urges us to define our lives, not in terms of past commitments, but in terms of present needs and future possibilities,"[47] while the ideal of the covenant-keeper is, on the contrary, that of a person who defines his or her life within the bonds of past commitments, as God is pictured as doing. As Lewis Smedes writes: "A Covenant-Keeper is loyal, trustworthy, committed, dependable. . . . He is the person who keeps faith with people who trust him, a person who holds relationships together and in the process keeps life humane and decent."[48]

Today's popular culture also sometimes emphasizes "love," which probably is thought to include generalized good will and sympathy and empathy for others. In a study by Samuel P. Oliner and Pearl M. Oliner of what distinguished people who aided Jews threatened by the Nazis from people who did not, it was found that rescuers tended to have empathy with the pain of others. But this was not enough. Rescuers were also the sort of people who were "more likely to get and stay involved because of their general sense of responsibility and tendency to make commitments."[49]

Smedes suggests that the covenant-keeper can be contrasted with a figure highly popular in modern society, the self-maximizer, and that the difference between these two kinds of people can be seen in their attitudes toward marriage and adultery.

> The self-maximizer evaluates relationships with others in terms of how they contribute to his own growth. . . . He marries in order to enrich his life, and

in analyzing his marriage, he is likely to ask: is my marriage giving me all I need to stimulate my growth? Probably the time will come in a self-maximizer's marriage when a sexual affair promises more than he is getting in the marriage, and he will grab at the promise.[50]

The covenant-keeper subordinates "the right to maximize his or her potential for sexual happiness to the responsibility for a covenanted partnership with another human being."[51] The different attitudes toward marriage and adultery are symptomatic of two different views of the meaning and purpose of human life, two different views of what human excellence looks like.

Virtue and Vice in Christianity

There is a formal similarity between Aristotle's account of virtue and the New Testament account, in that both are related to human beings' achieving their highest good. As far as the content of their accounts is concerned, however, the differences between Aristotle's conception of the ideal or virtuous person and that of Judaism and Christianity are evident. In the New Testament the highest good is being a child of God, or reflecting the nature of God (Matt. 5:43–48). There is nothing in Aristotle similar to the biblical ideal of compassion for the poor, the outcast, the sinner, and the enemy.

The various Greek words for love include *eros*, love that motivates striving for something desirable; *philia*, the sort of love embodied in friendship (the key concept for Aristotle); and *agape*, outgoing benevolence that is not based on the desirability or worthiness of the person loved, but that seeks to do good for the person loved. *Agape* is the most common word for love in the New Testament, where it refers to a kind of love that involves patience, kindness, generosity, and doing good, and that excludes rudeness, selfishness, taking offense, resentment, taking pleasure in other people's failings, and jealousy. (See 1 Cor. 13; Phil. 2:1–4; Col. 3:5–15.) The essential characteristic of Christian love or *agape* is sometimes thought to be self-sacrifice. It would seem, however, that what is valued is the willingness to sacrifice for the good of the other person, not self-sacrifice for its own sake.[52]

The Jewish and Christian ideal of humility seems to be the opposite of Aristotle's ideal of the great-souled man. The idea that one's achievements are due not to one's own excellence but to the grace of God is a common theme in the Hebrew Scriptures, as applied to the nation, and in the New Testament, as applied to the Church and the individual. Aristotle would probably not know what to make of the Apostle Paul's injunction: "In humility count others better than yourselves" (Phil. 2:3), or of the words of the Jewish author of *The Wisdom of Ben Sira*: "My son, go on with the business in meekness; the greater thou art, the more shalt thou humble thyself."[53] More will be said about pride and humility below.

Further Reflections on Religion and Virtue

Is the influence of religion on morality good or bad? The previously mentioned study of the differences between those who rescued Jews during the Nazi era and those who did not concludes that formal religious affiliation did not seem to be a major factor.[54] However, the nature of religious commitment did make a difference: "But rescuers did differ from others in their interpretation of religious teaching and religious commitment, which emphasized the common humanity of all people and therefore supported efforts to help the Jews."[55] So the sort of religion one has is a factor in virtue.

VICE, VULNERABILITY, VALUES, AND VIRTUE

We can ask, "Why do people act in certain ways?" They might act in certain ways because they have certain beliefs about how to achieve their goals. They might act differently if we showed them a better way of reaching those goals, or if we changed social conditions so that different ways of reaching those goals became available. Thus education and social engineering may be ways of improving human behavior. People might also behave differently if they acquire different character traits, if they come to have different values, or if they come to see that they are acting inconsistently with the values they have. Values and character traits are related. If we value kindness, for example, we are likely to act in a way that will tend to develop within ourselves the disposition to act kindly. So behavior might be changed by molding character in one way rather than another.

Does character make a difference? The authors of the study of Holocaust rescuers write: "Rescuers did not simply happen on opportunities for rescue; they actively created, sought, or recognized them where others did not. Their participation was not determined by circumstances but by their own personal qualities."[56]

We live in a century that has seen millions of people prevented from participating in a good life because they were tortured, maimed, murdered, or oppressed on account of their race, religion, or political beliefs, or because it was to the advantage of someone to treat them that way. We live in a society in which we are becoming ever more aware of the extent of gratuitous violence against children and women. We can ask what social institutions and arrangements lead to these evils and what changes could be made to prevent them (without leading to other evils). We might also ask what kind of psychiatric treatment might enable people to gain control of their passions. It is unlikely that social change or psychiatry, however, will solve all our difficulties. So we can and must also ask what personal qualities or character traits (vices) lead to such evils, and what personal qualities or character traits (virtues) might be correctives for them. Included among the prime candidates for these qualities would be the character traits of those who were rescuers.

Moral Insensitivity and the Vice of Cruelty

Cruelty is one contender to be put at the head of a list of vices. People are morally callous when they exploit the vulnerability of other people for their own ends and when they are indifferent to the suffering of others, especially the suffering of victims. These two things are closely related. As Mary Wollstonecraft said two centuries ago, "Those who are able to see pain, unmoved, will soon learn to inflict it."[57] We tend to call the exploitation of others cruelty when such exploitation causes physical or psychological suffering and/or when it exploits the vulnerability of another person for no further purpose, but only in order to express hatred, to gain some immediate enjoyment, or to confirm someone in a position of power.[58] We can certainly ask what social institutions should exist in society to protect the vulnerable from cruelty. But we can also ask about what character traits should be encouraged in individual human beings to avoid, counterbalance, and respond to cruelty.

Some Virtues and Vices

We will be concentrating on three virtues in particular: compassion, humility, and integrity. But before focusing on these, there are some others to be considered.

Group Loyalty.   One characteristic common among people who were rescuers of Jews during the Nazi era was a sense of obligation to the norms of their group.[59] Many people helped because they identified with a group in which helping was expected. Even if individuals were cut off from their groups, they still had internalized the norms of the group. When the Jewish people who fled Denmark during the German occupation returned, they discovered that the possessions they had left behind were all waiting for them, cared for by their neighbors. This was so because people had internalized the values of the group and had a sense of responsibility to live by them.[60] In many cases, these were religious norms. Abiding by and internalizing group norms is desirable, then, provided that the norms of the group are morally desirable.

The Vice of Cowardice and the Virtue of Courage.   If the compassionate are to oppose cruelty, they also need the courage to persist in the face of threats and obstacles. Those who did little or nothing to help the Jews when they were threatened by the Nazis tended to be people who were "overcome by fear, hopelessness, and uncertainty."[61] Some people who showed courage in other ways, however, were indifferent to the fate of the Jews.[62] So courage is a necessity in opposing cruelty, and it is a virtue provided that it is supplemented by other characteristics.

The Vice of Greed.   The Spaniards who colonized the Americas inflicted great cruelties on the vulnerable Indians. Why? One answer is greed or avarice. "Avarice is the inordinate love of temporal things, usually of riches, and it is inordinate 'if one is not guided by a reasonable end in view.'"[63] It can also be said that it is not so much love of possessions, because people acquire many more possessions than they could have any emotional attachment to, but the love of acquiring or the love of possessing. Greed does not necessarily lead to overt cruelty. Often it only leads to indifference. As Henry Fairlie writes:

> It is also avarice that leaves us no time or energy to care for our neighbors in our society, not just our neighbors but our fellow-citizens as well. . . . "Sins against the needy are, in an important sense, the exact opposite of those against the enemy," says William F. May. "The enemy occupies the center of attention. But the needy at the other extreme, barely exist."[64]

Between 1965 and 1980 the average American's buying power increased by 50 percent, but people's level of satisfaction was not 50 percent higher. Human beings have a natural tendency to recalibrate their expectations. The person whose buying power has only increased 40 percent is likely to feel deprived and to become insensitive to those who are really poor.[65] Here would seem to be a natural tendency toward greed that should be corrected by virtue.

Greed also gets in the way of pursuing a worthwhile life for ourselves because it obstructs the formation of a rational life plan. Fairlie writes: "Those who surround themselves with things that they do not need, and do not even really want, soon cease to know what they do need or want; and in a little more time they cease also to know or be able to be themselves."[66]

The Virtue of Concern for Justice and Equality.   "Justice" refers both to a characteristic of institutions and social, political, and economic systems, and to a characteristic of individuals. The just individual has the disposition to give people what they are entitled to and to act promptly on these entitlements. The unjust one does not.

Part of any standard of justice is the idea of fairness or equity. People are entitled to some things purely as human beings, including some sort of equal treatment. That is, they are not to be treated differently because of whim, caprice, prejudice, or irrelevant characteristics. Those involved in rescuing Jews sometimes gave a concern for such equity values as equality, justice, and respect as a reason for their actions.[67]

Moral Sensitivity and the Virtue of Compassion

But while rescuers of Jews made some reference to equity values and a concern for justice, "for most rescuers and rescued survivors the language of care dominated. *Pity, compassion, concern, affection* made up the vocabulary of 76 percent of rescuers and 67 percent of rescued survivors."[68]

Compassion would seem to be incompatible with cruelty. The Western world, under the influence of the Judeo-Christian tradition, generally regards love, of which compassion is a form, as one of the most important virtues. Philip Hallie writes: "The opposite of cruelty is not simply freedom from the cruel relationship . . . it is *hospitality*, . . . unsentimental, efficacious love."[69] One philosopher defines compassion as

> a complex emotional attitude toward another, characteristically involving imaginative dwelling on the condition of the other person, an active regard for his good, a view of him as a fellow human being, and emotional responses of a certain degree of intensity.[70]

Another defines compassion as "the disposition to help others who are suffering, to notice and recognize sufferers as sufferers, to judge them to be in some fundamental way similar to oneself, and to be sad to see suffering and glad to see it relieved."[71]

Part of these definitions of compassion have to do with a disposition to see, think, and judge in a certain way, that is, to think of other human beings as similar to oneself, to think that other people are important, to think that one has a duty to help others, and to see this duty as applying to all other human beings.[72] A Buddhist writer says, "Achievement in generosity and charity lies in the freeing of thought from avarice and the practicing of giving up things."[73] The idea of becoming virtuous through practice, by acting the way a person who has that virtue would act, reminds us of Aristotle. What is different, however, is the idea of becoming virtuous through changing one's way of thinking. In Buddhism, this goes further than seeing other people as important and as similar to oneself. Ultimately, partiality toward oneself depends on the illusion that one is a separate reality. Seeing things differently involves giving up that illusion.

The adherent of a theistic religion, or of no religion, is not likely to think that seeing oneself as a separate being is an illusion to be given up. Nevertheless, theists and secularists can learn from the Buddhist approach that it is important to learn to see things differently, and furthermore to have feelings that are appropriate to our way of seeing things. "We should cultivate our emotions so that we feel with others as if they were ourselves."[74] How is this done? By mentally identifying with others and by broadening the boundary of what we think of as our own. This sympathy and compassion for others is manifested outwardly in a reluctance to harm anyone. It has been said that "through this attitude, Buddhism can be said to have had an immense humanizing effect on the entire history of Asia."[75]

The Vice of Arrogance and the Virtue of Humility

A characteristic of the caring and compassionate person is a tendency to think of other human beings as similar to oneself and as important. Thus an obstacle to compassion is the tendency to think of others as not similar to oneself. Even people acting on greed often show restraint in dealing with people of their own race, nation, class, sex, or religion that they do not show in dealing with others.

Suppose people ask: "What gives me the right to play God with the lives of other people, to decide that someone should die or suffer?" Often the answer given is that I am superior and my victim is inferior. This was the rationalization the Spaniards (and the Americans) used to slaughter and enslave the Indians. This kind of arrogance can be a cause of cruelty when greed is not a factor at all. The Manson group, responsible for several notorious murders in California in the 1960s, justified killing because (they claimed) their victims were members of "the Establishment." The Nazis justified killing because their victims were Jews, gypsies, homosexuals, and communists. American slaveholders justified slavery because their victims were of a race they did not consider fully human. Sexism was and is rationalized on the grounds that women are inferior to men. In all of these cases, the victims are deprived of their humanity so that violence may be used against them with impunity.

Another answer to the question "What gives me the right to play God?" is "I am an agent of God." One author writes:

> Not equality but modesty is the cure for arrogance. And no form of arrogance is more obnoxious than the claim that some of us are God's agents, his deputies on earth charged with punishing God's enemies. It was, after all, in defense of the divine honor that all those heretics had been tortured and burned.[76]

It is true that institutional Christianity has carried out great cruelties in the name of God, even though Christians purport to be guided by a book, the New Testament, in which there is not one word sympathetic to the idea that they are supposed to carry out divine retribution or to use physical force in any way. Arrogance is possible with or without religious belief. Numerous psychological studies have shown that people have overwhelming tendencies to be far more certain of their virtue, their motives, and of the truth of their opinions than the facts entitle them to be.[77] Thus the virtue of humility, as a corrective to the strong tendency of human nature toward arrogance, would seem to be difficult to acquire. People readily exercise their cruelty in the name of a God who presumably forbids it, or in the name of some other god, such as communism, or anticommunism, or the master race, or their own wealth. Others exercise it purely in the name of self-expression, in the consciousness that there is no higher Being or cause or standard to which they are answerable. Victims being tortured in Latin American prisons have often been told by their torturers, "We are God in here." The cult of self-expression is such that each individual can regard himself as god. As Henry Fairlie writes concerning the Manson group:

> They murdered in the self-exaltation of Pride and from the incitements to it in our time. They had been taught to be pleased with themselves, with whatever they felt they were, felt they felt, and so felt they must do. They had been free to act as gods, wholly free from any human limitations.[78]

Perhaps what needs to be said is that any idea of being an agent of the divine, or of any substitute for the divine, expresses arrogance and feeds cruelty if that agency involves the use of force, violence, or coercion. Thus a commitment to nonviolence would seem to be a requirement of all who regard themselves as agents of any sort of divinity. If violence is ever to be used, it must be used for reasons other than holy crusades.

Arrogance is not only an opening to cruelty, but to the subversion of the social fabric. From the point of view of the arrogant, the moral and legal rules are made for other people; they do not apply to those who are sincerely dedicated to the good cause—sincere revolutionaries, or sincere supporters of the contras, or sincere patriots, or sincere communists, or sincere fellow believers, or sincere defenders of the Aryan race. The arrogant person regards all the actions of those who are fighting for the "right" cause to be justified.

There is a close connection between humility and truth. Human beings have very strong tendencies not to see themselves as they are.[79] The humble see themselves as they are. Kant says the most important of the duties to oneself is the duty to know one's own heart, one's own motivation.

Moral self-knowledge, which tries to fathom the scarcely penetrable depths of the heart, is the beginning of all human wisdom. . . . This moral self-knowledge . . . opposes that egotistical self-esteem of holding mere wishes to be proofs of a good heart; for even though they may occur with ever so great yearning, they are and remain in themselves not deeds.[80]

In conjunction with this is the virtue of humility. A person ought not to compare himself or herself with other people, but with the moral law. This is the secular version of the religious view of humility based on comparing oneself with Christ or God. Kant defines humility as "the limitation of the high opinion we have of our moral worth by comparison of our actions with the moral law. The comparison of our actions with the moral law makes us humble.[81]

So it would seem that for Kant self-knowledge and the honesty that allows us to achieve it are among the most important virtues. The humility that Kant talks about is obviously not the sort of humility that leads individuals to be unaware of or indifferent to their own rights, cringing and fawning or always deferring to the wishes of other people. That would be a disposition to violate the duty of self-respect. The duty of self-respect requires a person to treat himself or herself not merely as a means, but always also as an end, for whatever our honesty discovers about our own faults, "as representatives of mankind we ought to hold ourselves in high esteem."[82]

But humility is not only seeing oneself as one is, but also seeing for what they are the causes and interests for which one acts. Is it not an expression of arrogance for one generation to believe its political disputes to be so important that in pursuing them it risks destroying the existence of all future generations and the heritage of all past generations? Is it not a matter of a generation choosing not to see itself as one generation among many?

The Vice of Self-Deception and the Virtue of Integrity

The incredible mistreatment of women and children in our society is not caused only by the malevolent and the mentally disturbed. It is passively encouraged by a conspiracy of silence that fails to put a high priority on these problems.[83] The great political evils of our time were not perpetrated solely by Hitler, Stalin, and other tyrants, but by the millions of others who supported them and took orders from them. Why did people support them? Many, affected by arrogance and pride, agreed with their ideals, believing that they too were representatives of a superior race. Many lacked love or compassion for the victims of the tyrants, and/or the courage to take a stand against tyranny. Some, motivated by greed, saw opportunities for financial advantage in supporting them. Some were mired in sloth so that they did not care to do anything. But a goodly number of these supporters must also have lacked integrity. Many did not really believe in the doctrines and practices and propaganda of the tyrants, but, lacking integrity, they supported them anyway. They lied and they supported what they did not believe in. They did not put a high value on commitment to truth and moral duty.

These supporters of Hitler and Stalin may fairly be compared to people in our own society who, lacking integrity, allow themselves to believe that victims of sexual abuse and attack exaggerate the facts, or that they "asked for it." Many people tend to disbelieve reports of individual cases of rape and other sorts of violence against children and women, as well as statistics about these things. Presumably they believe what they believe because it is convenient for them to do so sometimes because other beliefs would challenge their ideologies, sometimes because it allows them to avoid taking responsibility, sometimes because it allows them to think that they are safer than other people.[84] Their readiness and willingness to believe these things shows a lack of intellectual integrity. This could be said to be a sin against the good of rationality.

Walter Kaufmann called the corrective for this vice "the new integrity," which he regarded as a cardinal virtue.[85] It would be impossible, Kaufmann maintained, for people to be followers of Hitler or Stalin if they asked themselves such questions as: "What counts for this belief? What counts against it? What alternatives are there? What counts for and against the alternatives?"[86] The new integrity involves asking such questions. It would seem to be a virtue (1) because of its good consequences, (2) because it respects the intrinsic good of truth, (3) because it embodies an appropriate aspect of life for humans as rational beings, (4) because it is an expression of humility, and (5) because it is a corrective to powerful human tendencies to form and sustain false beliefs.[87] I must respect the truth for what it is. The truth is not whatever I would like it to be.

VIRTUE AND DUTY

In some cases we can say that we have certain duties and that certain characteristics are virtues because they enable us to do our duty. For Kant, the strength-of-will virtues are important in enabling us to resist the temptation not to do our duty. We can also begin with certain character traits and relate duty to them. Lawrence Becker writes:

> If people have the dispositions that they ought, morally, to have, then they ought to do the morally justifiable things that will sustain and enhance those dispositions [e.g., such as expressing them in action]. . . . If people do *not* have the dispositions that they ought, morally, to have, then they ought to do the morally justifiable things that will generate those dispositions.[88]

Becker, who is concerned with the virtue of reciprocity, thus argues that we have a duty to reciprocate in appropriate ways for benefits we have received, and that other people may and should blame us if we do not. (He has much to say about what appropriate ways are.) Similar things could be said about the other virtues and other duties. A concern with being virtuous is fundamental. If we add the inserted words, Edmund Pincoffs seems to be correct when he writes: "We do not do our duty [only] because it is duty; we [also] do it because it is what, depending on the sort of duty it is, we must do if we are to be just, honest, properly grateful, and so on."[89]

If a person has no concern for being just, trustworthy, honest, and so on, no other moral considerations are of any importance. As we have a duty to enhance our own virtue, so also we have a duty to get rid of vices such as prejudice, greed, arrogance, and the inclination not to use our critical faculties.

It would seem then that we also have a duty to avoid servility, drug addiction, and whatever else seriously threatens our ability to be moral agents at all, and that we have a duty to preserve ourselves and develop ourselves as rational, self-determining beings (as discussed in the chapter on Kant). We also have a self-regarding duty to do those things that educate our emotions in ways that make us better moral agents, such as feeling appropriate compassion and not being influenced by inappropriate degrees of fear and anger.

MORAL EDUCATION AND MORAL VIRTUE

The Problem of Moral Education in a Liberal Society

A principal reason why people are disposed to act in certain ways is that they have certain values and certain character traits. Why did some people become rescuers when they saw others faced with the Nazi threat? To a significant extent, it was because of the values they were taught and the character traits they were encouraged to have.[90]

There are those who object to teaching values, or encouraging virtues that accord with particular values, in the public schools. One version of liberalism believes that individuals should freely choose their values without interference from the state.[91] Most students in the United States go to public schools run by the government. Does this mean that there should be no moral education or value education in the schools? Some have said so. Others have advocated as moral education the teaching of techniques for arriving at and applying general rules to situations, or techniques for sorting out one's own values, while the teacher remains neutral about the content of those rules or the nature of those values.[92]

The ideal of value neutrality as a government policy, however, is probably both undesirable and impossible to implement.[93] This is particularly true in the realm of education.[94] One problem with it is that "Americans tend to be highly other-directed and to gain much of their sense of right and wrong from what they see commonly done"[95] and are generally likely to assume that "anything that is commonly practiced" and "anything adults do not object to is permissible."[96] For example, whatever the intention of sex and drug education that attempts to be value-neutral, the message that adolescents receive is likely not to be neutral, but to be explicitly permissive and supportive of moral relativism. Such education is likely to be subversive of parents' efforts to pass on their values. Furthermore, to refrain from asserting influence when one can is not to be neutral, but rather to yield one's influence to whatever are the strongest cultural influences in society, which in the United States means the entertainment industry and the mass media, the leaders of which are neither elected by nor responsible to the people.[97] Whatever the defects of moral education in the public schools, they could hardly be worse than the defects of moral education by means of TV and the movies.

The Content of Moral Education

What then can and should be taught by the public schools in a pluralist society?

1. One philosopher writes that "We should call someone a moral being, if he has acquired the disposition to do what is morally required of him because he knows or thinks it is so required".[98] In other words, the moral person must *care* about morality and have the willingness to make sacrifices in order to abide by it, that is, have what Kant called "the good will." There is little point in teaching moral reasoning to those without any moral commitment.[99]

2. Second, a person must have the ability to abide by morality. This involves ability in practical reasoning. It also involves what we have called the strength-of-character virtues. There is little point in teaching moral reasoning to those without any self-restraint. As Amy Guttman writes, "Moral education begins by winning the battle against amoralism and egoism."[100]

3. Schools should also encourage those values and character traits, such as respect for truth and tolerance of others, that are crucial to the educational process itself. In order to encourage students to be open to truth, there need to be efforts to counterbalance the messages young people receive from the culture at large, especially from the mass media. One method for opposing cultural trends is what Neil Postman and Charles Weingartner call crap detection.[101] People more skilled at "crap detection"

would less likely become members of Nazi or other extreme ideological groups. "Crap detection" in sex education means "exposing selfishness, duplicity, and all the other games that young and not-so-young people play when sex is involved."[102] This method should encourage students to fulfill the duty of respecting the intrinsic values, in this case truth, and to acquire the virtue of intellectual integrity.

4. If public education is to prepare students for participation in a liberal democracy, then character traits should be acquired, and values supported, that tend to support free and democratic institutions. Thomas Jefferson "believed that the goal of schooling should be to help people protect themselves against tyranny" and he specified a curriculum that he believed would serve that purpose.[103] Some have argued persuasively that these traits and values include courage, independence, tolerance, and a strong attachment to truth.[104]

5. If public education is part of a democracy, then we should teach values and encourage character traits that meet two criteria: (a) they have wide democratic support within the society and (b) they are also rationally defensible[105] either as universal values or as values of a particular society that do not conflict with universal values. The claim that in American pluralist society there is too little agreement on values for much of anything to meet the first criterion is probably false. An educational official for the state of Massachusetts writes:

> I believe that very few American parents, of whatever political or religious persuasion, do not want their children to be kind and compassionate, respectful of the rights of others, and able to listen to different views while still standing up for their own convictions. I believe that American parents want their children to be truthful, loyal, and committed to the good of society. . . . We may differ vastly on "the highest good," but we agree more than we may think on what qualities we would like our children to have.[106]

6. Further, what needs to be taught in school is whatever resists the tendency of the culture to transmit values antithetical to those described above. The method of "crap detection" is one way of doing this. Emphasizing contrasting values is another. Insofar as our schools and society emphasize the successful acquisition of material goods over all other goals, they emphasize values related to self and are not neutral.

> Emphasis on economic competence can be conducive to a materialistic view of life often fostering a tendency to allow criteria of economic usefulness to dominate relationships. Less tangible concerns, feelings, abstract ideas, and moral issues are more likely to be considered a waste of time. As Bettelheim observed, "The more man is geared toward achieving 'practical' results, the more he may view the making of inner decisions that lead to no practical end as a total waste of energy."[107]

According to the Oliner study, one difference between those who were rescuers of the Jews and others is that the parents of rescuers apparently "emphasized values relating to self less frequently than nonrescuers."[108] Since it is hardly likely that schools and society in modern industrialized countries will stop emphasizing economic competence, or that parents or students would want them to do so, it is important that other emphases be there as well, including an emphasis on responsibility to others. (Here again the futility of the ideal of neutrality is illustrated.)

The Oliner study found that "others, rather than self, were the primary focus for rescuers. Rescuers brought to the war a greater receptivity to others' needs because they had learned from their parents that others were very important."[109] What is true for moral education from parents would likely be true for moral education from schools. One way of doing this would be to require units of community service from students, as some high schools and colleges are now doing, or are considering doing.

What further can be said about the communication of desirable values and character traits? Some of the major theories of moral education stress the process of arriving at and fairly applying abstract principles of equality and respect for persons.[110] Carol Gilligan has claimed that women tend to think in terms of human relationships and care for people, rather than in terms of principles. She has also claimed that the principle-oriented model of moral education developed by males needs to be balanced by the emphasis on care that is more common among women.[111] The difference between the two emphases has been described in this way:

> Whereas equity is directed toward the welfare of society as a whole, based on abstract principles of fairness, care is concerned with the welfare of people without necessary regard for fairness. Whereas equity is based on reciprocity, care endorses a willingness to give more than is received. Whereas equity emphasizes fair procedures, care insists on benevolence and kindness. Equity asks that we do our duty in accordance with reason, but care insists that we act out of concern.[112]

Gilligan would seem to be right about moral education. According to the Oliner study, during the Nazi era there was no significant difference between rescuers and nonrescuers with respect to the degree of emphasis their parents placed on equity values. However, those whose parents stressed generosity, expansiveness, and caring were much more likely to become rescuers.[113]

There are a few other factors that distinguished rescuers from nonrescuers, factors that could be emphasized in contemporary moral education. Compared to nonrescuers, rescuers tended to mention a greater number of groups toward whom they had duties. They saw moral concern as relevant to their relationship to all human beings.[114] In their childhoods, rescuers more often saw altruistic behavior modeled by their parents;[115]

heard fewer unfavorable references to minority groups;[116] and experienced less gratuitous and extreme punishment than nonrescuers, as their parents were more likely to reason[117] rather than demand obedience.[118] All of this should be relevant to the efforts of the community and the school to encourage young people to be morally sensitive and morally responsible.

While the moral characteristics that led people to become rescuers are not the only important characteristics, they would certainly form part of the picture of the morally desirable person. Oliner and Oliner describe such people thus:

> Involvement, commitment, care and responsibility are the hallmarks of extensive persons. Disassociation, detachment, and exclusiveness are the hallmarks of constricted persons. Rescuers were marked by extensivity, whereas nonrescuers, and bystanders in particular, were marked by constrictedness, by an ego that perceived most of the world beyond its own boundaries as peripheral. More centered on themselves and their own needs, they were less conscious of others and less concerned with them.[119]

POSTSCRIPT: FRIEDRICH NIETZSCHE

Friedrich Nietzsche (1844–1900), the nineteenth-century German philosopher, would have taken exception to some of the views set forth here. Nietzsche regarded the will to power as the dominant drive of human beings, a will that is expressed by overcoming internal and external obstacles.[120] While Kant saw morality as a matter of reason ruling human behavior instead of passion, Nietzsche saw morality as a matter of reason governing a person's choice of passions: life-furthering passions through which energy should be directed for the sake of one's self-perfection, and life-stultifying passions from which one's energy should be channeled away.[121] For Nietzsche, there is no objective standard of value by which to measure perfection. Good states of affairs are those that fulfill a person's desires and expectations. The "noble" person has the power to choose what will be of value and to attain it.[122] The "Viking" type of person, who with intense passion proudly asserts his will and passions, has the potential to become a noble person who pursues his goals with controlled intensity.

Morality that emphasizes meekness, thoughtfulness, equality, kindness, and respect for the rights of others—that is, the morality that is concerned with protecting the vulnerable—is the morality of socialism, democracy, Judaism, and Christianity. Nietzsche calls this "slave morality," morality designed by the weak and passionless for the sake of protecting themselves from the strong. Weak people, he says, made humility into a virtue because they did not have enough strength to live in any other way, and they made equality into an ideal to compensate for their natural inferiority. The strong man would not hesitate to sacrifice his own short-term interests for the sake of attaining great goals; neither would he hesitate to sacrifice the happiness of the defenseless for the attaining of those goals. The highest goals are the most spiritual because they involve the greatest amount of power over oneself and one's impulses. Societies are not to be judged by the happiness of the masses, but by the production of exceptional individuals. Nietzsche's ultimate goal is the production of a new kind of being who attains a level of manhood that has not yet been attained.[123]

What are we to say about Nietzsche's views? Nietzsche's concern for self-discipline, self-mastery, self-perfection, and what we have called the strength-of-character virtues would seem to be legitimate subjects for moral evaluation. This concern can be seen as a corrective to the prejudice that frequently surfaces in American society against those with superior intelligence or ability. Few would reject self-mastery, honesty, and courage as virtues, and many would agree that innocuousness, servility, conformity, and weakness are not virtues. But should pride, self-glorification, and callousness really be considered virtues? For Nietzsche they are virtues because they are signs of strength, while "bourgeois" and Christian virtues are signs of weakness.[124]

How might a Jew or Christian, or anyone else who shares a similar moral perspective, respond to Nietzsche? One can point out that part of Nietzsche's attack is not against Christian ethics, but against a nineteenth-century perversion of them, and that some of the things that Nietzsche teaches, such as the repudiation of vengeance, are similar to authentic Christianity. A second response might be to claim that true humility does not mean groveling in the dirt or self-flagellation, as Nietzsche pictures it, but rather means radical honesty before oneself, others, and (for the believer) God about one's limitations, one's true motives, and so on; as such, it is a sign of strength and not a sign of weakness, a sign of mastery over the strong human tendency toward self-deception and pride.

A third reply might challenge Nietzsche's views of compassion and equality. Compassion as a form of *agape* (love) is not sickly pity and a sign of weakness, but rather is the expression of the fullness, inner strength, and self-acceptance that enable a person to accept others and care about them. Furthermore, belief in human equality does not necessarily have anything to do with settling for an equality of mediocrity, but can be a recognition that all people should have the opportunity to live up to their potential, whatever that might be. The study of Holocaust rescuers seems to refute Nietzsche's views when it concludes that the "rescuers' sense of similarity to outsiders and empathy for the weak and the helpless" did not "emerge from their own feelings of personal vulnerability and weakness."[125] In fact, rescuers tended to be those who felt that they had power to influence events. Contrary to what Nietzsche suggests, the religiously motivated rescuers in particular did not see themselves as weak; rather

> rescuers of this type grew up feeling highly potent; they saw themselves as decisive, able to take responsibility, independent, and inclined towards adventurousness and risk taking. They had a positive attitude toward others generally.[126]

A fourth reply points to the consequences of Nietzsche's views. Although Nietzsche was not an anti-Semite or a racist himself, the Nazis found a great deal of comfort and inspiration in his writings. The moral atrocities of the twentieth century have thus become in themselves a refutation of much of his point of view.[127]

QUESTIONS

1. According to Aristotle, how does one become virtuous? Do you find his account convincing? What are the various arguments given as to why one should want to be virtuous? Do you find these convincing? Why or why not? What does the discussion of Buddhism add to the method of becoming virtuous?

2. Since a character trait such as courage can be used to enable a person to rob a bank as well as to rescue someone from a burning building, should it be regarded as a moral virtue? What reasons can you find in the chapter? What other reasons for or against can you think of?

3. Do you agree that our society has put a low priority on the strength-of-character virtues? If so, what have been the results of this? What have been the causes? How does this relate to the matter of ethical minimalism discussed in chapters 1 and 2?

4. Some TV preachers make all sorts of sweeping religious claims on the basis of highly debatable interpretations of obscure biblical verses. These same preachers make claims about what is going on in South Africa, Latin America, and other places, all on what seems to be the flimsiest of evidence. Astrologers advise people to make major decisions about their lives on the basis of unscientific gobbledygook. If these people do not believe what they are saying, are they morally deficient? If they do believe it, are they morally deficient? What does the author of the text think? If he is wrong, how would you argue against him? Are the people in the TV audience who applaud these preachers' dubious claims also morally deficient?

5. Why does Kant advise us to compare ourselves with the moral law and the ideal of perfection and not with other people? Is this the same reason Christians are advised to compare themselves with Christ? Are these reasons good reasons? Are there vices associated with comparing ourselves with other people (other than some ideal person)? What are they?

6. Can a person have the strength-of-character virtues and still be immoral? Can a person be a morally admirable person and not have the strength-of-character virtues? Can a person lead a fulfilling life without the strength-of-character virtues? Give reasons for your answers.

7. What are the different ways in which the author, in a number of different places, treats virtues as correctives? Is this a good way of thinking about many of the virtues? About all of them? Why or why not?

8. Did you recall receiving anything that could be called moral education in grade school or high school? How did what you experienced fit in with the views of the author? Do you agree or disagree with the author on moral education? Why?

9. What would Aristotle say about the Taoist view of getting in touch with one's natural goodness? What would Christianity say about it? What is your evaluation?

10. Does the Western world have something to learn from the Buddhist view of sympathy and its way of learning sympathy? Does the Buddhist view depend on believing that ultimately we do not really exist as separate selves, or can it be detached from that opinion? Can it be integrated into Western secular ethics? Can it be integrated into Christianity? Is it perhaps already in Christianity?

11. Aristotle believes that the highest sort of friendship can only exist between people of character. Edmund Pincoffs refers to virtues as "dispositional properties that provide grounds for preference or avoidance of persons."[128] What dispositional characteristics (virtues and vices) do you regard as most important when choosing people to be your friends? What is there about yourself that qualifies you to be a friend?

12. For various reasons, different vocations may require an emphasis on different virtues. Their goals may be different and the kinds and intensity of their temptations may be different. What virtues do you think are the most important for the vocation that you are in or are considering entering?

PROJECT

Find out about programs of moral education in schools in your area, or about such programs in general. Try to discover what values are reflected in such programs, and compare them to those suggested for moral education in this chapter. Information about various programs in moral education can be gotten from "Values," Box 1048, Santa Monica, CA, 90406. Perhaps you could seek to influence local schools to adopt one of the programs that you think is good. This project would be appropriate for anyone, but especially for education majors and for older students who have school-age children.

FURTHER READING

Aristotle's *Nicomachean Ethics* is available in many translations and editions. There are many general works on Aristotle and on Greek philosophy that can be consulted. The following are also useful:

Norman, Richard. *The Moral Philosophers: An Introduction to Ethics*. New York: Oxford University Press, 1983. See chap. 2.

Rorty, Amelie Oksenberg, ed. *Essays on Aristotle's Ethics*. Berkeley and Los Angeles: University of California Press, 1980.
Ross, W. D. *Aristotle*. 5th ed. New York: Oxford University Press, 1951.

Accounts of vice and virtue in Buddhism, Judaism, and Christianity can be found in the works listed at the end of chapter 3. For Judaism, see especially chapters 5–8 of Meyer Waxman's *Judaism: Religion and Ethics*, cited in chapter 3. For Christianity, see also:

Crossin, John W., O.S.F.S. *What Are They Saying About Virtue?* New York: Paulist Press, 1985.
Outka, Gene. *Agape: An Ethical Analysis*. New Haven: Yale University Press, 1972.

Introductory ethics anthologies with an emphasis on virtue and vice include the following:

Halberstram, Joshua, ed. *Virtues and Values: An Introduction to Ethics*. Englewood Cliffs, N.J.: Prentice-Hall, 1988.
Sommers, Christina Hoff, and Fred Sommers, eds. *Vice and Virtue in Everyday Life*. 2nd ed. New York: Harcourt Brace Jovanovich, 1989.

Important anthologies on virtue and vice, primarily for the more advanced student, are:

Kruschwitz, Robert C., and Robert B. Roberts, eds. *The Virtues: Contemporary Essays on Moral Character*. Belmont, Calif.: Wadsworth, 1988.
French, Peter A., Theodore E. Uehling, Jr., and Harold K. Wettstein, eds. *Midwest Studies in Philosophy*, vol. 13, *Ethical Theory: Character and Virtue*. Notre Dame, Ind.: University of Notre Dame Press, 1988.

Interesting books on the vices are:

Fairlie, Henry. *The Seven Deadly Sins Today*. Washington, D.C.: New Republic Books, 1978; Notre Dame, Ind.: University of Notre Dame Press, 1979.
Martin, Mike W. *Self-deception and Morality*. Lawrence, Kans.: University Press of Kansas, 1986.
Shklar, Judith. *Ordinary Vices*. Cambridge, Mass.: Harvard University Press, 1984.

Some book-length treatments of virtue by contemporary philosophers are:

MacIntyre, Alasdair. *After Virtue*. Notre Dame, Ind.: University of Notre Dame Press, 1984.
Pieper, Joseph. *The Four Cardinal Virtues*. Notre Dame, Ind.: University of Notre Dame Press, 1966.

Pincoffs, Edmund. *Quandaries and Virtues: Against Reductivism in Ethics.* Lawrence, Kans.: University Press of Kansas, 1986.
Wallace, James D. *Virtues and Vices.* Ithaca, N.Y.: Cornell University Press, 1976.
Warnock, J.G. The Object of Morality. Princeton, N.J.: Princeton University Press, 1969.

A work by psychologists that has influenced this chapter is:

Oliner, Samuel P., and Pearl M. Oliner. *The Altruistic Personality: Rescuers of Jews in Nazi Europe.* New York: Free Press, 1988.

Works on moral education include:

Almond, Brenda. *Moral Concerns.* Atlantic Highlands, N.J.: Humanities Press, 1987. See chaps. 6 and 7.
Chazan, Barry. *Contemporary Approaches to Moral Education.* New York: Teachers College Press, 1985.
Educational Leadership 43 (December 1985/January 1986). Most of the issue deals with moral education.
Oldenquist, Andrew. "'Indoctrination' and Societal Suicide." *Public Interest* (Spring 1981): 81–94.
Pincoffs, Edmund. *Quandaries and Virtues: Against Reductivism in Ethics.* Lawrence, Kans.: University Press of Kansas, 1986. See pt. 3 (chaps. 8 and 9).
Ryan, Kevin. "The New Moral Education." *Phi Delta Kappan* (November 1986): 228–33.
Sommers, Christina Hoff. "Ethics without Virtue: Moral Education in America." *American Scholar* 53 (Summer 1984): 381–89.
Taylor, Monica J., ed. *Progress and Problems in Moral Education.* Windsor, England: NFER, 1975.
Van Wyk, Robert N. "Liberalism and Moral Education." In *Inquiries into Values,* edited by Sander Lee. Lewiston, N.Y.: Mellen Press, 1988. See pp. 643–56.

Two works on moral education that have a religious orientation are:

Dykstra, Craig. *Vision and Character.* New York: Paulist Press, 1981.
Wolterstorf, Nicholas. *Educating for Responsible Action.* Grand Rapids, Mich.: Eerdmans, 1980.

NOTES

1. Aristotle, *Nicomachean Ethics* 1, 10:1101a14–17.
2. John Finnis, *Natural Law and Natural Rights* (New York: Oxford University Press, 1980), 88.
3. Aristotle, *Nicomachean Ethics* 6, 5:1144a1–3.
4. Ibid., 1, 10:1099b26–27, 13:1102a5–6.

5. See Alasdair MacIntyre, *After Virtue* (Notre Dame, Ind.: University of Notre Dame Press, 1984), 148.

6. Ananda K. Coomaraswamy, *Buddha and the Gospel of Buddhism* (London: Harrap, 1916; New York: Harper and Row, 1964), 140.

7. H. Saddhatissa, *Buddhist Ethics* (New York: Braziller, 1970), 24.

8. John Finnis, *Fundamentals of Ethics* (Washington, D.C.: Georgetown University Press, 1983), 56.

9. See Thomas Aquinas, *Summa Theologiae* 1, 2, Qu. 58, art. 4, and Aristotle, *Nicomachean Ethics* 6, 12:1144a7–10.

10. Aquinas, *Summa Theologiae* 2–2, Q. 47, art. 6.

11. G. H. von Wright, *The Varieties of Goodness* (New York: Humanities Press, 1963), 147ff.

12. James D. Wallace, *Virtues and Vices* (Ithaca, N.Y.: Cornell University Press, 1976), 83, 84.

13. Anthony Quinton, "Character and Culture," in *Vice and Virtue in Everyday Life*, ed. Christina Hoff Sommers (New York: Harcourt Brace Jovanovich, 1985), 440.

14. Wallace, *Virtues and Vices*, 87.

15. See St. Thomas Aquinas, *Summa Theologiae* 2–2, Qu. 47, art. 7.

16. Quinton, "Character," 440.

17. P. G. Geach, *The Virtues* (Cambridge: Cambridge University Press, 1977), 16.

18. L. A. Kosman, "Being Properly Affected," in *Essays on Aristotle's Ethics*, ed. Amelie Oksenberg Rorty (Berkeley and Los Angeles: University of California Press, 1980), 104.

19. Aristotle, *Nicomachean Ethics* 2, 6:1106b18–23.

20. Ibid. 2, 4:1105a26–1105b9; 6, 12:1144a14–20.

21. Ibid. 2, 4,1105a34.

22. Julie Annas, "Aristotle on Pleasure and Goodness," in Rorty, *Aristotle's Ethics*, 292.

23. Aristotle, *Nicomachean Ethics* 2, 3:1104b3–4.

24. Ibid. 10, 9:1179b27–29.

25. Ibid. 2, 1103b25–27.

26. Ibid. 2, 2:1104a35–12104b3.

27. Ibid. 2, 4:1105b10–13.

28. Ibid. 2, 9:1109a20–1110a27.

29. Yves R. Simon, *The Definition of Moral Virtue* (New York: Fordham University Press, 1986), 4.

30. *Chuanqtse*, trans. by Lin Yutang, in *The Wisdom of China and India*, ed. Lin Yutang (New York: Random House, 1942), 663–65.

31. Laotse, *Tau-Teh-Ching* 24, 29, 66, in Yutang, *Wisdom*, 596, 599, 617–18.

32. See Alasdair MacIntyre, *A Short History of Ethics* (New York: Macmillan, 1966), 78–83. See also A. H. Armstrong, *An Introduction to Ancient Philosophy*, 3d ed. (Totowa, N.J.: Littlefield, Adams, 1977), 104.

33. Elizabeth Telfer, *Happiness* (London: Macmillan, 1980), 55.

34. See Edmund Pincoffs, *Quandaries and Virtues: Against Reductivism in Ethics* (Lawrence, Kans.: University Press of Kansas, 1986), 86–87.

35. See J. L. Mackie, *Ethics* (Baltimore: Penguin, 1977), 191–92.

36. Pincoffs, *Quandaries*, 84–86.

37. Lawrence Becker, *Reciprocity* (New York: Routledge and Kegan Paul, 1986), 49.

38. Geach, *Virtues*, 162.

39. See Pincoffs, *Quandaries*, 89, 90.

40. Becker, *Reciprocity*, 90–92.

41. Peter Singer, *Practical Ethics* (New York: Cambridge University Press, 1979), 201–19.

42. Immanuel Kant, *Metaphysical Principles of Virtue*, trans. James Ellington (Indianapolis: Bobbs-Merrill, 1964), (395), 54.

43. Ibid., 53.

44. Ibid.

45. Ibid., 67–68.

46. Philippa Foot, "Virtues and Vices," in her *Virtues and Vices* (Berkeley: University of California Press, 1986).

47. Lewis Smedes, *Mere Morality* (Grand Rapids, Mich.: Eerdmans, 1983), 161.

48. Ibid., 160.

49. Samuel P. Oliner and Pearl M. Oliner, *The Altruistic Personality: Rescuers of Jews in Nazi Europe* (New York: Free Press, 1988), 174–75.

50. Smedes, *Mere Morality*, 160.

51. Ibid., 161.

52. See Gene Outka, *Agape: An Ethical Analysis* (New Haven: Yale University Press, 1972), 278–79.

53. *The Wisdom of Ben Sira* 3, 17; quoted in Meyer Waxman, *Judaism: Religion and Ethics* (New York: Thomas Yoseloff, 1958), 262.

54. Oliner and Oliner, *Altruistic Personality*, 156.

55. Ibid.

56. Ibid., 142.

57. Mary Wollstonecraft, *A Vindication of the Rights of Women* (1792; New York: Norton, 1967), 256; quoted by Mary D. Pellauer, "Moral Callousness and Moral Sensitivity: Violence against Women," in *Women's Consciousness, Women's Conscience*, ed. Barbara Hilkert Andolsen, Christine E. Gudorf, and Mary D. Pellauer (Minneapolis: Winston Press, 1985), 49.

58. Judith Shklar defines cruelty as "the willful inflicting of physical pain on a weaker being in order to cause anguish and fear," in her *Ordinary Vices* (Cambridge, Mass.: Harvard University Press, 1984), 8. Perhaps this definition is too narrow.

59. Oliner and Oliner, *Altruistic Personality*, 199.

60. Ibid., 203.

61. Ibid., 146.

62. Ibid, 149.

63. Henry Fairlie, *The Seven Deadly Sins Today* (Washington, D.C.: New Republic Books, 1978; Notre Dame, Ind.: University of Notre Dame Press, 1979), 137.

64. Ibid., 143–44.

65. See David G. Myers, *The Inflated Self* (New York: Seabury, 1980), chap. 1.

66. Fairlie, *Seven Deadly Sins*, 140.

67. Oliner and Oliner, *Altruistic Personality*, 166.

68. Ibid., 168.

69. Philip Hallie, "From Cruelty to Goodness," *Hastings Center Report* 11 (June 1981), 23–28.

70. Lawrence Bloom, "Compassion," in *The Virtues: Contemporary Essays on Moral Character*, ed. Robert C. Kruschwitz and Robert B. Roberts (Belmont, Calif.: Wadsworth, 1988).

71. Robert B. Roberts, "Will Power and the Virtues," in Kruschwitz and Roberts, *The Virtues*, 123.

72. Oliner and Oliner, *Altruistic Personality*, 149–70. In the Nazi era, what distinguished rescuers of Jews from nonrescuers was their tendency to notice and to be moved by the pain of others. "Sadness and helplessness aroused their empathy" (ibid., 174). Some people helped much more because of their empathetic emotional response, some people much more because of their conscious values. Compassion, however, is not always necessary for the disposition to help. Compassion and empathy bridge the gap between the nonsufferer and the sufferer. Where there is no gap because each person is sharing the same suffering, there is no need for the gap to be bridged. Terrence Des Pres, who studied the literature of the survivors of the Nazi terror, found that while there was much readiness to help others, empathy and compassion, especially as expressed in words of sympathy, were almost by definition absent where everyone was sharing the same suffering. See his *The Survivor: An Anatomy of Life in the Death Camps* (New York: Oxford University Press, 1976), 131, 147.

73. H. Saddhatissa, *Buddhist Ethics* (New York: Braziller, 1970), 24.

74. Edward Conze, *Buddhism: Its Essence and Development* (Oxford: Cassirer, 1951; New York: Harper and Row, 1959), 61–62.

75. Ibid., 62. It is the inner state of sympathy that is emphasized. The outward expression of compassion in positive actions, except for teaching others the way of liberation, seems to be less important than in the Western religious tradition. Mahayana Buddhism says

that the person who only seeks *nirvana* for himself has not reached the ideal of obliterating self. The ideal person is the one who with compassion seeks *nirvana* for all and who postpones entering that state himself in order to guide others. Compassion is here valued equally with wisdom (ibid., 128). Ultimately the highest ideal is nonattainment or self-extinction, "forgetting oneself in complete self-surrender" (ibid., 135).

76. Shklar, *Ordinary Vices*, 29.
77. Much of this is summarized and discussed in Myers, *Inflated Self*, chaps. 1–9.
78. Fairlie, *Seven Deadly Sins*, 47.
79. See Myers, *Inflated Self*, chaps. 1–3.
80. Kant, *Metaphysical Principles of Virtue* (441), 104.
81. Kant, *Lectures on Ethics*, trans. Louis Infield (New York: Harper and Row, 1963), 127. See also his *Metaphysical Principles of Virtue* (435–436), 97–98.
82. Kant, *Lectures on Ethics*, 126. See also his *Metaphysical Principles of Virtue* (434–437), 96–99.
83. See Pellauer, "Moral Callousness," in Andolsen et al., *Women's Consciousness*, 36.
84. Ibid., 44.
85. Walter Kaufmann, *Without Guilt and Justice* (New York: Wyden, 1973), 180–89.
86. Ibid.
87. These tendencies are discussed in Myers, *Inflated Self*, chaps. 4–9.
88. Becker, *Reciprocity*, 168.
89. Pincoffs, *Quandaries and Virtues*, 65.
90. Oliner and Oliner, *Altruistic Personality*, 113–41, 142.
91. See Ronald Dworkin, "Liberalism," in *Private and Public Morality*, ed. Stuart Hampshire (New York: Cambridge University Press, 1978), 127.
92. See John Wilson, "Teaching and Neutrality," in *Progress and Problems in Moral Education*, ed. Monica J. Taylor, 113–22 (Windsor, England: NFER, 1975). His position is criticized by Mary Warnock in "The Neutral Teacher," in Taylor, *Progress and Problems*, 107–8, 110. Values clarification viewpoints are set forth in many places, including Howard Kirschenbaum, "Clarifying Values Clarification: Some Theoretical Issues," in *Moral Education: It Comes with the Territory*, ed. D. Purpel and K. Ryan, 122 (Berkeley, Calif.: McCutchan, 1976). They are also criticized in many places, including John S. Stewart, "Clarifying Values Clarification: A Critique," *Phi Delta Kappan* (June 1976): 694–95.
93. See Robert N. Van Wyk, "Liberalism, Religion, and Politics," *Public Affairs Quarterly* 1 (July 1987): 59–76.
94. See Robert N. Van Wyk, "Liberalism and Moral Education," in *Inquiries into Values*, ed. Sander Lee (Lewiston, N.Y.: Mellen Press, 1988), 643–56.
95. Kenneth Strike, *Educational Policy and the Just Society*. (Urbana: University of Illinois Press), 107.
96. Ibid., 107, 108.
97. Neil Postman, *Teaching as a Conserving Activity* (New York: Dell, 1979), 12, 113.
98. Kurt Baier, "Ethical Pluralism and Moral Education," in *Moral Education: Interdisciplinary Approaches*, ed. C. M. Beck, B. S. Crittenden, and E. V. Sullivan (Toronto: University of Toronto Press, 1971), 96.
99. For a critique of moral education without virtue, see Christina Hoff Sommers, "Ethics Without Virtue: Moral Education in America," *American Scholar* 53 (Summer 1984): 381–89.
100. Amy Guttman, *Democratic Education* (Princeton, N.J.: Princeton University Press, 1987), 62.
101. Neil Postman and Charles Weingartner, *Teaching as a Subversive Activity* (New York: Dell, 1969), 1–15.
102. See James DeGiacomo, "All You Need Is Love," *America* (February 14, 1987), 129.
103. Postman, *Teaching as a Conserving Activity*, 109.
104. Kenneth R. Minogue, *The Liberal Mind* (New York: Random House, 1963), 167–76. See also Kenneth Spragens, *The Irony of Liberal Reason* (Chicago: University of Chicago Press, 1981), 383.
105. Baier, "Ethical Pluralism," in Beck et al., *Moral Education*, 110–12.
106. Charles Glenn, *Reformed Journal* 36 (September 1986): 16.

107. Oliner and Oliner, *Altruistic Personality*, 160. Quote is from Bruno Bettelheim, *The Informed Heart: Autonomy in a Mass Age* (New York: Avon, 1971), 69.

108. Oliner and Oliner, *Altruistic Personality*, 160.

109. Ibid., 161.

110. See some of the many writings of Laurence Kohlberg.

111. Carol Gilligan, *In a Different Voice* (Cambridge, Mass.: Harvard University Press, 1982).

112. Oliner and Oliner, *Altruistic Personality*, 163.

113. Ibid., 164–65.

114. Ibid., 165.

115. Ibid., 144.

116. Ibid., 150.

117. Ibid., 179–80.

118. Ibid., 162.

119. Ibid., 186.

120. See Friedrich Nietzsche, *Thus Spake Zarathustra*, pt. 2, section entitled "About Self-Mastery," and pt. 1, section entitled "About a Thousand and One Aims." In the translation by Marianne Cowan (Chicago: Regnery, 1957), these are on p. 132 and p. 63.

121. See chap. 4, section entitled, "Morality, Reason, and Passion," in Robert Solomon, *From Rationalism to Existentialism* (New York: Harper and Row, 1972), 120–25.

122. Nietzsche, *Zarathustra*, pt. 1, sections entitled "About the Three Transformations," "About the Tree on the Mountainside," and "About a Thousand and One Aims," pp. 24–25, 45, and 65 in the Cowan translation.

123. The idea of the *Übermensch* first becomes important for Nietzsche's thought in *Thus Spake Zarathustra*. See the prologue, pp. 1–19 in Cowan translation.

124. Nietzsche, *Beyond Good and Evil*, pt. 260, and *The Genealogy of Morals*, first essay, sections 10 and 11; in *Basic Writings of Nietzsche*, trans. and ed. Walter Kaufmann (New York: Random House, 1966), 394–98, 472–79.

125. Oliner and Oliner, *Altruistic Personality*, 176–77.

126. Ibid., 184.

127. For further evaluation of Nietzsche, see Solomon, *From Rationalism*; Bertrand Russell, *A History of Western Philosophy* (New York: Simon and Schuster, 1945), 760–73; and Walter Kaufmann, *Nietzsche: Philosopher, Psychologist, Antichrist*, 3d ed. (New York: Knopf and Random House, 1968). For one kind of response to Nietzsche from a Christian writer, see Nicholas Berdyaev, *The Destiny of Man* (New York: Harper and Row, 1960), 114–17.

128. Pincoffs, *Quandaries and Virtues*, 82.

11

The Morality of
the Social Order:
Social Justice and
the Good Society

THE IMPORTANCE OF THE IDEA OF JUSTICE

We have been dealing with questions about the moral life of human beings. We can also ask about the moral nature of institutions, governments, and societies. Larger social arrangements are judged in terms of how people are treated under them, and the question most asked is whether that treatment is just, and thus whether the institutions and social arrangements are just. Chaim Perelman writes that "justice is one of the most highly respected notions in our spiritual universe. All men—religious believers and nonbelievers—invoke justice, and none dare disavow it."[1] In the name of justice the Hebrew prophets Isaiah, Jeremiah, Amos, and Hosea attacked the social practices of their time. In the fourth century B.C., Plato devoted most of his *Republic* to analyzing the concept of justice, and Plato's pupil Aristotle devoted a book of his *Nicomachean Ethics* to the same task. Justice is sometimes thought to be embodied in the ancient phrase "To each his own" (or "To each what he or she is entitled to"). But where we go from there depends on what it is that determines what is one's own.

Justice and the Rule of Law

The first answer is that the law determines what each person is entitled to, or what each person's rights are. According to Aristotle, the term "unjust" is held to apply both to the person who breaks the law and to the person who takes more than his due, the unfair man. "Hence it is clear that the law-abiding man and the fair man will both be just. 'The just' therefore means that which is lawful, and that which is equal and fair, and 'the unjust' means that which is illegal and that which is unequal or unfair."[2]

Of course, insofar as it is the law that determines one's fair share, these amount to the same thing. Thomas Hobbes would agree that what is unjust is what is against the law. One is entitled to what the law or the ruler says one is entitled to. John Stuart Mill wrote,

> In the first place, it is mostly considered unjust to deprive anyone of his personal liberty, his property, or any other thing which belongs to him by law. Here, therefore, is one instance of the application of the words "just" or "unjust" in a perfectly definite sense, namely that it is just to respect, unjust to violate the legal rights of anyone.[3]

One of the great values of justice in the sense of the rule of law is that, with its requirement of uniformity, it leads to predictability and thus to security. It permits the coherent and stable functioning of the judicial system.

Other Criteria of Justice

If the only criterion for deciding whether something is just is whether it is in accordance with the law, then we cannot ask whether the law itself is just. But as John Stuart Mill writes: "The legal rights of which [a person] is deprived may be rights which *ought* not to have belonged to him; in other words, the law which confers on him these rights may be a bad law."[4] The law may also fail to ensure people certain rights that it should ensure them. It is the concern of ancient philosophy, of traditional religion, and of natural law theory to provide criteria for making such judgments about whether the law itself is just or unjust.

Mill points to the following criteria for standards of justice.

1. It is just for people to be treated according to what they deserve (e.g., the winner gets the prize, the guilty are punished).
2. It is unjust to break faith or violate an agreement. So it is unjust to break a contract (as Hobbes emphasized) or to change the rules in the middle of the game.
3. It is unjust, as Aristotle indicated, to show partiality for oneself or one's friends in areas where personal preference should not apply.
4. Related to impartiality is the idea of equality. It is often felt that the more equally people are treated, the more justly they are treated.

Many controversies among different political points of view have to do with which of these criteria are most important, especially between those who emphasize equality above all and those who emphasize inequalities proportional to what people deserve.

An additional problem is that there are different ways in which the criteria of impartiality and equality can be applied. How much should a just tax system take from each individual? The various answers include:

1. The same absolute sum (like membership dues in a club or the occupation taxes some communities have).
2. The same percentage of income (e.g., a flat-rate income tax, such as many states have).
3. A graduated income tax (which many nations have).
4. An amount in accordance with how much people of each class benefit from the state's services.
5. An amount in accordance with what the state in the past has led people to believe to be their share.

We can also ask how any social system should determine the distribution of benefits. Again there are various answers:

1. Flat equality for those who are members of the relevant community. All state residents may have their tuition at a state university subsidized to the same degree, regardless of their wealth.
2. In terms of need. Eligibility for food stamps, welfare benefits, and some scholarship help is based on need.
3. In terms of usefulness. Students going into teaching may have loans forgiven.
4. In terms of merit. You may be paid in terms of how much it is judged that you deserve, or you may receive a merit scholarship.

THE UTILITARIAN VIEW OF JUSTICE

Classical Utilitarianism

Which of these criteria are correct? An intuitionist theory of justice, which is one possibility, might simply attempt to balance these various sorts of criteria intuitively. The utilitarian answer, which is another possibility, is that any of them may be appropriate. Whichever criteria produce the most good for the most people in given circumstances are the correct ones in those circumstances.

Sometimes people claim that they have a right to be treated in a certain way—equally, or according to need, or according to merit. We see appeals to these conflicting criteria when the issue of affirmative action is discussed. But which rights do people in fact have? John Locke[5] and Thomas Jefferson (in the Declaration of Independence) tried to answer that question by making inferences about the intention of the Creator.

John Stuart Mill gave the utilitarian answer: "To have a right, then, is, I conceive, to have some thing which society ought to defend me in the possession of. If the objector goes on to ask why it ought, I can give him no other reason than general utility."[6]

Suppose the government forces me to sell my property so that it can build a dam for a flood-control project that will benefit many people. Have my property rights been violated, and consequently, have I been treated unjustly? Jeremy Bentham's utilitarian answer to this was that "There is no right, which ought not to be maintained so long as it is upon the whole advantageous to the society that it should be maintained, so there is no right which when the abolition of it is advantageous to society should not be relinquished."[7]

To take a look at a contemporary issue, we can ask what utilitarians would say about the practice of giving members of minority groups that have in the past been discriminated against preference over others in admissions to law schools, medical schools, and certain kinds of jobs. A person who fails to get into medical school because of such preferential treatment might claim that his or her right to be chosen on the basis of merit has been violated. But, as we have just seen, for the utilitarian, if such a right is not advantageous for society, then it cannot serve as the basis for a moral argument. If accepting more members of minority groups is advantageous to society, for instance by producing more doctors or lawyers who are more likely to serve in areas where doctors and lawyers are in short supply, or by breaking down the pattern of racism for the benefit of future generations, then the individual who loses out has no legitimate complaint.

We have already criticized the utilitarian view of justice in chapter 7. Perhaps the individual just referred to has no legitimate complaint, but are there cases in which the individual does have a legitimate complaint? Whether Bentham's assertion that rights no longer advantageous to society should be abolished is true or false depends at least in part on how the phrase "advantageous to society" is understood. As some versions of utilitarianism understand it, the implication is that the individual may be vulnerable to being sacrificed for the sake of maximizing the pleasure or desire-satisfaction of others, no matter how trivial the pleasure or how indefensible the desire.

Cost-Benefit Analysis

Bentham regarded the interest of society as the sum total of the interests of the individuals who make it up. His preference-utilitarianism is a "liberal" theory, in the sense that it leaves each individual at liberty to decide for himself or herself what is really good or worth pursuing in life. It also embodies another liberal ideal, equality, in that when calculating the total, the pains, pleasures, and preferences of every individual are counted equally.

One application of the preference-utilitarian approach to public policy is cost-benefit analysis. The costs and benefits of various options are measured in terms of dollars. For example, the amount of money it costs to clean up a polluted bay is weighed against the amount of money the pollution is costing the fishing industry. But then nonfinancial factors, such as desires people have that nature not be despoiled, need to be translated into dollar equivalents to introduce them into the equation that determines policy. So the strength of people's preferences might be weighed in terms of how much they would be willing to pay to see them realized. This view has been popular with many economists, but it has been an object of ridicule by some philosophers. Mark Sagoff writes:

> It should be possible, following the same line of reasoning, to decide whether creationism should be taught in the public schools, whether black and white people should be segregated, whether the death penalty should be enforced, and whether the square root of six is three. All of these questions depend upon how much people are willing to pay for their subjective preferences or wants or none of them do. This is the beauty of cost-benefit analysis; no matter how relevant or irrelevant, wise or stupid, informed or uninformed, responsible or silly, defensible or indefensible wants may be, the analysis is able to derive a policy which is legitimate because, in theory, it treats all of these preferences as equally wise and good.[8]

Preferences and Democracy

Furthermore, preference-utilitarianism as a way of making public policy has antidemocratic implications, since the preferences that are counted are not the preferences people reveal in the way they vote (e.g., voting to outlaw nonreturnable beverage bottles) but the preferences they express in the market by their allocation of income (e.g., buying beverages in nonreturnable bottles). The calculations of economic experts can on this view take policy formation away from the people and their elected representatives. Insofar as only certain preferences count and not others, or the preferences that experts think people would have if people were different from what they are now, the results are even more antidemocratic, as policy is taken even further away from the people and their elected representatives and put into the hands of supposed experts.[9]

LIBERAL AND SOCIAL CONTRACT
VIEWS OF JUSTICE

Traditional Contract Views

The formal demand for justice is that each person get what he or she is entitled to, however that is defined in a particular society. It has often been believed that people should have more wealth, political power, or authority in accordance with some natural entitlement. In villages in India, it used to be considered an injustice for a person of a certain caste to get more or less grain than a person of that caste was entitled to.[10] *Liberalism* has to do with the rejection of the idea that there is some natural order of things by which some people are entitled to more wealth or power than other people; rather, it considers all people "equal and independent."[11]

Liberals such as Locke maintain that the only way that any person or any social system can have authority over an individual is if that individual consents to that authority.[12] Since people would not consent to be in a situation in which they were worse off than they would be otherwise, government and the social system must provide some benefit for people. The benefit that Locke emphasized was the protection of the individual's rights to life, liberty, and property.[13] But as Jean-Jacques Rousseau (1712–1778) vehemently pointed out, a social contract between those unequal in wealth and power was hardly likely to be fair, and was likely to be nothing but a way in which the rich and powerful made their advantageous positions permanent.[14] Rousseau's alternative was to envision a social contract between people who were truly equal in power and wealth.[15] It was only possible to envision such a contract, however, for small, independent, homogeneous, relatively nonindustrial communities.

Another alternative is to base justice not on any real contract or real act of consent, but on an imaginary or hypothetical contract that people *would* have been willing to consent to if they had been in a position where they were all free and equal. This approach is discussed in the next section.

John Rawls's Hypothetical Social Contract

One of the most influential academic books of the second half of the twentieth century is *A Theory of Justice* by the Harvard University philosopher John Rawls, published in 1971.[16] Rawls believes that there are two basic principles of justice. His first principle is that "each person is to have an equal right to the most extensive basic liberty compatible with a similar liberty for others."[17] This principle requires equality in basic rights and duties and declares that it would be unjust to deprive a person of "political liberty . . . together with freedom of speech and assembly, liberty of conscience and freedom of thought."[18]

The second principle has two parts. The first part will be described below. The second part says that everyone should have equal opportunity to attain the preferred positions in society. Equality of opportunity is a basic ingredient of liberalism. The opportunity to get ahead in life should not depend on one's race, religion, sex, or the social status of one's parents. But suppose all laws and practices that discriminate on these grounds are abolished. In many countries, including the United States, it is still possible to go into a maternity hospital and predict with a high degree of accuracy, purely on the basis of such things as sex, race, and the social and economic status of the parents, what sorts of education, income, and medical care each of the children will get during their lifetimes. One could say that there is formal equality of opportunity, but not substantive equality of opportunity. Rawls insists that justice requires more than formal equality of opportunity.

> The thought here is that positions are to be not only open in a formal sense, but that all should have a fair chance to attain them. . . . Assuming that there is a distribution of natural assets, those who are at the same level of talent and ability, and have the same willingness to use them, should have the same prospects of success regardless of their initial place in the social system, that is, irrespective of the income class into which they are born.[19]

Many people in the United States say that welfare-state liberals and socialists are trying to assure people of equality of results when all that justice demands is equality of opportunity. But when one thinks about this for a moment, it is obviously absurd. Suppose we are in a society in which most of the available jobs pay wages that leave 90 percent of families below the poverty level while 10 percent of the population is exceedingly rich. Can it really be claimed that if each person has an equal opportunity to get one of the better jobs, then this society is just? Obviously not. Something must also be said about the extent of the inequalities between the various positions and how those inequalities are justified. This is what the first part of Rawls's second principle deals with. It says that social and economic inequalities are to be arranged so that they are "reasonably expected to be to everyone's advantage."[20]

This principle, which Rawls calls the *difference principle*, can be illustrated in the following way: Suppose the economy of a society of ten people could be arranged in three ways.

1. In the first arrangement, everyone makes $20,000 a year, for a gross national product (GNP) of $200,000.
2. In the second arrangement, two people make $15,000, three people make $22,000, three people make $25,000, and two people $40,000, for a GNP of $251,000.
3. In the third arrangement, four people make $21,000, four people make $24,000, and two people make $30,000, for a GNP of $240,000.

The first arrangement embodies the most equality. However, in Rawls's view, since changing from the first to the third would benefit everyone, even the worst off, it would be irrational not to make that change. Assuming these are the only three alternatives, the inequalities in the third one are therefore acceptable. A utilitarian would claim that the second was preferable, either because it provides the most benefit or because it benefit the most people, since eight people would be better off under the second arrangement than they would be in either the first or the third. Accepting the inequalities in the second, however, would violate Rawls's principle, since two people would be worse off under the second arrangement than they would be under the first. As Rawls puts it, "The principle excludes, therefore, the justification of inequalities on the grounds that the disadvantages of those in one position are outweighed by the greater advantages of those in another position."[21]

Rawls might justify affirmative action as a means of improving the position of the most disadvantaged in the society and in order to give individuals a fair chance that their social background had deprived them of. He would not accept as a legitimate objection to affirmative action that the people who are being passed over for the sake of benefiting others are being deprived of something they deserve, since for Rawls we do not deserve our natural abilities or the advantages they give us.[22]

Why does Rawls think that these are the correct principles? One justification for them involves imagining people deciding on a set of rules of justice (and then on a constitution, and then on specific laws). Since people would tend to pick principles that would benefit people of their race, their sex, their abilities, or their economic class, we have to imagine these people having temporary amnesia about these factors. Rights and duties are determined by a social contract, as they were with Hobbes, but it is not any contract anyone has ever made. It is the contract that would be made under certain ideal conditions designed to ensure fairness, where none of the contractors are in a disadvantageous position. Rawls calls this "deciding behind the veil of ignorance." Of course, we cannot imagine the contractors to be ignorant about everything, otherwise they would have no reason to select any principles at all.

One thing they would have to be ignorant of, according to Rawls, would be what they really believe to be the highest good or the most worthwhile kind of life. So when they are thinking about the distribution of good things, they would have to limit their considerations to what Rawls calls "the primary goods," those things that are presumed to be useful to people whatever their views are of the ultimate good of life. This includes such things as liberty, wealth, status, and self-respect. So Rawls's theory is a liberal theory first in its basic egalitarianism, second in its emphasis on liberty, third in its acceptance of the ideal of equality of opportunity, fourth in its basic neutrality among different ideas that people have of the good life, and fifth in its respect for the autonomy and voluntary choice of the individual. As Rawls writes:

> A society satisfying the principles of justice as fairness comes as close as a society can to being a voluntary scheme, for it meets the principles which free and equal persons would assent to under circumstances that are fair. In this sense its members are autonomous and the obligations they recognize are self-imposed. [23]

Criticisms of Rawls's Views

There are many ways in which Rawls's views have been criticized. Some have claimed that the method of deciding behind the imagined veil of ignorance is a good method, but that it would yield a different set of principles. Some have claimed that there is a problem of specifying what would have to be known and what not known by people behind the veil of ignorance. Some have attacked the whole method for various reasons. Those who believe that human society should serve some higher good than individual self-interest doubt whether principles adopted by individuals calculating their self-interest in fair circumstances is all that much superior to principles adopted by individuals calculating their self-interest in unfair circumstances. [24] Some have pointed out that there are conceivable situations when no alternative would pass the difference principle test, such as when the economic situation worsens. Some challenge Rawls's difference principle, asking why a small deprivation for some could not be justified by a large benefit to many. Some believe that the difference principle, given appropriate circumstances, could justify extremes of wealth and poverty. Others see it as demanding too much redistribution of wealth. One reason for this last position is the claim that the difference principle does not take into consideration the extent to which people are in favorable or unfavorable positions because of their own choices. [25]

THE LIBERTARIAN THEORY OF JUSTICE

Robert Nozick's Libertarian Theory

Rawls's book was followed in 1974 by another influential work by a Harvard philosopher, Robert Nozick's *Anarchy, State, and Utopia*, which set forth a very different view known as *libertarianism*. [26] Suppose that a man with three children is making his will and trying to decide how to distribute his wealth among them. The eldest child has the greatest need because of medical problems; the second child, having done a lot for his father in his old age, is the most deserving; the youngest child is a derelict playboy who deserves little, has no unmet financial needs, and will probably gamble all the money away. Suppose he decides to give everything to the youngest child. Is this unjust? If we look at it from the point of view of the result, then whether we favor equality, or reward according to merit, or distribution according to need, the result is unjust. Nozick calls the theories that take the viewpoint of the recipients "end state" theories, or "time slice" theories.[27] They are also "patterned" theories in that justice means distribution according to a pattern—each equally, or each according to his merit, or each according to his need.

Nozick, however, looks at it from the point of view of the man making the will. It is his money and he does not violate the rights of anyone else however he chooses to distribute it. If the distribution comes about by his choice, and not by one of the children stealing the money or defrauding him of it, then whatever distribution results is a just distribution. We can ask whether it is just that some people have billions and some unemployed people in the slums have nothing. According to utilitarianism, and according to Rawls, we look at the present distribution of wealth in the society (using a "time slice" principle) and compare it to some ideal distribution, such as the most good for the most people. According to Nozick, this is not the way to discover whether a certain distribution is just. "Whether a distribution is just depends upon how it came about."[28] Thus Nozick's theory is a "historical" theory rather than an end-state theory or time-slice theory.

Nozick criticizes "time slice" principles in the following way. Suppose today we redistributed wealth in society according to Rawls's principles, or utilitarian criteria, or some other formula. By tomorrow some people would begin to get wealthier and others poorer. What is the government to do? Should it forbid people to work on their own time? Should it forbid capitalist acts between consenting adults? As Nozick writes, "No end state principle or distributional patterned principle of justice can be continuously realized without continuous interference with people's lives."[29]

Nozick's view is based on the idea that people have a negative right not to be coerced. It would be a violation of such a right, and therefore wrong, for the government to take a kidney from a person who has two kidneys in order to give it to a person who needs one. Similarly it would be a violation of property rights, and therefore wrong, for the government to use the tax system to take five dollars from a millionaire entitled to his money to give it to a person who is starving to death. Whether the millionaire really is entitled to the money is determined by tracing the history of his wealth. If it came to him through gifts or exchanges that involved no force or fraud, and if the first person who had that wealth got it legitimately (that is, by mixing his or her labor with the natural resources), then he is entitled to it.

To take it from him would be violating his right to do what he wants with what is his. Of course, others might say that the millionaire's property rights cannot be absolute because they must be balanced against the hungry person's positive right (or subsistence right, or economic right) to be provided with the means of survival, but Nozick's moral universe is not populated by any such rights.

What would Nozick say about justice and medical care? It would be an interference with the freedom of doctors to force them to offer services to the poor and it would be an interference with the property rights of other people to tax them to provide medical care for the poor. So it would seem that there is nothing unjust about letting them go without. It would be nice if private charity would help, but there is no injustice if there is no help. What would Nozick say about affirmative action? Generally, he would take the position that the government should neither require nor forbid affirmative action to benefit groups in society, since an employer would be entitled to do with its jobs, or a school would be entitled to do with its facilities, whatever it pleases. The exception would be where it could be shown that a specific individual's rights were violated in the past, and that some act of preference now would compensate that individual, or perhaps his or her heirs, for that past injustice. At the same time, no deprivations should be imposed on anyone other than those who benefited from the past injustice.[30] For the libertarian who is true to this position, rather than one who chooses this position merely because he or she desires the government to stay off his or her back, there would seem to be very strong duties not to violate the negative rights of future generations, but of course no duty to benefit future generations.

Nozick's theory is egalitarian only because negative rights belong to everyone equally. It is also a liberal theory because it supports liberty to the extent that it minimizes government interference in people's lives and because it claims to be built on complete neutrality toward the question of what things are ultimately worth pursuing in life. Each individual is free to make such decisions for her- or himself within the constraints of not interfering with the rights of others.

Criticisms of Nozick's Theory

It is hardly surprising that the literature criticizing Nozick's theory is immense.[31] Some of the main points of that criticism are discussed in this section.

Libertarianism cannot be based on a respect for liberty. Perhaps libertarianism values rights. But where do the natural rights claimed by libertarians come from? Do they just drop from the sky, or do they serve some human interest?

We have already (in chapter 8) criticized rights-based ethics. Rights must be in the service of human interests. What human interest, then, does libertarianism value? Presumably, it values liberty or the right to liberty. But, as James Sterba asks,[32] why then should it not value the liberty of the poor to take from the rich what they require in order to survive, as much as it values the liberty of the rich to use their riches to enjoy luxuries? If the answer appeals to the need to protect property rights, then we can ask why people should accept a view of property rights that will seem totally implausible to large numbers of people, namely the poor. Would it not be irrational to expect the poor to see the point of or to acknowledge an absolutist view of property rights that requires them passively to starve? If the poor are numerous enough, the only way to get them to conform to such norms of justice would be by brute force. This is a strange consequence for a position that is based on a concern for liberty.

Libertarianism's view of property rights is implausible and conflicts with its concern for liberty. One problem with Nozick's view of property rights is that it seems to many people much more plausible to regard property rights as things created by a government and a legal system, rather than as preexisting things that a government was created to protect.[33] Second, it can be argued that approaches such as Nozick's, which see no problem with unlimited accumulation of and unrestricted use of wealth, do not value liberty very much. The libertarian who says that no one has a right to economic resources would probably agree that everyone has a right to a fair trial. But there is a contradiction here because the kind of trial one gets is dependent to a great extent on the sorts of lawyers one can afford and thus on the distribution of economic resources.[34]

If the economic sphere had no influence on other spheres, the political sphere for example, then unlimited accumulation might not threaten anyone and so might not be a problem. As Michael Walzer writes, "If we succeeded absolutely in barring the conversion of money into political power, for example, then we might not limit its accumulation . . . at all."[35] But we have not succeeded in doing so, nor is it likely that we, or anyone else, will. Thomas Scanlon writes: "If a supposed right turns out to give the person holding it an obviously unacceptable degree of control over other people's lives, then that is ground for saying that there is no such right."[36]

But a right to unlimited accumulation of wealth would do just that, so there is a good reason—the protection of the vulnerable—for saying there is no such right. Similarly, as another author puts it: "If property rights derive their importance from the right to liberty, then if the accumulation of property has negative threshold effects on liberty, then the right to liberty not only does not prohibit end-state theories of justice, it demands them!"[37]

Nozick disagrees with all redistributive schemes on the grounds that they ignore the fact that "things come into the world already attached to people who have entitlements over them" and not "nowhere out of nothing."[38] A third problem with Nozick's view of property is that although kidneys do, of course, come into the world attached to people, the vast majority of natural resources on which wealth is based did appear out of nothing unattached to anyone. This is a fact that could legitimately set limits on all later claims on that wealth, whether those claims are based on labor, gift, purchase, or some other foundation. It would seem that any believer in a theistic religion should agree with the traditional Native American view that no one can actually own the land and that people can legitimately regard it only as something they hold in trust. If there are already duties connected to the resources of this earth, then government coercion may be seen, not as interfering with individuals' legitimate freedom, but simply as requiring them to fulfill duties they already have.

Libertarianism is implausible because it is based on a monistic view of human good. If liberty rights are valued because they are based on genuine human interests, why should anyone think that human beings have only one significant interest, namely liberty, and thus have rights based only on that one interest? It seems completely arbitrary for the libertarian to reject positive rights or subsistence rights (such as a right to food) while making the security-oriented right not to be interfered with into an absolute, since, as Henry Shue argues, the same sorts of reasons that can be given in favor of regarding people as having security rights (rights not to be harmed) can be given in favor of regarding them as having subsistence rights.[39] Both are based on the need of the vulnerable to be protected. (The right to private property was first stressed by people who were vulnerable to having their livelihoods threatened by an autocratic government that could arbitrarily seize the property on which that livelihood depended.) Both involve taxing some people to benefit others, whether these others are those most in need of food or those most in need of police protection.

James Fishkin argues that a policy choice is an unacceptable instance of tyranny if it imposes severe deprivations on some people despite the availability of an alternative policy that would impose no severe deprivations on anyone. But policies based on Nozick's principles, which overlook all human interests except one, could clearly impose such deprivations, so they are tyrannical and unjust.[40] It has also been argued that Nozick's view that government should protect certain liberty rights while totally ignoring all needs seems to go against universal precedent, for, as Michael Walzer writes:

> There has never been a political community that did not provide, or try to provide, or claim to provide, for the needs of its members as its members understood those needs. And there has never been a political community that did not engage its collective strength—its capacity to direct, regulate, pressure, and coerce—in this project.[41]

The whole libertarian argument seems to be arbitrary. Those traditional moral considerations that can be appealed to to support the interests of the "haves" are made into absolutes; those that can be appealed to to support the interests of the "have-nots" are rejected.

Libertarian views, even if true in theory, have no application to the real world. Suppose we could start again on a previously uninhabited island or planet. Perhaps there we could apply Nozick's theory. In the real world, however, almost everyone has benefited from injustices in the past, as well as suffered from them. There is no plausible way of sorting out the causal chains involved and discovering the degree to which people are entitled to what they have today. Furthermore, in the real world, wealth is not produced purely by individuals. Since we do not now live in a completely libertarian society, whatever wealth individuals have been able to accumulate is the product not only of their own effort but of their community's institutions and regulations—for example, of the public schools they attended, the roads they use, and the infrastructure of their whole society.

OTHER LIBERAL THEORIES: MIDDLE WAYS BETWEEN NOZICK AND RAWLS

Various writers in the liberal tradition have formulated views of justice that have a place for "end state" or "patterned" principles of justice, but which, in order to avoid having government constantly interfering with individual freedom (among other reasons), also have a place for historical principles. According to these writers, everybody could be assured a certain minimum level of well-being based on certain positive rights, such as a right to adequate medical care, a right to food, or "a right to a fair share of society's scarce resources."[42]

One philosopher who takes such a position, James Sterba, writes that each person should be "guaranteed the primary social goods that are necessary to meet the *normal* costs of satisfying his basic needs in the society in which he lives."[43] This end-state principle might require considerably less transfer of wealth from the rich to the poor than Rawls's difference principle would require. This is the first of four principles that Sterba thinks would be approved of by people behind Rawls's veil of ignorance. The second is a historical principle that allows for private appropriation and voluntary agreement and exchange. The third is a principle of contribution that basically says that the rich can be required to pay taxes to benefit the poor and the able-bodied poor can be required to work. The fourth is a principle of saving that has to do with preserving resources for future generations.[44] An advantage of such a view is that since it does not call for maintaining a specific pattern of distribution, it does not require constant interferences with liberty. A disadvantage that some would see is that this approach would still allow for extreme inequalities in wealth, and therefore extreme inequalities in power. This might be a threat to areas of life in which wealth should not be the determining factor.

What would advocates of this sort of view say about medical care? Probably they would say either that government should make sure that all citizens have a minimum income high enough so that they can afford health insurance,[45] or it should see to it that a *basic* level of medical care is provided to all citizens regardless of their ability to pay. This would not necessarily include particularly expensive care, such as heart transplants. Those who have the money, however, should be free to buy whatever additional care they wish.[46]

What might advocates of this sort of view say about preferential hiring or admission to schools? In addition to those cases in which a preferential scheme is clearly correcting a past injustice to a particular individual, such a scheme might be acceptable if it is necessary for the sake of guaranteeing to each person "the primary social goods that are necessary to meet the *normal* costs of satisfying his basic needs in the society in which he lives," to use Sterba's formulation. So this position might agree with utilitarianism in allowing for preference among applicants to law and medical schools to go to those, such as members of minority groups, who will most likely be willing to serve in areas of greatest need.

THEORIES OF JUSTICE BASED ON CONCEPTS OF THE GOOD

Liberalism, Justice, and Human Good

Most of the modern positions considered here are liberal in one or more senses. Liberalism was born in an age when people had experienced the power of autocratic rulers who claimed to be superior to others; thus it emphasized human equality, the rights of individuals against the state, and the necessity for the state to be constituted with the actual or probable consent of the people. It was also born in an age that saw the horrors of civil war and religious strife, so it valued religious freedom and tolerance.[47] It was also born at the beginning of the capitalist age, so it emphasized individualism and saw economic freedom as a source of prosperity; furthermore, it saw autocratic government and religious strife as threats to prosperity.[48] The liberal tradition later came to emphasize the ideal of personal freedom and the autonomy of each individual freely choosing his or her own way of life.[49]

Utilitarianism embodied the emphasis on human equality and hoped to provide consequentialist arguments for the other emphases.[50] We see all of these concerns in Rawls's theory. Libertarians emphasize individualism, individuals' rights against the state, and their religious, economic, and personal freedom. Some modern liberals (including preference-utilitarians, Rawls, and Nozick, among many others) extend the emphases on religious and economic freedom to the point of claiming that government should be totally neutral with respect to what kinds of lives are worth living, either because of moral skepticism or because they regard such matters as outside the proper area of concern of government.[51] In fact, however, liberalism is often based, not on neutrality, but on the belief that the good life is the life in which an individual, as much as possible, makes free and autonomous choices.

The author of this text believes that such neutrality is neither possible nor desirable. If we reject the idea of value neutrality, then justice, or the distribution of benefits and burdens in a society, is not the only criterion of a good society. A society, by means of government action, may protect the environment, further scientific research, promote the arts, and so on because these are good things to do, without having to show that they satisfy the most preferences or conform to some principle of justice.

The advocacy of government neutrality is seen as a way of avoiding totalitarianism. An alternative protection against tyranny is moral pluralism.[52] William Galston writes: "The fundamental argument for a diverse society is not—as some believe—that our reason is incompetent to judge among possible ways of life. It is rather that the human good is not one thing but many things."[53] A liberalism that believes that certain goals and ways of life are intrinsically worthwhile will value freedom of choice—not necessarily freedom of choice among all ways of life, but only among desirable ways of life.[54] A view of justice based on a pluralistic conception of the good must reject the views of Rawls and Nozick that freedom without regard to how it might be used (for good or ill) is something intrinsically valuable or something to which we have an absolute right.[55]

Michael Walzer's Democratic Theory of Justice

Another noteworthy book on justice is Michael Walzer's *Spheres of Justice*. As title indicates, he sides with the pluralistic conception of the good. The various criteria of justice mentioned earlier, including need, merit, and equal provision, may each be appropriate in various spheres of life and with respect to various social endeavors. The kind of good that is being distributed determines the criteria for its distribution. For many goods, especially economic ones, the first criterion is need. So Walzer would agree to some extent with James Sterba's position, which allows for the satisfaction of basic needs without the abrogation of economic freedom. However, he begins in a different way, with a discussion of membership and of what people who are members of the same community owe to each other. This idea of membership does not seem to play any role in noncontract views such as utilitarianism and libertarianism, in which all that seems at issue is what human beings owe other human beings purely as human beings. Nor does Walzer appeal to abstract principles that are valid for all societies for all eternity, since justice has to do with "what citizens owe one another, given the community they actually inhabit."[56]

> The social contract is an agreement to reach decisions together about what goods are necessary to our common life, and then to provide those goods for one another. . . . [The contract signers] owe mutual provision of all those things for the sake of which they have separated themselves from mankind as a whole and joined forces in a particular community.[57]

What do people owe each other in a democratic society? He answers with this rhetorical question: "Is it not the purpose of the democratic state, rightly understood . . . to sustain equally the lives and minimal well-being of all its citizens?"[58] Walzer goes on to write that since "every political community must attend to the needs of its members,"[59] goods must be distributed according to need, and that this "distribution of goods must recognize and uphold the underlying equality of membership."[60] A basic requirement of distributive justice is "communal provision of security and welfare,"[61] including "care for the ill, the aged, the infirm, the destitute, the unemployed, and so on."[62] Thus a "safety net" is created for the protection of the group. The idea of the "safety net"

> means that the first commitment of the welfare state is to its weakest members; nothing else can be done until their position is secure. . . . The crucial point is that the safety net be constructed so as to secure for everyone whatever it is we collectively believe to be the central values of our culture, the needs that must be met if we are to stand to one another as *fellow citizens*.[63]

Therefore, according to Walzer, if it is really true that the United States must cut back on public expenditures in order to reduce its budget deficit, then it should begin with those expenditures that help the better off. This is in accordance with the view of this book that some of our most fundamental moral duties have do with protecting the vulnerable.

Walzer accepts the view that the good of society is not equal to the sum total of the interests of individuals, as Bentham maintained, but has a collective element. He is concerned with such interpersonal factors in society as "culture, religion, and politics."[64] He is also concerned with

> a shared economic, social, and cultural infrastructure, a public sector that both enlarges the scope of and gives some determinate shape to our private lives: roads, bridges, mass transit, national parks, communications systems, schools, museums, and so on. . . . The purpose of the infrastructure is to enable the mass of citizens to participate in necessary or valued social activities. . . . The decay of the infrastructure [which he thinks is now happening] and its replacement by private facilities has the effect of disabling or excluding some citizens, but not others, from participating in that way of life.[65]

What needs must justice meet beyond basic security and welfare, and to what extent? Walzer writes, "Clearly we can't meet, and we don't have to meet, every need to the same degree or any need to the ultimate degree."[66] Well, then, which ones do we have to meet? For example, how should expenditures be divided between medical care and education? Preference-utilitarianism and those who emphasize individual liberty would say that we should meet people's needs as each individual understands them. Other utilitarians might say that we should meet people's needs as they are determined by the standards of some expert economist, philosopher, or physician. Libertarians would say that we have no duty to meet the needs of others. Rawls says we should first meet what he calls basic needs.

Walzer's answer is that there is no *a priori* stipulation of which needs ought to be met; rather, people's needs should be met as the members of the community *collectively* understand those needs. So he supports the view that the state should provide those in need with specific things, such as medical care and food stamps, rather than simply distributing money, which people are free to spend as they wish. Neither does Walzer see any "*a priori* way of determining appropriate levels of provision."[67] Determining the needs that should be met and the degree to which they should be met is what the democratic political process is for, and presumably that process will decide in a way that reflects the basic values of the society. "Any philosophical effort to stipulate in detail the rights or the entitlements of individuals would radically constrain the scope of democratic decision making."[68]

But whatever is seen by the group to be a proper subject of communal provision, whether it is more money for medical care or more money for education, it must be provided in a way that treats people equally.

> Perhaps the most telling statistic about contemporary American medicine is the correlation of visits to doctors and hospitals with social class rather than with degree or incidence of illness. . . . Were medical care a luxury, these discrepancies would not matter much; but as soon as medical care becomes a socially recognized need, and as soon as the community invests in its provision, they matter a great deal. For then deprivation is a double loss—to one's health and to one's social standing. . . . So long as communal funds are spent, as they currently are, to finance research, build hospitals, and pay the fees of doctors in private practice, the services that these expenditures underwrite must be equally available to all citizens.[69]

Walzer and others with a theory of justice based on a view of the good society would not think that the issue of affirmative action could be settled by an appeal to absolute rights. If affirmative action is helpful in getting the basic needs of people met, including access to physicians and lawyers, then it would be morally permissible. Whether it should be preferred over some other method would depend on what the political process decides in light of other value considerations.

When American society, through its legislators, chose to give preference to veterans over nonveterans, this was not considered a violation of the rights of nonveterans.[70] Colleges also practice selective admissions in order to get a diverse group of students; a school in Pennsylvania may accept an out-of-state student with a mediocre record over a local student with a better record, or a student with a poor record who wants to major in ancient history (where there are few majors) over a student with a better record who wants to major in business (where there are many). It is doubtful that anyone's rights are violated here. Societies have a right to value and reward service to the country. Schools have a right to value diversity. So no *a priori* answer can be given on the question of preferential treatment. Various claims may have to be weighed against each other and settled by the political process. Alan Brown writes:

> It would seem, then, that there is no principled consideration which rules out reverse discrimination. It is something we may employ if it is an efficient means to the desirable end of a society characterized by good social relations. By the same token there can be no principled consideration which makes reverse discrimination morally obligatory. . . . It is clear, then, that to operate a practice of reverse discrimination is to conduct a social experiment. And one can only be certain of the success of an experiment in retrospect.[71]

Walzer would probably justify "reverse discrimination" in places where it is necessary to bring people into fully equal participation in the society.

Evaluation of Walzer's Views

Many of Walzer's specific proposals seem reasonable. It is also reasonable to believe that there is no one eternally valid, detailed idea of justice by which we can judge all societies. It is useful, up to a point, to criticize injustices in the United States not by appealing to eternally valid principles, but by appealing to the highest ideals of the shared values of the American tradition and American society. However, how does one decide which of the ideals in the American tradition, or any other tradition, should be emphasized and which should be deemphasized? Must there not be some criteria for what is good and bad for human beings that transcend the traditions of particular societies?[72] Walzer's approach needs to be supplemented by an appeal to a transcultural view of human good. While justice may have to do with meeting human needs as they are understood in a particular society, some ways of understanding the good for human beings, and thus what human beings need, are better than others. Absolute justice cannot provide one right way to organize society, but it can determine that some ways are wrong ways. This is, of course, what versions of the natural law theory seek to do.

ADDITIONAL CONCERNS OF JUSTICE

Justice and Power: One Concern of Democratic Justice

After people's basic needs are met, should justice be concerned any further with distribution of wealth or economic equality? We can take an indirect approach to answering that question. In chapter 8 we referred to Philip Hallie's views on cruelty and power and the necessity of either getting a person out of an unbalanced power relationship or of balancing the power.[73] Insofar as we live in the same society, we cannot flee from such an imbalance. It must either be prevented from occurring or corrected. That means that the power of the government itself must be limited by a system of checks and balances and by accountability to and replacement by the people. But the government is not the only wielder of power and potential exploiter of the vulnerable. For a social system to be worthy of consent, it must prevent extreme inequalities of wealth from occurring or it must prevent inequalities of wealth from becoming inequalities of power in spheres in which wealth should not be relevant (e.g., in election campaigns, in the courts). This is what Walzer means by "spheres of justice." Insofar as a society cannot achieve one goal, it must seek to achieve the other. Insofar as it successfully achieves neither, it is morally defective by the standards of absolute justice. Since it is likely that neither of these goals is going to be achieved in more than a very partial way, it is morally important that opportunities be taken to work toward both of them.

Absolute Justice, Distributive Justice, and the Principle of Desert

So we can judge practices in terms of whether they live up to the ideals of a society, but we can also look beyond the ideals of that society to "absolute justice." One of the ideals within our society is the principle that what people get should not be out of line with what they deserve (known as the principle of *desert*). Utilitarians, Rawls, and Nozick have all been criticized because the principle of desert is missing from their theories. Writers who base their view of justice on a view of human good are more likely to have a place for a principle of desert. If the members of a society share a view of what is worthwhile, then people can be regarded as deserving to the degree that they contribute to the good of society, especially when they sacrifice to do so. William Galston, for example, regards desert as the most important consideration after need.

To what degree should the principle of desert be used and where, that is, in what spheres? Individual excellence and contributions to the community, both of which involve an idea of what is intrinsically worthwhile, are relevant to the distribution of public honors.[74] Desert would not seem to have a positive role to play in the question of the distribution of medical care, but perhaps it would have a negative role. It would justify putting more of the costs of the system on people who take greater risks with their health (e.g., smokers and alcoholics).

How much should the principle of desert, or contribution, apply to the question of economic distribution, and in what way should it apply? According to Galston, the criteria of desert that are relevant to economic distribution are those related to one's contribution to economic production: sacrifice, duration, effort, productivity, and quality,[75] although other criteria of desert apply elsewhere. Many Americans would appeal to the contribution principle to justify the great difference in income between doctors and janitors, or the difference in income between policemen, who risk their lives, and clerks working for the same city, who do not.

But there is also the question of whether the principle of contribution should count for as much as it does in the American value system, or even whether it should count at all. Charles Taylor supports Rawls's difference principle, which makes no reference to any desert or contribution principle, on the grounds that such a principle would be based on the myth that most of what an individual contributes is due to his or her own efforts. He writes:

> First of all, the talented individual who makes a valuable contribution owes much of his or her capacity to society. It is not just that the training without which this capacity could not flourish is often provided by the larger society, but also that the very fact that someone with this capacity can make a large contribution may depend on a given mode of economy or social life. Someone with great mathematical gifts is much in demand in an age of computers, not at all perhaps in prescientific society.[76]

This is, of course, true, and it does show that the principle of contribution has limited applicability. But it is also true that some of what an individual contributes is due to his or her own effort. There are people who have great talents and the potential to make great contributions to society who never use these talents. What seems to be mistaken is not so much the principle of contribution as the assumption that this principle justifies the distribution of income that now exists.

Many of the inequalities in society have little to do with desert or contribution. The principle of contribution can be a valuable tool to criticize such inequalities. Many people surely feel that it is a violation of this principle when people who contribute little or nothing to society make much more money than people who contribute much. The former category includes drug dealers, sleaze publishers, and lawyers whose primary function is to find ways to enable corporations to avoid paying their fair share of taxes or to avoid paying for their crimes; the latter category includes teachers and nurses. In many cases it may not be possible to do much about such realities without violating other values, such as freedom. However, such inequalities still offend most people because they violate the principle of desert that is deeply imbedded in their sense of justice. Even if it is impossible to apply the principle of contribution throughout society, it can still be applied in limited contexts, such as to argue for higher pay for teachers, or in the example of the policemen and the clerks. Of course, the principle of contribution should not take precedence over the principle of need.

If equality of opportunity does not exist, then claims of desert have little validity. An emphasis on a principle of desert would seem not only to permit but even to require *selective* affirmative action intended to restore people to the position they would have occupied if it had not been for past discrimination that hindered their efforts to make a contribution to society, and designed to deprive other people only of advantages to which they were not entitled.[77]

MARXISM, ETHICS, AND JUSTICE

Karl Marx, Marxism, Morality, and Justice

Karl Marx (1818–1883), the German economist, sociologist, and political philosopher, was one of the most influential figures of all time. The ideas advanced by Marx and his associate Friedrich Engels gave rise to the communist and socialist movements and radically affected the practical and economic developments of the twentieth century.

In Marx's view, as history progresses, the means of production change (for example, manual techniques of separating picked cotton are replaced by the cotton gin; horse power is replaced by the steam engine). As the means of production change, new relations come into existence between economic groups (serfs and lords of the manor, slaves and plantation owners, free workers and owners of industry). These developments produce new religious, philosophical, and legal ideas, such as freedom of contract, the right to private property, the ideal of the free market, and so on.[78] So the ideas, including moral ideas, that are held by different societies, and by different classes within a society, are by-products of their differing economic structures, which are themselves by-products of differing levels of technological development.[79] Friedrich Engels wrote:

> We maintain . . . that all former moral theories are the product in the last analysis, of the economic stage which society had reached at that particular epoch. And as society has hitherto moved in class antagonism, morality was always a class morality; it has either justified the domination and the interests of the ruling class, or, as soon as the oppressed class has become powerful enough, it has represented the revolution against the domination and the future interests of the oppressed.[80]

This would seem to be a kind of pure relativism. If the morality in my society is nothing but something constructed to protect the interests of the controlling class, why should I pay any attention to it? Principles of justice might claim to represent some impartial point of view, but they in fact do not. Is there some impartial standard of justice beyond those that serve the interests of various groups and classes? Marx predicted that inevitably the oppressed working classes would rise up and overthrow the capitalist system by which they were kept in poverty. No doubt he regarded this as not only inevitable, but also a good thing. Nevertheless, when criticizing the social system and defending its opponents, he refused to appeal to impartial standards of justice (which supposedly took into consideration the interests of all people), but rather appealed only to the class interests of the proletariat (working class).[81] On the other hand, some Marxists argue that serving the interests of the proletariat is morally justified on the grounds that it furthers the interest of the most people.[82] Some also claim that socialism is morally superior to its alternatives. Such a claim implies the existence of an objective standard of morality.[83]

Marxist Morality

In fact, however, contemporary societies that consider themselves Marxist, like the Soviet Union, have turned against relativism.

> At first the exclusion of eternal, suprahistorical laws was held to warrant amoralism, ethical indifference, or at least some experimentation in new ways of living. Soviet authorities found that attitude socially inconvenient, and eventually Stalin formally condemned all applications of historical relativism that suggested that the new polity could have a new ethics (or a special new logic).[84]

What then would be the basis of morality in Marxist societies? Since Stalin condemned relativism, Marxist philosophy has accepted "the ethical ideals preached in other contemporary societies but adds that only a communist nation can escape hypocrisy by living up to those ideals."[85] In fact, Marxists do not seem to have any distinctive idea of the human good. Some Marxists would say that the good is the realization of distinctive human potential, which is to live as rational, self-conscious beings who understand what they are doing.[86] Others see the good as the happiness of the individual. What Marxism has to offer is not a new view of human good, but a way of doing away with the obstacles to the achievement of human good (however it is defined) that have been created by other social and economic systems.[87]

Marxism and Achieving the Human Good

What are these obstacles? For Marx, it is characteristic of human beings to be productive, but in past and present societies what workers produce primarily increases the wealth of employers and gives those employers even more control over the lives of the workers. The goal of history is achieved when human beings not only free themselves from the tyranny of their overseers (by taking control of the means of production for their own benefit), but also free themselves "from the tyranny of nature and fashion the world after their own plans."[88] The obstacles to this movement toward freedom are economic. One is the insufficient production of goods for human benefit, perpetuated, even after technological advances, by the wastefulness of the capitalist system (a system based on private property and the unrestricted acquisition of wealth). The other is the conflict between self-interest and the common good in capitalist society, which encourages envy, greed, and egoism. Overthrow the capitalist system with its wastefulness and useful production will increase, enabling human beings to have more of what enriches life, including free time to use in creative ways. Overthrow the capitalist system and "the split between the particular interests of the individual and the common interest of society would disappear."[89] In the Soviet Union, this system was overthrown, but the realization of this promise of abundance was left for the future. And since the obstacles to happiness were primarily material, the duty for the present was to obey the now all-powerful Communist Party in its effort to build a more productive economy.[90] (So long as the good was seen as a goal for the future, it was possible for communist governments to try to use utilitarian considerations to justify, at least to themselves, incredible horrors against human beings in the present.)

Justice in Marxist Society

As we have seen, many people think of injustice in terms of a violation of rights, whether these are regarded as natural, as based on a contract, or as based on utility. Justice, which has to do with the distribution of burdens and scarce resources, is regarded by Rawls and others as the most important moral virtue of institutions. Marxists, however, dispute this on the grounds that the need for justice depends on characteristics of society that could be changed.

> Marx apparently believes that reliance on principles of justice is necessary only because of egoistic interaction rooted in the conflict of classes over unnecessarily scarce resources. Secondly he believes that scarcity will be greatly reduced with the abolition of classes and that egoistic strife will give way to communal harmony.[91]

So on the Marxist view, if we do away with any reluctance on the part of people to bear necessary burdens, we do away with one part of the need for principles of justice, and if we do away with scarcity, we do away with another part. In order to do away with reluctance to bear burdens, we would have to change human nature. But for Marx human nature is not something fixed, but something that is a by-product of economic and social conditions.

> Marx expected the abolition of private property and the institution of common ownership of the means of production and exchange to bring about a society in which people were motivated more for a desire for the good of all than by a specific desire for their own individual good. In this way individual and common interests could be harmonized.[92]

This is a vision of a society in which ideas of justice and individual rights are unnecessary because all its members willingly work for a common good that they see as their own good and cooperate in the production of abundance. Critics have pointed out a number of problems with this view. First, there are other reasons for talking about rights that do not have to do with the distribution of scarce resources, such as setting limits on ways of doing things for the common good.[93] Second, it is not likely that egoism will pass away if society is reorganized or if abundance occurs. People have ways of discovering new "needs."[94] Third, even without egoism there is not likely to be abundance, because there are projects that can have a potentially unlimited drain on resources, such as medical research, medical care, and space exploration.[95] Fourth, as Allen Buchanan notes: "For Marx to say that capitalism is wasteful of resources is presumably to say that it is wasteful in comparison with communism. But Marx says little about how communism would work as a system of social coordination."[96]

According to Marx, since the state exists to protect the interests of the most powerful class, once a classless society comes into existence the state will have no more purpose, coercion will no longer be needed. Thus, the state will "wither away." Since human beings have a natural desire to work when they can work where and when and how they wish, they will continue to work with energy at those things they themselves choose to work at, producing more abundance than was produced when they reluctantly worked for the good of the capitalist class. But there are problems with this.

> The difficulty is that Marx's assumption that the communist individual will enjoy tremendous freedom and flexibility in choosing and scheduling his own particular activities greatly enhances the problems of efficiently coordinating large numbers of individual activities through the use of democratic, non-oppressive planning techniques, in the absence of even a limited role for the market as a coordinating device.[97]

If coordination is needed, coercion will no doubt be needed. It is hard so see how various sorts of public goods, such as pollution control and population control, can be attained without the use of coercion. Even in a society of thorough-going altruists in which no group has exclusive control over the means of production, there may be violent disagreements over what the common good is and over how it is to be achieved, so some people may have to be forced to conform to public policy.[98] In fact, societies that regard themselves as Marxist are among the most coercive in the world.

Marx's Contributions

Marx helped us become aware of how moral and other ideas can be conscious or unconscious rationalizations for inequalities of power, and how power is almost inevitably abused to benefit the few at the expense of the many. One of his weaknesses was to fail to see that the sins of human nature, including the tendencies toward cruelty and the abuse of power, would reassert themselves in people whether they were called "capitalists" or "managers in a workers' cooperative." In the process he also takes away one of the tools people have to defend themselves against the abuse of power, namely, the idea of rights. While Marxists have appealed to ideas of the good common to other societies, they have not accepted the ideas of justice of Western liberalism. The negative side of Marx's attack on the idea of rights and justice is seen in the reality of actual Marxist societies. In the Soviet constitution of 1977, "Numerous rights of the citizen are soberly listed, but each is 'qualified' with the condition that it may be overridden for the sake of the common good, where the latter is equated with the power of the state."[99] So rights have withered away, but not the state.

The positive side of Marx's own ideal is the challenge it gives to the liberal concentration on justice as resolving conflicts between the claims of various parties while largely ignoring ways of structuring society so that the reasons for conflict do not arise in the first place.[100] The construction of a more free and equal society may be a way of reducing (certainly not eliminating) such reasons, but, as Peter Singer writes, that has turned out to be "a more difficult task than Marx realized."[101]

JUSTICE AND SOCIAL CHANGE

Approaches to Social Change

The Extreme Conservative Approach.   There are different approaches to the question of justice and to the creation of a good society. An extreme conservative approach advocates leaving things as they are. That approach could satisfy preference-utilitarian ideals by simply convincing (or brainwashing) everyone to prefer the way things are at any given time. However, such an approach is morally unacceptable because it calls on people to refrain from making moral evaluations of society, and to refrain from caring about whether anything worthwhile is achieved or whether the vulnerable are protected.

Radical Approaches.   A radical approach is to settle on some definition of the ideal society, perhaps derived from some principle of justice. One may then propose to take whatever steps are necessary to bring about that ideal society. The Nazi Holocaust and the killing fields of Cambodia are examples of what *can* happen when that approach is taken. Kantians are sure to note that in these cases millions of people were treated as nothing but the means to some utopian social goal, and not as ends in themselves. Perhaps the homeless poor in the United States are the product of a limited attempt to put Nozick's ideal into practice.

Some philosophers begin with a certain principle of equality and then ask how society should be changed to fit that ideal. Some kinds of radical feminists, for example, have, in the name of equality, called for such things as constructing a genderless society; either doing away with legal marriage or allowing for and encouraging legal marriages between various numbers and combinations of men and women; allowing and encouraging people to choose their mates with no more concern about the sex of that mate than about the color of their eyes; doing away with any restriction on the sexual activity of children; doing away with natural insemination, pregnancy, and childbirth; and in fact doing away with the family as we now know it.[102]

A problem with many proposals for radical change is that the people who are supposed to be benefited by such changes do not want them. Most women in the United States do not favor the conservative approach. They desire specific social changes (called for by "liberal" feminists) that they think will make their lives better and happier, such as better educational and job opportunities, the elimination of sexual discrimination and harassment, flexible working hours that would allow parents to spend more time with their children, arrangements that would allow wives to share parenting and housekeeping activities more evenly with their husbands, affordable day care, and paid maternity leaves. On the other hand, most women do not want the extensive changes proposed by the radical feminists. Generally, they prefer to be in stable families, to have husbands rather than roommates, and to bear children in the usual way. Many take time out from their jobs or careers to be with their children; many others choose to be full-time mothers and homemakers until their children reach a certain age.

What can the radical feminist say to the woman who does not desire the changes that radical feminism proposes? Presumably, she would say, "If you were to be freed from the conditioning you have received in the present sexist society, you *would prefer* life in the new society we wish to create. So your present preferences do not count, since they are unenlightened preferences." Christina Hoff Sommers writes that as far as these radical feminists are concerned, "The actual concerns, beliefs and aspirations of the majority of women are not taken seriously *except* as illustrations of bad faith, false consciousness, and successful brainwashing."[103]

How do proponents of radical change know what people *would prefer* if they were liberated or enlightened, or if they lived in a kind of society that has never existed? Advocates of a new society have to argue in terms of how satisfied they think people *would be* in the new society as compared to the old, and thus whether they *would* prefer it to the old. How would they go about arguing this? One answer claims that all the problems and misery in our present society are due to one particular cause, so we can predict that when this cause is removed, a new society will inevitably emerge that will automatically produce little misery. Marx held the view that most misery is due to factors that are ultimately the product of the class structure of society. Remove the class structure through revolution and most sources of misery will dissipate. Marxist feminists agree. Some radical feminists, on the other hand, see the fact that women bear children as a major cause of social evils. Do away with natural childbearing and sources of misery will dissipate as "new women and men emerge, . . . different from any people who have previously existed."[104] To the unconvinced, these answers seem to say, "The new society will be wonderful, this I know, for my ideology tells me so." The antidemocratic and totalitarian potential of this point of view should be obvious.

Moderate Approaches.   Moderate or liberal approaches tend to look at society and ask what steps should be taken next to improve the lives of individuals and serve the general good. ("Liberal" here refers to an attitude or approach and not to a body of doctrine, as earlier in the chapter.) How do we decide what changes are improvements? The position taken in this book rejects preference-utilitarianism and the idea that all preferences should be treated with equal respect. The liberal, like the radical, may appeal to preferences that people do not now have, saying, "If you make these changes, you will see that they are for the better." For example, suppose we are trying to encourage a battered housewife to leave her situation. At the moment, facing economic uncertainty, she does not think she wants to leave. We say, "Once you get out of this situation, you will discover that you are glad that you made the break. If you leave, you will not desire to go back."

When John Stuart Mill was faced with the question as to which pleasures were superior to others, his answer was that when people have experienced two pleasures and all or most prefer one to the other, then that is the superior one.[105] So all or most people who have acquired the capacity really to experience great music prefer a life in which great music plays a part to a life in which it does not. Similarly, all or most people who have experienced life as a battered spouse and were freed from that experience prefer the new situation. So here we have a middle way between the idea that all the preferences that people now have are worthy of equal respect and the idea that the preferences people now have can be swept aside in favor of claims about what preferences they would have if conditions were different. On this view, the preferences that count the most are those that continue to be held by those who have experienced alternative ways of life. This is compatible with what was said in chapter 2 about appealing to an ideal consensus.

Mill's approach to social reform involves seeing what changes have in fact decreased human misery, have increased people's satisfaction with their lives, and have led them to revise, or not to revise, their preferences.[106] The position of this book is that the desires that are worthy of the most respect are desires for what is really worthwhile. Mill's approach may not be an infallible guide to what is intrinsically worthwhile, but it would certainly seem to be a more reliable guide than the two alternatives of either treating all preferences as equally worthy of respect, or sweeping aside the preferences of a large segment of people in the name of the preferences that ideologies think they should have.

Feminism, Radical Change, and the Family

As we have seen, the proposals of some radical feminists call for eliminating the family as we are familiar with it. If equality between the sexes means that when a person gets married, society in general should not be concerned with whether his or her partner is a man or a woman, or with how many partners there are in the relationship, then the traditional family is eliminated. What happens to children seems to be of secondary importance for these feminists than the implementation of an abstract principle.

Even less radical proposals can threaten the existence of the family. At some points, Rawls indicates that an ideal society would be one in which a person would not be able to predict anything about the future educational or economic success of a child from knowing anything about the race and social class of his or her parents. The only way to realize that ideal fully would be to do away with the family as we know it, since as long as children are raised in different families, their parents will inevitably have different incomes, different values, and different life situations generally, hence there will be fundamental ways in which children do not have equal life prospects.[107] It seems that all such proposals are very questionable, for the following reasons.

1. Radicals have proposed replacing the traditional family with communal arrangements. But it seems that the individual "infant is 'bonded' with individual adults, in small numbers, and not with a large anonymous collectivity."[108] They have also proposed group arrangements into which people enter or leave as spontaneous love determines. But in reply it can be claimed that

> The family permits an individual to develop love and security—and most important the capacity to trust others. Such trust is the prerequisite for any larger social bonds. . . . In the words of the German ethologist Eibl-Eibenfeldt, "The human community is based on love and trust; and both are evolved through the family."[109]

When the person on whom a child might place his or her primary allegiance may choose to contract out of the child-raising community, it is hard to see how trust is to develop. Laurence Houlgate writes that although changes need to be made in marriage contracts so that they embody more equality, still "it is important to retain those features of marriage that conduce to successful child-rearing."[110]

2. Another argument has to do with the fact that the weakening of the family as an institution, and the weakening of its influence on the raising of children and the transmission of values, has great totalitarian potential, because the power and influence of government are thereby increased.[111] Taking power away from families and parents means giving it to someone else. Brenda Almond writes:

> In the special area of sexual relationships the liberal's desire to resist totalitarianism in the sense of state domination of the life of the individual seems to conflict with the demand, potentially totalitarian in its consequences, for the state to take over the traditional role of the family. In particular, feminist demands for *female* freedom may run counter to traditional liberal demands for a reduction in the involvement of state agencies in personal and private life. In this case, the price paid for the freedom of one sex may be too high if bought at the cost of important freedoms of both sexes. Given the permanent tendency of human beings to construct hierarchies of power, and given pressures for conformity, the value of institutions that cut across political, economic, and social hierarchies is inestimable. Of these institutions, the family as a biological and natural network must be one of the most powerful. . . . The fact is that any totalitarian scheme, starting with that of Plato's *Republic*, seems necessarily to involve the elimination of the family as a source of subversion.[112]

3. Every way in which traditional families and long-term marriages have been weakened has been detrimental to children (and often to women) and thus to society. A man's income a year after a divorce is 80 percent of the former family income, while the average ex-wife, who usually cares for the children, has an income that is only about 32 percent of the previous family income.[113] Family disruption and disintegration are a major factor in teen suicide.[114] Numerous studies contribute to the conclusion that "children and adolescents will frequently use drugs in a society characterized by divorce, cohabitation, out-of-wedlock births, and men and women giving highest priority to activities and interests outside the home."[115]

Girls from households headed by single mothers are much more likely than girls from intact families to become single mothers themselves and to be on welfare,[116] and boys from such households are much more likely than boys from intact families to father illegitimate children, who are likely to be poor.[117] The further results are disastrous and well known. Sol Gordon writes:

> Almost every index of disturbance or pathology in our society is positively related to being born to or being a teenage mother—low birth-weight, infant mortality, physical disabilities, or retardation. The chances of a baby born to

a teenager being physically abused, becoming delinquent or drug-addicted are much greater than if born to an older woman. The life-script of teenage mothers is also grim. Their chances of finishing school, obtaining good jobs, or having marriages that will last for more than a few years are minimal. In this context, it seems almost trivial to point out that in the next 20 years the American taxpayer will pay in excess of $100 billion (at current prices) for the net results of teenage childbearing. . . . Many of the 600,000 babies born each year to teenagers end up on the welfare rolls.[118]

The duty to protect the vulnerable should take precedence not only over an unduly reverential attitude toward the status quo, which usually defends the interests of those with power, but also over an attachment to utopian schemes for reform. For this reason, and for reasons given above, the author generally supports the liberal or moderate approach to social change, as opposed to the radical or conservative approach. The considerations which support the liberal or moderate approach to social change would also tend to support liberal feminist proposals for change as against both radical feminist and anti-feminist points of view. Concern with protecting the vulnerable focuses concern on the interests of children and consequentially on the interests of families. Some academic feminists may not have paid enough attention to the connections between the welfare of children, the stability of families, and excessive individualism. However, the greater threats to such stability, and thus to children's welfare, would seem to come from the unwillingness of men and social institutions to accommodate change, and the unwillingness of society and government to deal adequately with fundamental problems of employment, education, and housing. The interests of children are threatened when working conditions and schedules are not designed to accommodate working mothers and when men abandon their families when their wives are no longer willing to fit some predetermined mold. They are threatened among the poor most of all, when, as Marian Edelman writes, there are too few "young males who are potentially good providers."[119] This is a threat that needs to be countered with "improved education, training and employment opportunities," support for a "value system that prepares young people for work,"[120] and the devising of ways "that the family and the private sector and the government can interact positively for all families, regardless of income."[121]

CONCLUSION

The author has no overall theory of justice to offer. There ought to be a concern about the distribution, use, and abuse of power, and anything, like money, that can be translated into power. There ought to be more concern with meeting the needs of human beings than with trying to force society to fit some theoretical pattern, whether it be that of libertarianism, a scheme intended to promote radical equality, or whatever. Beyond this, there may be a broad range of morally permissible ways of arranging society. As Mark Sagoff has pointed out, if we have a theory of justice that answers all the questions about what governmental policies should be, then there is nothing left for the democratic process to do.[122] Societies may, for example, legitimately choose to reward certain kinds of contributions to the general good. However, the principle of protecting the vulnerable must be central. If James Fishkin's claim that a policy choice is morally unacceptable if it imposes severe deprivations on some people even though an alternative policy would have imposed no severe deprivations on anyone is correct,[123] then the United States has made tyrannical policy choices that have led to, or not prevented, the increase of poverty and hopelessness among children, our most vulnerable and politically powerless citizens.[124]

QUESTIONS

1. In spite of the extreme differences between utilitarianism (particularly preference-utilitarianism), Rawls's liberalism, and libertarianism, the text points to some features they, and perhaps some other views, have in common. What are these common assumptions or common conclusions? Are what these views have in common more basic than their differences?

2. Members of the religious right wing claim to accept the authority of the Bible, which has much to say about protecting the vulnerable, loving one's neighbor, and realizing that the earth belongs to God. Some of its members are allied with members of the secular right wing, whose views are somewhat similar to Nozick's on questions of economic justice. Is there something inconsistent in this?

3. If you are using an anthology of readings in introductory ethics or moral problems that includes essays on the question of preferential treatment or affirmative action, read some of the essays and see if their positions can be identified with any of the theories of justice described here. Which views do you think are most justifiable?

4. How much should desert count in questions of justice? Rawls's view is that since we don't deserve the additional ability, energy, or self-discipline that our heredity and environment give us, we don't deserve whatever we achieve through that ability, energy, or self-discipline, so desert is not a relevant criterion for justice. Charles Taylor's view is somewhat similar. Do you agree or disagree? Why?

5. Compare the views that the various positions take on the just distribution of medical care. Which would you support and why? Should medical care be treated separately from other services paid for out of an individual's general income? Should merit enter into the picture? For example, should subsidized medical care be withheld from or rationed for those whose ill health is self-caused (e.g., by drugs or alcohol)?

6. Some of the views in this chapter are based on social contract principles, which involve the idea of a social contract between equals. Belief in the equality of

human beings is thought by some to be a product of the influence on British and American society of Judaism and Christianity (both of which assert that all people are created equally in the image of God). These commentators fear that as that influence wanes, we will end up with equality taking a back seat to technological utility, so that whatever social contract view we are left with "will exclude liberal justice from those who are too weak to enforce contracts—the imprisoned, the mentally unstable, the unborn, the aged, the defeated and sometimes even the morally unconforming."[125] What is your opinion of that fear? Are positions such as Galston's, which seek to base justice on a conception of the human good beyond a social contract, a protection against that development?

7. Many people in the United States, including whole families, do not have any decent place to live, owing to a variety of factors—among them the widespread conversion of apartment buildings into expensive condominiums that most people cannot afford and the lack of economic incentives for developers to build low- and middle-income housing. Is there any theory of justice discussed in this chapter according to which these people are not being treated unjustly? Do you think that view is defensible? If they are being treated unjustly, whose responsibility is it to see to it that the situation is changed? If the government should encourage housing by subsidizing rents, where should the money come from? What theory of justice would you appeal to? Defend your choice.

8. William Galston wishes to combine the principle of need (first of all) with a principle of desert or contribution. There are those who believe that the United States to some extent successfully combined these two principles in times of economic growth. In such times, there was enough money in the economy to provide benefits for the poor and at the same time to allow the incomes of the educated and industrious to rise. There is the fear, however, that in times of economic recession society may be torn apart by the conflict between the well-off, who resent the sacrifices they must make to support the poor and who feel that the principle of merit is being violated, and the poor, who resent government cutbacks in social programs and who feel that the principle of need is being violated. People in the middle may use the principles alternately as they resent both the rich and the poor. Is this a real problem? Do you see any way out of it? Do we need to find some way to deemphasize the principle of contribution?

9. What are some of the problems involved in treating each of the preferences that people have as having an equal claim to be satisfied? What are some of the problems involved in disregarding such preferences and appealing to preferences people would have if they were more rational, more enlightened, less brainwashed, and so on? Can one avoid both sets of problems? If so, how?

10. Compare liberal feminism and radical feminism. If you disagree with the author's criticisms of radical feminism, set forth your arguments.

FURTHER READING

The most relevant works of the major figures discussed in this chapter are:

Galston, William. *Justice and the Human Good*. Chicago: University of Chicago Press, 1980.

Mill, John Stuart. *Utilitarianism*. (1861) Indianapolis: Hackett, 1979.

Nozick, Robert. *Anarchy, State, and Utopia*. New York: Basic Books, 1974.

Rawls, John. *A Theory of Justice*. Cambridge, Mass.: Harvard University Press, 1971.

Sterba, James. *The Demands of Justice*. Notre Dame, Ind.: University of Notre Dame Press, 1980.

_____. *How to Make People Just*. Savage, Md.: Rowman and Littlefield, 1988.

Walzer, Michael. "Justice Here and Now." In *Justice and Equality Here and Now*, edited by Frank S. Lucash, 136–50. Ithaca, N.Y.: Cornell University Press, 1986.

_____. *Spheres of Justice*. New York: Basic Books, 1983.

Discussions of various theories of justice can be found in:

Buchanan, Allen. "Justice: A Philosophical Review." In *Justice and Health Care*, edited by Earl E. Shelp, 3–22. (Boston: Reidel, 1981).

Campbell, Tom. *Justice*. Atlantic Highlands, N.J.: Humanities Press, 1988.

Fishkin, James. *Tyranny and Legitimacy: A Critique of Political Theories*. Baltimore: Johns Hopkins University Press, 1979.

Lebacqz, Karen. *Six Theories of Justice*. Minneapolis: Augsburg Publishing House, 1986.

Pettit, Philip. *Judging Justice: An Introduction to Contemporary Political Philosophy*. Boston: Routledge and Kegan Paul, 1980.

Sterba, James P. "Recent Work on Alternative Conceptions of Justice." *American Philosophical Quarterly* 23 (January 1986): 1–21.

There are a very large number of books and articles presenting, developing, criticizing, and presenting alternatives to the views of justice discussed in this chapter. Four anthologies of articles are:

Arthur, John, and William H. Shaw, eds. *Justice and Economic Distribution*. Englewood Cliffs, N.J.: Prentice-Hall, 1978.

Social Philosophy and Policy 1 (Autumn 1983). Entire issue on the subject of distributive justice.

Sterba, James, ed. *Justice: Alternative Political Perspectives*. Belmont, Calif.: Wadsworth, 1980.

Stewart, Robert M., ed., *Readings in Social and Political Philosophy*. New York: Oxford University Press, 1986. See pt. 3.

Justice in health care has been widely discussed. There are numerous anthologies of writings on biomedical ethics, each of which has a section on justice in health care and each of which has an extensive bibliography. A few additional works are:

Churchill, Larry R. *Rationing Health Care in America: Perceptions and Principles of Justice*. Notre Dame, Ind.: University of Notre Dame Press, 1987.

Daniels, Norman. *Just Health Care*. New York: Cambridge University Press, 1985.

Outka, Gene. "Social Justice and Equal Access to Health Care." *Journal of Religious Ethics* 2 (Spring 1974): 11–32.
Shelp, Earl E., ed. *Justice and Health Care.* Boston: Reidel, 1981. See pp. 213–30.

A short critique of the libertarian point of view is found in:

"Is the Least Government the Best Government?," *QQ: Report from the Center for Philosophy and Public Policy* 1 (Spring 1981).

An interesting critique of Rawls as representative of modern liberal views is found in:

Grant, George Parkin. *English-Speaking Justice.* Notre Dame, Ind.: University of Notre Dame Press, 1974.

Critiques of cost-benefit analysis are found in:

Raz, Joseph. "Liberalism, Autonomy, and the Politics of Neutral Concern." In *Midwest Studies in Philosophy*, vol. 2, *Social and Political Philosophy*, edited by Peter A. French, Theodore E. Uehling, Jr., and Howard K. Wettstein, 89–120. Minneapolis: University of Minnesota Press, 1982. See section 4, 98–102.
Sagoff, Mark. "At the Shrine of the Lady of Fatima, or Why Political Questions Are Not All Economic." In *Ethics and the Environment*, edited by Donald Scherer and Thomas Attig, 221–34. Englewood Cliffs, N.J.: Prentice-Hall, 1983.
———. *The Economy of the Earth.* New York: Cambridge University Press, 1988.
———. "The Limits of Cost-Benefit Analysis." *QQ: Report from the Center for Philosophy and Public Policy* 1 (Summer 1981): 9–11.

For Marx, primary sources can be found in:

McLellan, David, ed. *Karl Marx: Selected Writings.* New York: Oxford University Press, 1977.

The literature on Marx and Marxism is huge. The following are a few mostly introductory-level works, particularly relevant to the concerns of this book:

Buchanan, Allen. *Marx and Justice.* Totowa, N.J.: Rowman and Allanheld, 1982.
Campbell, Tom. *Justice.* Atlantic Highlands, N.J.: Humanities Press, 1988. See chap. 7.
Elster, John. *An Introduction to Karl Marx.* New York: Cambridge University Press, 1986.
Kamenka, Eugene. *Marxism and Ethics.* New York: St. Martin's Press, 1969.
Norman, Richard. *The Moral Philosophers: An Introduction to Ethics.* New York: Oxford University Press, 1983. See chap. 9.
Singer, Peter. *Marx.* New York: Oxford University Press, 1980.

The views of various sorts of feminists are discussed in the following writings. For additional sources, follow the references given in these writings:

Jagger, Alison. "Political Philosophies of Women's Liberation." In *Today's Moral Problems*, 3d ed., edited by Richard Wasserstrom. New York: Macmillan, 1988.

Sommers, Christina Hoff. "Philosophers against the Family." In *Person to Person*, edited by Hugh LaFollette and George Graham, 106–24. Philadelphia: Temple University Press, 1989.

Storkey, Elaine. *What's Right with Feminism*. Grand Rapids, Mich.: Eerdmans, 1985.

The problem of the conflict between commitment to the family and commitment to various principles of justice is discussed in:

Fishkin, James. *Justice, Equal Opportunity, and the Family*. New Haven: Yale University Press, 1983.

NOTES

1. Chaim Perelman, *Justice* (New York: Random House, 1967), 3.
2. Aristotle, *Nicomachean Ethics* 5, 13:1129a32–34.
3. John Stuart Mill, *Utilitarianism* (1861), ed. George Sher (Indianapolis: Hackett, 1979), chap. 5, 42–43.
4. Ibid., 43.
5. John Locke, *Second Treatise of Civil Government* (1690), ed. C. B. Macpherson (Indianapolis: Hackett, 1980), chap. 2, paragraph 6, p. 9.
6. Mill, *Utilitarianism*, chap. 5, p. 52.
7. Jeremy Bentham, "Anarchical Fallacies," in *Human Rights*, ed. A. I. Melden (Belmont, Calif.: Wadsworth, 1970), 32.
8. Mark Sagoff, "At the Shrine of the Lady of Fatima, or Why Political Questions Are Not All Economic," *Arizona Law Review* 23 (1982): 1283; reprinted in *Ethics and the Environment*, ed. Donald Scherer and Thomas Attig (Englewood Cliffs, N.J.: Prentice-Hall, 1983) , 231.
9. Ibid., 224–27. See also Sagoff, *The Economy of the Earth* (New York: Cambridge University Press, 1988), chap. 2.
10. This is referred to by Michael Walzer in *Spheres of Justice* (New York: Basic Books, 1983), 313.
11. Locke, *Treatise*, chap. 2, paragraph 6.
12. Ibid., chap. 8, paragraph 95, 52.
13. Ibid., chaps. 2, 7, 8.
14. Jean-Jacques Rousseau, *Discourse on the Origin of Inequality* (1755), in Rousseau, *Basic Political Writings*, trans. Donald Cress (Indianapolis: Hackett, 1987).
15. Rousseau, *The Social Contract* (1762), trans. Donald Cress (Indianapolis: Hackett, 1988).
16. John Rawls, *A Theory of Justice* (Cambridge, Mass.: Harvard University Press, 1971).
17. Ibid., 60. See also p. 302.
18. Ibid., 61.
19. Ibid., 73.
20. Ibid., 60.

21. Ibid., 60–61. See also p. 302.

22. Ibid., 102–4.

23. Ibid., 13.

24. See George Parkin Grant, *English-Speaking Justice* (Notre Dame, Ind.: University of Notre Dame Press, 1974).

25. See James Sterba, *The Demands of Justice* (Notre Dame, Ind.: University of Notre Dame Press, 1980), 38–39.

26. Robert Nozick, *Anarchy, State, and Utopia* (New York: Basic Books, 1974).

27. Ibid., 155–56. Not all "patterned" theories are "end state" or "time slice" theories.

28. Ibid., 155.

29. Ibid., 163. Rawls does have a reply to Nozick, namely, that his principles of justice are meant to be used to decide on a constitution and on the basic structure of the society. They are not meant to be applied on a day-to-day basis.

30. See William Bradford Reynolds, *QQ: Report from the Center for Philosophy and Public Policy* 5 (Winter 1985): 6–8.

31. See the works mentioned in notes 32–36, 38, and 39. Numerous essays are collected in *Reading Nozick*, ed. Jeffrey Paul (Totowa, N.J.: Rowman and Allanheld, 1983). Additional works include John Granrose, "Review: Robert Nozick, *Anarchy, State, and Utopia*," *Social Theory and Practice* 3 (Fall 1975): 487–96; A. M. Honore, "Property, Title and Redistribution," in *Property, Profits, and Economic Justice*, ed. Virginia Held (Belmont, Calif.: Wadsworth, 1980), 84–93; Hal Varian, "Distributive Justice, Welfare Economics, and the Theory of Fairness," *Philosophy and Public Affairs* 4 (Spring 1975): 223–47; and J. R. Kearl, "Do Entitlements Imply That Taxation is Theft?," *Philosophy and Public Affairs* 7 (Fall 1977): 121–28.

32. James Sterba, "A Libertarian Justification for a Welfare State," *Social Theory and Practice* 2 (Fall 1985): 285–306.

33. See Sagoff, *Economy of the Earth*, chap. 8.

34. See "Is the Least Government the Best Government?," *QQ: Report from the Center for Philosophy and Public Policy* 1 (Spring 1981): 5.

35. Walzer, *Spheres of Justice*, 127.

36. Thomas Scanlon, "Nozick on Rights, Liberty, and Property," *Philosophy and Public Affairs* 1 (Fall 1976): 13.

37. Jeffrey H. Reiman, "The Fallacy of Libertarian Capitalism," *Ethics* 92 (October 1981): 92.

38. Nozick, *Anarchy, State, and Utopia*, 160.

39. Henry Shue, *Basic Rights* (Princeton, N.J.: Princeton University Press, 1980), chaps. 1 and 2.

40. James Fishkin, *Tyranny and Legitimacy: A Critique of Political Theories* (Baltimore: Johns Hopkins University Press, 1979), chaps. 1, 3, and 8. He makes the same claim about utilitarianism and Rawls's views as well.

41. Walzer, *Spheres of Justice*, 68.

42. Charles Fried, *Right and Wrong* (Cambridge, Mass.: Harvard University Press, 1978), 110. Others who defend similar points of view are Sterba, *Demands*, 55, and Baruch Brody, "Redistribution without Egalitarianism," *Social Philosophy and Policy* 1 (Autumn 1983): 71–87.

43. Sterba, *Demands*, 55. See also Charles Fried, "Distributive Justice," *Social Philosophy and Policy* 1 (Autumn 1983): 52. The word "normal" is included here to deal with a case in which a person with a catastropic illness might have a need to be kept alive that could be met, for example, by the expenditure of a billion dollars a year on medical care. Society does not have an obligation to meet that need. Charles Fried's reference to a "fair share" also seeks to take such a situation into account.

44. Sterba, *Demands*, 57–58.

45. See, for example, Baruch Brody, "Health Care for the Haves and the Have-nots: Toward a Just Basis for Distribution," in *Justice and Health Care*, ed. Earl E. Shelp (Boston: Reidel, 1981), 151–60.

46. See Charles Fried, "Equality and Rights in Medical Care," *Hastings Center Report* 6 (February 1976): 29–34.

47. See Locke, *A Letter Concerning Toleration* (1689), ed. James Tully (Indianapolis: Hackett, 1983).

48. See Hume, *Treatise of Human Nature*, ed. L. A. Selby-Bigge (Oxford: Oxford University Press, 1988), 3. 3. 7.

49. See Mill, *On Liberty* (1859), ed. Elizabeth Rapaport (Indianapolis: Hackett, 1978), chap. 3.

50. Ibid., chaps. 1–3.

51. Another advocate of the ideal of neutrality is R. M. Dworkin. See his "Liberalism," in *Private and Public Morality*, ed. Stuart Hampshire (New York: Cambridge University Press, 1978), 113–43.

52. See Robert N. Van Wyk, "Liberalism, Religion, and Politics," *Public Affairs Quarterly* 1 (July 1987): 59–76.

53. William Galston, "Equality of Opportunity in Liberal Theory," in *Justice and Equality Here and Now*, ed. Frank S. Lucash (Ithaca, N.Y.: Cornell University Press, 1986), 94.

54. This view of liberty and liberalism is set forth, for example, by H. J. McClosky, "Liberalism," *Philosophy* 49 (January 1949): 22–24, and Joseph Raz, *The Morality of Freedom* (New York: Oxford University Press, 1987), 381.

55. See Galston, *Justice and the Human Good* (Chicago: University of Chicago Press, 1980), 97–99.

56. Walzer, *Spheres*, 85.

57. Ibid., 65.

58. Walzer, "Justice Here and Now," in Lucash, *Justice and Equality*, 142.

59. Walzer, *Spheres*, 84.

60. Ibid.

61. Ibid., 64. See also Walzer, "Justice Here and Now," in Lucash, *Justice and Equality*, 139.

62. Walzer, "Justice Here and Now," in Lucash, *Justice and Equality*, 139.

63. Ibid., 142–43.

64. Walzer, *Spheres*, 65.

65. Walzer, "Justice Here and Now," in *Lucash, Justice and Equality*, 137–38.

66. Walzer, *Spheres*, 89–90.

67. Ibid., 91.

68. Ibid., 66–67.

69. Ibid., 67n.

70. This point is made by Robert Fullinwider in "The Equal Opportunity Myth," *QQ: Report from the Center for Philosophy and Public Policy* 1 (Fall 1981): 8–9.

71. Alan Brown, *Modern Political Philosophy* (New York: Penguin, 1986), 199.

72. This and other points are made by Joshua Cohen in his review of Walzer's *Spheres of Justice* in *Journal of Philosophy* 43 (October 1986): 457–68.

73. See Philip Hallie, "From Cruelty to Goodness," *Hastings Center Report* 11 (June 1981): 25.

74. Galston, *Justice and Human Good*, 274. Galston agrees with Walzer that need is the first consideration.

75. Galston, *Justice and Human Good*, 197.

76. Charles Taylor, "The Nature and Scope of Distributive Justice," in Lucash, *Justice and Equality Here and Now*, 56.

77. This is the approach taken by George Sher, "Justifying Reverse Discrimination in Employment," *Philosophy and Public Affairs* 4 (Winter 1975): 159–70.

78. See Peter Singer, *Marx* (New York: Oxford University Press, 1980), 37.

79. Allen Buchanan, *Marx and Justice* (Totowa, N.J.: Rowman and Allanheld, 1982), 132.

80. Quoted in Eugene Kamenka, *Marxism and Ethics* (New York: St. Martin's Press, 1969), 39–40.

81. Kai Nielsen, "Arguing About Justice: Marxist Immoralism and Marxist Moralism," *Philosophy and Public Affairs* 17 (Summer 1988): 216.

82. Ibid., 222.

83. See Kamenka, *Marxism and Ethics*, 40.

84. Neil McInnes, "Marxist Philosophy," in *Encyclopedia of Philosophy*, 5:174 (New York: Macmillan and Free Press, 1967).

85. Ibid.

86. For an example, see John Somerville, *The Philosophy of Marxism: An Exposition* (New York: Random House, 1967), 162–63.

87. See Kamenka, *Marxism and Ethics*, 47–48.

88. Singer, *Marx*, 42–43.

89. Ibid., 60.

90. Kamenka, *Marxism and Ethics*, 63–64.

91. Buchanan, *Marx and Justice*, 157.

92. Singer, *Marx*, 73.

93. Buchanan, *Marx and Justice*, 157.

94. Singer, *Marx*, 73.

95. Buchanan, *Marx and Justice*, 157.

96. Ibid., 171.

97. Ibid., 172.

98. Ibid., 167.

99. Ibid., 177.

100. Ibid., 178.

101. Singer, *Marx*, 76.

102. These proposals are pointed out and discussed by Christine Hoff Sommers in "Philosophers against the Family," in *Person to Person*, ed. Hugh LaFollette and George Graham (Philadelphia: Temple University Press, 1989), 82–105. They are made in a number of writings, including Ann Ferguson, "Androgyny as an Ideal for Human Development," in *Feminism and Philosophy*, ed. Mary Vetterling-Braggin, Frederick A. Elliston, and Jane English (Totowa, N.J.: Littlefield Adams, 1977), 45–69, and Carol Gould, "Private Rights and Public Virtues: Women: The Family and Democracy," in *Beyond Domination*, ed. Carol Gould (Totowa, N.J.: Rowman and Allanheld, 1983), 3–18.

103. Sommers, "Philosophers against Family," in LaFollette and Graham, *Person to Person*, 90.

104. Alison Jagger, "Political Philosophies of Women's Liberation," in *Today's Moral Problems*, 3d ed., ed. Richard Wasserstrom (New York: Macmillan, 1988), 51.

105. Mill, *Utilitarianism*, chap. 2.

106. This discussion is indebted to Sommers, "Philosophers against Family," in LaFollette and Graham, *Person to Person*.

107. This issue is discussed in James Fishkin, *Justice, Equal Opportunity, and the Family* (New Haven: Yale University Press, 1983).

108. Brigitte and Peter L. Berger, *The War over the Family: Capturing the Middle Ground* (Garden City, N.Y.: Anchor Press/Doubleday, 1983), 153.

109. Ibid., 174.

110. Laurence Houlgate, *Family and State* (Totowa, N.J.: Rowman and Littlefield, 1988), 68.

111. See Peter L. Berger and Richard John Neuhaus, *To Empower People: The Role of Mediating Structures in Public Policy* (Washington, D.C.: American Enterprise Institute for Public Policy Research, 1977), chap. 3. Berger and Neuhaus assert: "Totalitarian regimes have tried—unsuccessfully to date—to supplant the family in [its] function [of transmitting values]. Democratic societies dare not try if they wish to remain democratic. Indeed they must resist every step, however well intended, to displace or weaken the family institution" (p. 20).

112. Brenda Almond, *Moral Concerns* (Atlantic Highlands, N.J.: Humanities Press, 1987), 38.

113. Lenore Weitzman, *The Marriage Contract* (New York: Free Press, 1981), 47; cited by Bert N. Adams, "The Family: Problems and Solutions," *Journal of Marriage and the Family* 47 (August 1985): 526.

114. John S. Wodarski and Pamela Harris, "Adolescent Suicide: A Review of Influences and the Means for Prevention," *Social Work* 32 (November/December 1987): 477–84.

115. Alan C. Carlson, "Between Parents and Pushers: Resolving America's Drug Crisis," *Family in America* 2, (7): 8.

116. Sara S. McLanahan, "Family Structure and Dependency: Early Transitions to Female Household Headship," *Demography* 26 (February 1988): 1–16.

117. William Marsiglio, "Adolescent Fathers in the United States: Their Initial Living Arrangements, Marital Experience and Educational Outcomes," *Family Planning Perspectives* 19 (November/December 1987): 240–51.

118. Sol Gordon, "Preteens Are Not Latent, Adolescence Is Not a Disease," in *Sex Education in the Eighties*, ed. Lorna Brown (New York and London: Plenum Press, 1981), 93.

119. Marian Wright Edelman, *Families in Peril: An Agenda for Social Change* (Cambridge, Mass.: Harvard University Press, 1987), 14.

120. Ibid.

121. Ibid., 83.

122. Sagoff, *The Economy of the Earth*, 161–67.

123. Fishkin, *Tyranny and Legitimacy*, chaps. 1, 3, and 8.

124. Edelman, *Families in Peril*, 25–26.

125. Grant, *English-Speaking Justice*, 84–85.

Index

social, 161–163, 167–171
strength-of-character, 156–158,
    163–164, 181
Vocation, vocations. *See* Careers
Voluntarism, 10, 13
Von Wright, G. H., 156
Vulnerable, protecting the, 129–137,
    138, 139, 148, 167, 170, 205,
    220

Wallace, James, 156, 157, 184
Walzer, Michael, 75, 76, 200, 202,
    205–208
Waxman, Meyer, 50, 52, 53
Weapons of mass destruction, 2
Weingartner, Charles, 176, 177
Wesley, John, 50, 117
Wolgast, Elizabeth, 14, 141
Wollstonecraft, Mary, 168

W

Well-being, welfare, 118–125, 135,
    204

Y

Yoder, John Howard, 38, 51